KILLING THE MOB

KILLING THE MOB

The Fight Against Organized Crime in America

BILL O'REILLY

AND

MARTIN DUGARD

ST. MARTIN'S PRESS

NEW YORK

First published in the United States by St. Martin's Press, an imprint of St. Martin's Publishing Group

www.stmartins.com

Design by Meryl Sussman Levavi

Library of Congress Cataloging-in-Publication Data

Names: O'Reilly, Bill, author. | Dugard, Martin, author.
Title: Killing the mob / Bill O'Reilly and Martin Dugard.
Description: First edition. | New York : St. Martin's Press, 2021. |
Series: Killing | Includes bibliographical references and index.
Identifiers: LCCN 2020033805 (print) | LCCN 2020033806 (ebook) | ISBN 9781250273659 (hardcover) | ISBN 9781250273666 (ebook)
Subjects: LCSH: Organized crime—United States—History—20th century. | Mafia—United States—History—20th century.
Classification: LCC HV6446 .O727 2021 (print) | LCC HV6446 (ebook) | DDC 364.1060973—dc23
LC record available at https://lccn.loc.gov/2020033805
LC ebook record available at https://lccn.loc.gov/2020033806
Our books may be purchased in bulk for promotional, educational, or business use. Please contact your local bookseller or the Macmillan Corporate and Premium Sales Department at 800-221-7945, extension 5442, or by email at MacmillanSpecialMarkets@macmillan.com.

First Edition 2021

1   3   5   7   9   10   8   6   4   2

This book is dedicated to my late father and mother, who always obeyed the law and passed that dedication on to their children.

KILLING THE MOB

PROLOGUE

MARCH 3, 1934
LAKE COUNTY JAIL
CROWN POINT, INDIANA
9:15 A.M.

The man with four months to live is about to bust out of jail.

This is a cold and rainy Saturday morning. Thirty-year-old John Dillinger, America's most famous bank robber, has finished his meager prison breakfast and now mills around with fourteen other inmates in a jailhouse corridor. He enjoys his only "exercise" of the day but has much more on his mind.

Dillinger is a charming celebrity inmate, standing five feet, seven inches, with a crooked smile, trim athletic build, and thinning brown hair. He is well known as a ladies' man. A career criminal from Indianapolis whose only legitimate job was a short stint in the U.S. Navy, Dillinger has spent his adult life in and out of prisons. Nevertheless, he has become famous. Such is Dillinger's notoriety that the prosecuting attorney and sheriff in his current court case both demanded to have a picture taken with their arms around his shoulders.

It has been five weeks since authorities in Tucson, Arizona, arrested Dillinger and his gang. The four gangsters had committed eight bank robberies throughout the Midwest in the previous year and had gone farther west to escape the law. Additionally, state police arsenals were brazenly raided to steal machine guns, pistols, and ammunition.

*John Dillinger (1903–34), a prominent bank robber
in the midwestern United States during the 1930s.*

"The Dillinger Gang," as they are known, plans heists with great sophistication, utilizing detailed getaway maps and high-horsepower vehicles to outrun law enforcement. They also brandish Thompson submachine guns. Each man plays a specific role in the robberies, whether as a driver, lookout, or vault man, but it is the self-assured Dillinger who strides into a bank, opens a leather case containing his Thompson, and yells, "This is a stickup," to the tellers and bank customers. Dillinger makes no attempt to hide his handsome face, and as the numbers of robberies mount between June 21, 1933, and January 15, 1934, his legend grows.

It is bad luck that gets Dillinger and his band captured in Tucson. Two of the men are staying at the Hotel Congress when a broken furnace leads to a fire, forcing an evacuation of all rooms. Rather than let their belongings burn, gang members Russell Clark and Charles Makley bribe firefighters to climb back up the ladders to retrieve their luggage. Tucson is a small town with a population of just over thirty thousand. The suspicious behavior of these strangers catches the attention of firefighter William Benedict, who identifies Makley and Clark from a photo he remembers in *True Detective* magazine. Benedict then notifies the Tucson police, and over the course of the next four days the gang is carefully tracked and eventually captured.

John Dillinger is the last man arrested. He is carrying $7,000 in cash, some of which can be traced to a recent robbery in East Chicago, Indiana. There, police officer William Patrick O'Malley was killed in cold blood, shot dead with eight bullets to the chest by Dillinger himself. So when it comes time for Tucson prosecutors to extradite the gang to the scenes of their many crimes, Makley, Clark, and Pete Pierpont are first flown in handcuffs to Ohio—there to stand trial for a deputy murdered while the three were breaking John Dillinger out of a small town jail in October 1933.*

But Dillinger does not go to Ohio. He is extradited here to Crown Point, located fifteen miles south of Lake Michigan, where he will be tried for the killing of Officer O'Malley.

The electric chair looms if he is convicted.

But John Dillinger has no intention of standing trial.

✦

The second floor of the Lake County Jail is considered "escape proof." Since his arrival in early February, Dillinger spends most days alone in his barred cell, with its simple bed and small bucket for a toilet. On those occasions when Dillinger's jailers allow him to step outside, it is either to eat, exercise, or empty "slop jars" of human waste from his cell and those of other prisoners. The wardens and deputies take great pride in making the legendary John Dillinger perform this grim duty—a way of reminding the famous captive that he is now powerless.

---

* All three men will be convicted. Russell Clark receives a life sentence. Charles Makley and Pete Pierpont will be sentenced to death. However, on September 22, 1934, all three will attempt to escape from the Ohio State Prison in Columbus. Clark has a change of heart and returns to his cell. Makley is shot dead. Pierpont is captured alive. Still wounded from his failed prison break, the thirty-two-year-old Pierpont must be carried to the electric chair, where he is executed on October 17, 1934.

Dillinger plays along, pretending to be unbothered. "I played the good fellow with all the guards at the jail," Dillinger will later recall. "I patted them on the back and told them what fine fellows they were. I volunteered for all the distasteful jobs that had to be done."

In this way, Dillinger convinces the guards that he is no longer a threat. His daily habit of whittling a piece of wood has not drawn suspicion. Instead, the guards have made this another point of mockery, calling him "John the Whittler."

But on this Saturday morning, as sixty-four-year-old jailhouse trustee Sam Cahoon slips into the exercise area carrying soap for the showers, the end result of Dillinger's whittling becomes quite obvious. The block of wood has been carved into the shape of a small pistol. Now, before Cahoon can close the prison door behind him, Dillinger presses the fake weapon hard into the trustee's torso. "I'll blow you apart," the bank robber snarls, any vestige of sweet disposition now vanished.

Using Cahoon as a shield, Dillinger works his way through the jail, not only convincing his guards that he possesses a gun but ordering them to lock themselves inside cells. Finally, Dillinger arrives at the warden's office, where one of the guards sleeps soundly in a desk chair. Gliding quietly across the room, Dillinger removes an automatic weapon from a gun rack and presses the barrel into the back of the guard's head.

"This is Dillinger," says the bank robber. "If you move a muscle, I'll blow your head off your shoulders."

Dillinger then leaves the jailhouse a free man, stealing the sheriff's personal vehicle to make his getaway. The jail is affixed to the sheriff's house, so the theft is an easy one. There is no two-way radio in the car, or in any other law enforcement vehicle, so the Crown Point sheriff has no way of alerting police officers on the interstate that a wanted criminal is heading their way. Thus John Dillinger drives at a furious pace toward Chicago.

Roughly ten miles after fleeing the redbrick building housing the Lake County Jail, Dillinger drives the stolen vehicle across the Indiana-Illinois state line. In so doing, he violates the National Motor Vehicle Theft Act. To this point in his bank-robbing career, Dillinger had only

J. Edgar Hoover, head of the U.S. Bureau of Investigation,
addresses the National Crime Conference in Washington, D.C.,
on December 11, 1934.

broken state and local laws. But by committing an offense against what
is also known as the Dyer Act, John Dillinger has violated a federal law
for the first time.

Unbeknownst to him, a special unit from the Department of Justice will now take control of the hunt for John Dillinger. It was first
known as the Bureau of Investigation—BOI for short—and then Division of Investigation, or DOI. Its leader is a thirty-nine-year-old lawyer
named J. Edgar Hoover.

And Hoover will stop at nothing to catch his man—no matter how
long it takes.

PART I

THE GUNNERS

CHAPTER ONE

May 26, 1934
Aspin Hill Memorial Park
Silver Spring, Maryland
Morning

Violence is plaguing America.

Throughout 1933 and the first half of 1934, dozens of vicious and heavily armed gangsters are creating carnage in rural parts of the United States. It is the middle of the Great Depression. The average national individual income has been cut in half. The nationwide unemployment rate is 21.7 percent. The homicide tally is the highest of the century due to rampant poverty and the clash of immigrant and traditional cultures as America becomes increasingly urban.

In addition, half of all home mortgages are delinquent, and more than one thousand home loans are foreclosed every day. As more and more American families are evicted, the banks are viewed as predatory villains—more intent on making a dollar than helping poor people survive.

So it is no surprise that some criminals in the United States are actually becoming popular public figures, especially the handful of men and women who rob banks for a living. The Division of Investigation calls these people "Public Enemies," but to many they are Robin Hoods, exacting revenge on bankers and fat cats from Portland, Maine, to Portland, Oregon.

On this warm Saturday morning, the man who has just been handed the enormous responsibility of stopping the Robin Hoods is momentarily unconcerned about fighting crime. John Edgar Hoover is in a state of deep mourning as he watches his beloved dog lowered into a grave in this Washington suburb.

Hoover has lived in the District of Columbia his whole life. He began his career of public service at eighteen, a high school class valedictorian who landed work as a clerk at the Library of Congress while attending college and then law school. Hoover's employment ended when he passed the bar in 1917. He took a job with the Justice Department the very next morning. Within two years, the young lawyer's work ethic saw him promoted rapidly. By 1924, at the behest of President Calvin Coolidge, twenty-nine-year-old J. Edgar Hoover was placed in charge of a corrupt federal agency known as the Bureau of Investigation.*

The promotion appears to be a career dead end for the hard-charging young lawyer with the receding hairline, permanent scowl, and the habit of talking too fast in order to hide a stutter. Founded in 1908, the Bureau of Investigation is America's first national law enforcement agency. However, there is widespread fear in Congress that the BOI might become a secret police—"spying upon . . . the people, such as has prevailed in Russia."

So Congress has intentionally limited the BOI's power. The original thirty-four agents are forbidden to carry a weapon—and even prevented from making arrests. When it comes time to take a suspect into custody, the agents have a choice: either call in U.S. Marshals or the local police.

Hoover devotes himself to his new job, eschewing any semblance of a personal life in favor of complete commitment to law enforcement. Immediately, the new director cleans house, firing any agent accused

---

* Hoover was actually appointed by Coolidge's attorney general, Harlan Fiske Stone. Hoover was assistant director of the bureau at the time. Director William Burns was accused of involvement in the Teapot Dome Scandal, leading to his resignation and Hoover's appointment as director. Burns's leadership was symptomatic of the bureau's pre-Hoover corruption, a period that included collusion with bootleggers, selling protection, selling sensitive bureau files, and swapping employment in the agency for political favors.

of taking bribes. He sets up a rigorous training program to ensure that his agents are mentally and physically fit. Also, his investigators are expected to be of high moral character, with training in accounting or law. There is no such thing as paid overtime. Hoover raises the BOI's profile by establishing the first nationwide database for fingerprints.

And yet, the BOI is powerless to prosecute the bank robberies and the random murders plaguing America during the Great Depression. State and local police have complete authority in such cases, despite the frustrating reality that these agencies do not communicate with one another, nor can they chase criminals across state lines. John Dillinger has made an art of escaping this way.

✦

There is no question that J. Edgar Hoover is a strange man. He has few friends and lives at home with his seventy-five-year-old mother, Anna Marie.

The director's most trusted confidante is his Airedale terrier, Spee De Bozo. It is Spee who fetches the paper each morning and eats the soft-boiled egg that Hoover gives him for breakfast. J. Edgar loves Spee so much that he not only keeps the animal's framed photo on his office desk but also hangs a painting of the Airedale on a wall at home. Hoover may be a tough boss with his agents, but he never disciplines his dog.

Spee De Bozo passes away on May 24 at the age of eleven, and now his shroud-covered body is being lowered into the grave at this pet cemetery. "This is one of the saddest days of my life," the grief-stricken Hoover explains to a groundskeeper. His display of emotion is unnerving to the three DOI agents who have been asked to accompany him to the burial, for Hoover is normally a closed vault of privacy.

At the same time, the director is actually becoming one of the most powerful men in the country. On May 18, Congress recognizes that state and local law enforcement agencies are powerless to stop the bank-robbing epidemic. This is a reaction to the 1933 Kansas City Massacre, where criminals led by a robber known as "Pretty Boy" Floyd shot and killed four federal agents in cold blood. Thus, the Crime Control Acts of 1934 were passed—now if a person kills or assaults a federal officer,

From left, Charles Arthur "Pretty Boy" Floyd; his son, Charles Dempsey Floyd; and his wife, Ruby Floyd, circa 1930.

transports kidnapped persons, or robs a bank, they are subject to federal law. They will be charged with federal crimes.

State troopers and local sheriffs will no longer have jurisdiction in these matters. That power now goes to the newly renamed Division of Investigation. Just as important, Congress is about to pass another important piece of legislation allowing DOI agents to bear arms and make arrests.

As Spee De Bozo's burial comes to an end, J. Edgar Hoover promises himself that he will soon buy another dog.*

The time for mourning quickly passes.

The time for catching violent bank robbers is about to begin.

And there will be blood.

---

* J. Edgar Hoover would have eight more dogs after Spee De Bozo, many of which were interred in the same plot. The tombstone and gravesite can still be found at the Aspin Hill Memorial Park.

CHAPTER TWO

May 23, 1934
Bienville Parish, Louisiana
9:15 A.M.

Twenty-three-year-old Bonnie Parker sits in the passenger seat of a stolen Ford V-8. On her lap rests a bacon, lettuce, and tomato sandwich on white bread wrapped in a napkin. Thick forest and bushes line the dusty country road on both sides. Bonnie's lover, Clyde "Champion" Barrow, is at the wheel, pushing sixty-five miles per hour because the couple is late for a rendezvous. Clyde, twenty-five, has already finished his fried bologna sandwich purchased during the couple's recent stop at Ma Canfield's Café in the nearby Louisiana town of Gibsland.

Clyde loves the high-powered V-8 so much, he wrote a letter to automotive manufacturer Henry Ford praising its "speed and freedom." The bank robber wears wire-rim sunglasses, and a blue shirt and suit with a matching hat, but drives in his stocking feet. Long ago, the convicted criminal asked a fellow inmate to cut off two of his toes with an ax to escape hard labor in prison. As a result, Clyde walks with a limp, and driving while wearing shoes is extremely uncomfortable. Ironically, prison officials had already decided to parole young Clyde before the ax dropped. He limped out of prison a free man just six days after the mutilation.

Bonnie's hat, her trademark tam, has been tossed into the back seat.

An undated photo of bandits Bonnie Parker and Clyde Barrow.

The poetry-writing criminal wears a wedding ring—though she left her unfaithful husband years before falling for Clyde. She is a petite four feet, eleven inches tall, chain-smokes Camel cigarettes, and has her ex-husband's name still tattooed inside her right thigh. A long red dress reveals Bonnie's hourglass figure but hides her legs because they were badly burned by battery acid after crashing during a high-speed car chase one year ago. As a result, Bonnie Parker also walks with a limp, just like Clyde. Sometimes her pain is so bad that she cannot walk at all, and he must carry her. Yet Bonnie wears high heels rather than flat soles, even though they will make it more difficult for her to run from the law should the need arise.

Widely known as Bonnie and Clyde, the young couple has robbed banks since beginning their crime spree in February 1932. But as they moved through Missouri, Louisiana, Texas, New Mexico, and even north to Minnesota—taking advantage of poor communications between state and local authorities to stay ahead of the law—bank robbery is just one of the crimes they commit. They have stolen cars and robbed stores and gas stations at gunpoint for as little as five dollars. On the violent side, they have kidnapped people and shot dead at least thirteen men and women. All told, the couple has committed more than one hundred felonies in two years.

Bonnie and Clyde first met in January 1930—she, a recently unemployed waitress, and he, a poor laborer from the slums of Dallas. Other than petty theft, Clyde Barrow had no criminal record at the time. But just months later, he is arrested for burglary and sent to the Eastham Prison Farm, where after being routinely sexually assaulted, he commits his first murder: Clyde kills another prisoner with a lead pipe to avenge his prison rapes.

Thus, the mild-mannered Barrow is forever changed by Eastham Prison—"from a schoolboy to a rattlesnake" in the words of one fellow inmate. Despite his two years behind bars, Bonnie has waited for him. Upon release, and fueled by a hatred for the law, the couple begins committing crimes throughout the Midwest. Theirs is a simple life of robbing for money and food whenever they need it, and killing the hated police when they can. Other criminals join them as part of a small gang. But while these men come and go, the partnership of Bonnie and Clyde remains steady.

The couple were essentially small-time southern hoods, forever in the shadow of bigger criminal names like John Dillinger and his cronies Baby Face Nelson and Pretty Boy Floyd. But just one year ago—April 13, 1933—police surprised Bonnie and Clyde at a hideout in Joplin, Missouri. The aftermath was gruesome, with two police officers shot dead. The couple escaped by driving more than six hundred miles through the night into the heart of Texas. But in the ruins of the Missouri hideout, police discover a roll of undeveloped film. Wishing to familiarize the public with descriptions of Bonnie and Clyde, Joplin police develop the film and give the pictures to the Joplin *Globe* newspaper, which wires the photos nationwide.

The result is instant celebrity. Images of Bonnie poking a grinning Clyde with a sawed-off shotgun, and Bonnie posing alone with a cigar in her mouth and pistol in her hand make the two as famous as movie stars. Not only does the American public clamor for more information about Bonnie and Clyde, but their exploits soon became fodder for movie newsreels as an excited nation cheers for them to outfox law enforcement.

The criminal couple could not be happier. Both have nursed dreams of fame—Bonnie through her writing and quiet dreams of being a famous actress, and Clyde as a musician who plays the saxophone.

On May 21, 1934, just three days after Congress passes the new crime legislation to expand federal law enforcement, J. Edgar Hoover decides to go to war with Bonnie and Clyde. His first move: an 8″ x 8″ wanted poster bearing their images and listing their crimes is circulated nationwide. Unlike the Joplin photos, there is nothing glamorous about these images.

Yet that only enhances the legend of Bonnie and Clyde. However, Bonnie Parker somehow knows the truth of what is to come, writing flowery verse predicting that she and Clyde will die horribly.*

✦

As they drive down the rural Louisiana road, Bonnie and Clyde are fifteen minutes late for a meeting with a member of their gang on this muggy Wednesday morning. The stop for Bonnie's BLT to go at Ma Canfield's Café has put them behind schedule.

All seems well. Rounding a bend in the road, a flatbed truck belonging to Ivy Methvin, father of the convicted criminal they are due to meet, can be seen on the shoulder. Methvin kneels by the jacked-up

---

* The verse goes this way: "Some day they'll go down together; And they'll bury them side by side; To a few it will be grief, to the law a relief; But it's death for Bonnie and Clyde."

vehicle, changing a tire. A logging truck approaches from the other direction.

Clyde shifts into first gear. His window is already rolled down. Bonnie places the sandwich, still in its napkin, on her lap. In the back seat, under a blanket, are a pile of guns, a suitcase full of cash, and Clyde's personal saxophone.

Suddenly, Ivy Methvin rolls under his truck.

✦

The hidden posse is armed and dangerous.

Frank Hamer of the Texas Rangers has been tracking Bonnie and Clyde for four months. He has followed the pair to Bienville Parish with three other Texas lawmen. J. Edgar Hoover and his agents are not taking part in the posse but have provided crucial information on the couple's whereabouts. The Division of Investigation has pinpointed this region of Louisiana as a regular hiding place for Bonnie and Clyde.

In order to obtain the necessary jurisdiction to capture the criminals, the Texas Ranger has enlisted the aid of local sheriff Jordan Henderson and his young deputy, Prentiss Oakley. Together, the lawmen set a trap, believing the criminals will eventually go to the home of gang member Henry Methvin.* Ranger Hamer has promised Henry's father that his son will not receive the death penalty for his crimes in exchange for betraying Bonnie and Clyde. Thus, Ivan "Ivy" Methvin's flatbed pickup, specially designed for hauling pulpwood, is now strategically positioned to block the road on which the criminals are driving.

After nearly thirty hours of hiding, the posse is irritated and exhausted from waiting in the woods as thick clouds of mosquitoes swarm them. The day is already sweltering. Strung out in the forest, each man clutches his favorite weapon. Loaded and cocked backup guns are scattered on the pine straw. The collection of rifles, pistols, and

---

* Ivan Methvin is forty-nine when he volunteers to work as a decoy in the hunt for Bonnie and Clyde. Despite Ivan's efforts to help his son, Henry Methvin later went to prison for his role in the murder of an Oklahoma policeman. Ivan, who died in 1949, was predeceased by his son, who was crushed while drunkenly trying to crawl under a moving train.

automatics is formidable—the trademark of men quite comfortable in the art of killing.

Frank Hamer personally believes that a simple .45-caliber round to the gut is the best way to immobilize a suspect. Just to be sure, the relentless lawman is also armed with a Remington Model 11 shotgun and Colt Monitor Machine Rifle—a powerful World War I relic capable of killing a man from a mile away.

As the posse shifts restlessly, they see in the distance a Ford V-8 racing down the road at top speed.

The men cock their weapons.

The plan is simple: when Clyde Barrow slows down to approach the disabled truck, posse member Ted Hinton will confirm if the individuals in the vehicle are indeed Bonnie and Clyde. Hinton is from Dallas and knows Bonnie from her waitressing days. Once visual recognition is achieved, Hamer will step forward, Colt Monitor Rifle leveled, and demand their surrender. Frank Hamer is six foot two and solidly built, a thickset man with the gravitas and assumed legal authority expected from a Texas Ranger. Hamer is renowned for his marksmanship and even instructs new Rangers on the art of shooting. He will have no trouble opening fire should Bonnie and Clyde refuse to step out of the car and raise their hands in the air.

The only question in the mind of Frank Hamer is whether or not he can shoot a woman.

As the Ford V-8 draws closer and Ivy Methvin assumes his position as a decoy on the ground, Hamer steels himself for the confrontation. His current location is a hillside overlooking the road. There is every chance *he* will be shot if Bonnie or Clyde sees him making his way onto the road.

The Ford V-8 is flying down the road in a cloud of dust. As hoped, Hamer and the posse hear the telltale sound of downshifting and watch as the car slows to a stop alongside Methvin's truck.

Hamer looks at Ted Hinton, just to make sure the young couple in the car are Bonnie and Clyde.

Suddenly, without being given permission, Deputy Oakley opens fire with a Remington Model 8 borrowed from a local dentist. He stands fifty feet to the right of Hamer. Oakley has a clear shot at

Clyde through the open window. But several of his bullets miss, hitting the doorframe. However, one two-inch casing passes neatly through the left side of Clyde Barrow's skull, blowing open a gaping wound as it kills him.

Bonnie Parker, sandwich still on her lap, knows she is about to die as well. She screams in terror, a feral howl so mournful that the lawmen will remember it the rest of their lives.

The scream ends as the posse opens fire.

The brutal shooting lasts sixteen seconds. Bonnie and Clyde die immediately, but the firing does not stop until the frame and windows of the Ford are riddled with 167 bullets.

When it is done, as the smell of gunpowder carries through the Louisiana countryside, Frank Hamer steps onto the road clutching his Colt automatic. As leader of this posse, it is his obligation to make sure the job is complete.

The Ranger loosens a burst into the rear window.

Just to be sure.

Clyde is not visible, so Hamer's shots are focused on Bonnie, whose head still can be seen inside the car. Any doubts that he can shoot a woman have been answered.

The Texas Ranger then walks to the front of the Ford and takes direct aim at Bonnie from point-blank range. The legendary criminal is already dead, her head riddled with bullets as blood pours from wounds across her torso.

Frank Hamer squeezes the trigger anyway. The Colt kicks backward as he fires a final burst into the dead woman.

Just to be sure.

Two thousand miles away, J. Edgar Hoover is unaware that the federal fugitives he has been chasing have been slaughtered.

They will not be the last.

CHAPTER THREE

May 28, 1934
Chicago, Illinois
7:30 p.m.

John Dillinger is almost dead.

As "anesthesiologist" Harold Cassidy removes the towel soaked in ether from the killer's face, he is appalled to see that the unconscious gangster is turning blue. Dillinger has swallowed his tongue and cannot breathe—all because he is being chased. The Division of Investigation has been tracking the bank robber ever since his Indiana jailbreak two months ago. Every day, J. Edgar Hoover's G-men come closer to capturing Dillinger and sending him to the electric chair. But Cassidy's incompetence might deny the feds their execution.

John Dillinger knows his end may be near. So he is desperately trying to change his appearance. That has led to disaster.

Working frantically, surgeon Wilhelm Loeser wedges a pair of forceps into the criminal's mouth. Using both hands for leverage, he clamps the instrument around the tongue in an effort to pull it forward and open the airway.

As Cassidy looks on helplessly, the ether towel still clutched in his hands, Loeser extricates the tongue. A still-blacked-out John Dillinger vomits all over himself and the small bed on which he rests.

Dr. Loeser is a German-born immigrant who did his medical training at the University of Kansas and Northwestern. He recently lost his license to practice medicine after a narcotics conviction that sent him to Leavenworth Penitentiary.* When killers on the lam like John Dillinger are in need of medical care, law-abiding physicians will usually not cooperate. But Dr. Loeser, who practices his trade in secret, is happy to accept $5,000 for the procedure he is about to perform—all the while knowing that *his* life is in danger from Dillinger's gang should any harm befall the boss.

There is no operating theater. Instead, Loeser performs his work in the small bedroom of a cottage belonging to a sixty-six-year-old petty criminal and former prizefighter named Jimmy Probasco, who makes thirty-five dollars a day allowing fugitives to hide in his Chicago home. Both Loeser and Probasco will soon pay dearly for their actions—with the doctor spending more time in prison, and Probasco dangled outside the window of a Chicago high-rise by federal agents. He will then plunge nineteen stories to his death, which the Division of Investigation will claim to be a suicide.

But that is all to come. As Dillinger vomits once more, Loeser assures himself that his patient is capable of enduring the operation. Satisfied that this is the case, Loeser puts down his forceps and picks up a scalpel.

Then, slowly and patiently, Dr. Wilhelm Loeser begins cutting away at John Dillinger's face, beginning the plastic surgery intended to make the wanted criminal completely unrecognizable to J. Edgar Hoover and his agents.†

✦

Dillinger moved in to Jimmy Probasco's cottage just last night. There was no advance notice. The arrangements were made through mutual friends. He simply walked through the front door carrying a machine

---

* In 1931, Loeser was convicted under a 1914 federal statute known as the Harrison Narcotics Tax Act, which prohibited the selling of opiates and products of the coca plant.

† The term *plastic surgery* is taken from the Greek word *plastike*, which means to sculpt flesh. It was first applied to the alteration of physical appearance in the medical vernacular in 1839, seventy years before petroleum-based materials were engineered into a new product that was given the name "plastic."

George "Baby Face" Nelson, Public Enemy Number One. In 1934 he was wanted for the murder of three federal agents.

gun, two pistols, a bulletproof vest, and several hundred rounds of ammunition and made himself at home. Dillinger is friendly, if reserved.

This is unusual for the bank robber. John Dillinger is a gregarious man. He likes to attend baseball games, go to the movies, and drink in nightclubs. People are drawn to his upbeat personality, not knowing they are talking to a cold-blooded killer. The idea of laying low and not going out in public feels claustrophobic, and Dillinger cannot wait until his recovery from plastic surgery is complete so that he can once again walk the streets of Chicago.

But the killer is troubled. Twice in the last two months, the DOI manhunt has come within moments of capturing him alive. The first time came in Minneapolis, where Dillinger fled after the Indiana jailbreak in early March. Working with another famous bank robber, Lester Gillis—known as "Baby Face" Nelson—Dillinger and his cohort stole $49,500 from the Security National Bank in Sioux Falls,

South Dakota. The robbery came just three days after Dillinger escaped prison in Indiana. Three days after that, on March 13, Dillinger and Nelson stole another $52,344 from the First National Bank of Mason City, Iowa.* The pair then split up, with Nelson driving west to Reno, Nevada, while Dillinger rented Unit 303 at the Lincoln Court Apartments in Minneapolis with girlfriend Evelyn "Billie" Frechette.

John Dillinger is normally fond of showing off the twenty-seven-year-old half-French, half-Indian Frechette. But the gangster was slightly wounded in the Mason City heist. So the two remain in their apartment most of the time. Their brand-new Hudson sedan is parked outside. But when the pair go out, they leave only through the back door. Noting this behavior, landlord Daisy Coffey grows suspicious, especially after they refuse to allow a handyman inside to fix a bathroom fixture.

For reasons known only to the nosy Coffey, her first instinct is not to confront the couple but to pay a visit to the Division of Investigation's St. Paul field office, where she files a report. At 10:15 the next morning, agents knock on the door of Unit 303. It is Frechette who answers, telling the agents she needs a few moments to get dressed, before closing the door.

This event takes place two months before DOI agents are legally allowed to carry weapons or make arrests. But, as citizens of the United States, Hoover's men are entitled to the same freedoms of the Second Amendment as all other Americans, and thus use this loophole to bear arms. So it is that DOI agent Rufus Coulter stands outside Unit 303 carrying a loaded revolver. St. Paul police detective Henry Cummings is on hand to make any arrests. He is also armed.

But the officer's pistols are no match for John Dillinger's Thompson submachine gun.

Seeing no other way to escape, Dillinger fires through the door, scattering the agents. He and Frechette race down the stairs to their Hudson, then drive off—though not before Detective Cummings fires five shots, one of which hits Dillinger in the left calf. Making use of the same illicit underground medical network he would utilize for

---

* The equivalent of $947,708 and $1,002,235, respectively, in modern currency.

his plastic surgery in Chicago, Dillinger has his wound treated by a Minneapolis physician, who hides the criminal and his girlfriend for five days.

But J. Edgar Hoover's agents are relentless. Even after Dillinger and Billie Frechette flee to Indiana in the early days of April, the DOI has compiled a list of their potential hiding places and is thus anticipating their movements. By April 9 the couple are in Chicago, where agents arrest Frechette in a bar on State Street. She had entered the establishment to see if it was safe. Dillinger, who had a hunch authorities were near, waits outside and can only watch from a distance as his girlfriend is taken into custody.

Despondent over losing his companion but knowing he must flee, Dillinger drives north the length of Wisconsin to a remote vacation camp. Baby Face Nelson, recently returned from Reno, joins him.

There, at an idyllic lodge known as Little Bohemia, John Dillinger will meet the man who will kill him.

✦

Agent Melvin Horace Purvis II is small in stature, standing just five feet, four inches. But he is known to be vicious, questioning suspects with such intensity that many claim their broken bones and bruises are a result of his interrogation. The thirty-year-old South Carolina native runs the DOI's Chicago bureau but has recently alienated his boss, J. Edgar Hoover, who believes Purvis is not doing enough to capture John Dillinger.

So it is with great delight that Purvis receives a tip placing Dillinger and several members of his gang at a remote location in upstate Wisconsin. With a reward of $10,000 for Dillinger's capture, it was only a matter of time before such a break came Purvis's way. The agent triumphantly phones Director Hoover to tell him that Dillinger will soon be surrounded. Then, mindful of Hoover's wrath, Agent Purvis immediately takes extreme measures to make sure Dillinger does not get away.

Little Bohemia is eight hours north of Chicago—actually longer now that winter is lingering and the roads of Northern Wisconsin are

Melvin H. Purvis of Chicago, chief of the bureau of investigation of the U.S. Department of Justice in the Midwest, who on April 25, 1934, became the target of an ouster movement in Wisconsin over the failure to capture John Dillinger.

still covered in ice and snow. Instead of driving, Purvis further risks the anger of the tight-fisted Hoover by chartering two airplanes to fly agents from Chicago and St. Paul, Minnesota, into the town of Rhinelander.

It is Sunday afternoon, April 22. Little Bohemia is a vacation lodge consisting of a two-story main log building with eight guest rooms and a number of adjacent cabins. The sign out on the main highway touts Little Bohemia as a place to "Dine, Dance & Swim," and local residents often visit to take advantage of the restaurant in the main lodge, which offers a dollar dinner special on Sunday night. So the resort is packed as the agents arrive by car from the airport, armed with machine guns and wearing bulletproof vests. In addition, some men carry tear gas to immobilize the gangsters. As the agents turn off Highway 51 into the lodge's gravel driveway, Purvis orders two vehicles to block the drive, preventing Dillinger and his gang from escaping. A strict order of silence is enforced as agents fan out into the woods, stepping lightly through the snow-covered forest surrounding the main lodge. Dogs chained outside the main building begin barking at their scent. Dillinger is known to be in the company of perhaps a dozen gang members, including Baby Face Nelson and his wife. The agents are relieved that there is no one outside to inquire about the barking. In fact, John Dillinger will later remember hearing the yapping dogs as he played cards but thought nothing of it.

Which is strange. The criminal underworld in which Dillinger thrives is founded upon suspicion and paying attention. Using the hotel's telephone, for instance, is a grave risk because there is no privacy on the party lines that dominate rural American telephone systems. Better to locate a public pay phone when coordinating a rendezvous with gang members. Paying loyal intermediaries or family members to set up a meeting and arrange a quiet place to settle down for a few days is another tactic Dillinger often uses. There is also the strategy of leaving messages for other known criminals at "safe houses"—common hideouts used by gangs and wanted men. In this way, the underworld has its own informal post office. This involves trusting others with life and freedom. Even the choice of Little Bohemia as a hideout was made through criminal connections—forty-six-year-old owner Emil Wanatka was once closely connected with the Chicago underworld. But Dillinger is feared and he knows it. So betrayal is not a factor. Nevertheless, the bank robber is usually very alert to potential danger.

Not tonight.

As federal agents slowly cinch the noose tighter around the Little Bohemia Lodge, Dillinger feels as if he is completely safe. Northern Wisconsin is hundreds of miles from a major city. The thought of federal agents traveling across icy, snow-covered roads to ambush him seems an impossibility. But the killer is wrong.

In fact, Emil Wanatka has furtively alerted federal agents about the bank robber's location.

Wanatka wants the $10,000 reward.

Meanwhile, Dillinger ignores the barking dogs and deals another hand of cards.

✦

The Wisconsin night is completely dark. It is almost 8:00 p.m. at Little Bohemia.

Things now go horribly wrong.

Three local men have just finished dinner and are walking together to their car. Northern Wisconsin is a hunter's paradise, and each man carries a rifle, arousing the suspicion of the hidden agents. As the men step into the car, driver John Hoffman blasts the radio loudly as he begins to drive away.

Therefore, Hoffman and his friends John Morris and Eugene Boisneau do not hear the agents shouting for them to stop the car. The windshield is fogged from the cold, so they do not see the officers now leveling automatic weapons at their vehicle. An oblivious John Hoffman continues barreling toward the restaurant exit.

Melvin Purvis will later defend his agents, stating that they were aiming for the vehicle's tires. But the hard truth is that the DOI men were shooting to kill—machine-gunning the car's body and windows. Miraculously, only Boisneau dies. The other two men, not knowing who is shooting at them, are wounded but manage to run into the woods.

But the death of Eugene Boisneau is the least of Purvis's worries. Machine-gun fire can be heard as far as a mile away. Instantly, John Dillinger knows those gunshots are not for hunting. Dillinger and the other members of his gang race to their rooms to get their automatic weapons.

In the chaos, the Dillinger group flees into the woods, eluding Purvis and his agents. Baby Face Nelson shoots and kills a DOI agent before making his own escape. The dark and dense forest makes it impossible for the federal men to pursue because of the potential hostile fire.

Hoover, a man addicted to adulation, had foolishly alerted certain media that Dillinger's demise was at hand. In an attempt to elevate his personal profile, the director has released a personal statement to the press, letting them know that he is completely in charge of the manhunt—and deserves all credit for Dillinger's arrest. Four hours later in Washington, a furious and embarrassed J. Edgar Hoover announces to the media that once again, John Dillinger has eluded capture.

✦

One month later, in Jimmy Probasco's house at 2509 Crawford Avenue on the north side of Chicago, John Dillinger is covered in blood and vomit as Dr. Wilhelm Loeser completes the plastic surgery. Gone are three prominent moles above the gangster's eye, as well as the dimple in his chin, which has been filled with tissue removed from his cheek. Loeser has tightened the muscles of Dillinger's face, giving him a mild lift. The gangster's nose has been slit open, then completely reconstructed.

Loeser will soon pour lye on Dillinger's fingertips to burn off the fingerprints. But that painful procedure can wait. For now, it is enough that the brazen bank robber looks markedly different. Despite the DOI manhunt, and the fact that Melvin Purvis and agents of the Chicago office are literally just a few miles away, Dillinger is filled with the false sense of confidence that he can walk the streets unrecognized. He also has a new birth certificate and falsified identification cards.

But John Dillinger is mistaken about being secure. On the bank robber's thirty-first birthday, June 22, 1934, J. Edgar Hoover announces that a new category of criminal is now being hunted. This label applies to just one individual at a time. The term is *Public Enemy Number One*.

And until he is either dead or incarcerated, that label now belongs solely to John Dillinger.

CHAPTER FOUR

Public Enemy Number One is feeling the heat.

Chicago is enduring its hottest summer on record. The thermometer will spike to 109°F tomorrow, an all-time high. At 101°F, today is slightly cooler but no less daunting—since the sun rose this morning, twenty-three Chicagoans have died from the extreme temperatures.

Like many city residents, John Dillinger is spending this Sunday evening in a "refrigerated" movie house. He chooses the air-conditioned Biograph Theater on Lincoln Avenue, where William Powell, Myrna Loy, and Clark Gable are starring in *Manhattan Melodrama*. The Biograph is right around the corner from his rented hideout apartment at 2420 Halsted Street.

For company, the bank robber brings along a redhead named Polly Hamilton, a lookalike of his recently incarcerated girlfriend, Billie Frechette. Hamilton works as a waitress at the S&S Sandwich Shop, but in her younger years, as a teenage runaway from North Dakota, she worked as a prostitute for a Romanian madam named Ana Akalieva. Hamilton eventually made a new life but remained friends with Ana—who is also Dillinger's landlady. The robber has invited both women to the movie tonight, not at all worried that Ana's lover is an East Chicago detective. Foolishly, Dillinger is trusting his landlady.

Though a man squiring two women might draw attention, the wanted criminal is also unconcerned about that. A night on the town is nothing new since his plastic surgery, despite the federal manhunt. Dillinger is flush with cash, thanks to yet another bank robbery three weeks ago in South Bend, Indiana. Working with the equally notorious Pretty Boy Floyd and Baby Face Nelson, the gang robbed the Merchants National Bank of almost $30,000—shooting a policeman dead in the process. After dividing the money and escaping to Chicago, Dillinger moved out of Jimmy Probasco's cottage on the edge of town and rented an apartment on the city's North Side to be closer to the action.*

Since then, John Dillinger has attended several Chicago Cubs games at Wrigley Field, visited the 1933–34 World's Fair, and enjoyed lunches at the Seminary Restaurant. The bank robber makes sure to drink moderately and not be flashy with money, although he always insists on picking up the check. Through it all, John Dillinger is quietly planning one more big heist. However, instead of a bank, he will knock off a mail train—mail trains are known to carry a fortune in cash. Then Dillinger plans to turn away from his life of crime and escape to Mexico.

Now, dressed in gray slacks, white shirt, and red tie, the bank robber purchases three tickets at the Biograph box office. Clark Gable's part is that of a ruthless gangster named Blackie Gallagher—a character said to be based on Dillinger himself.

An intrigued John Dillinger steps into the theater. He has plans to make a movie of his own one day and is eager to witness his depiction on the screen. Dillinger quickly rushes Polly Hamilton and Ana Akalieva through the crowded lobby to take their seats.

As the cool of the theater takes the edge off the heat for John Dillinger, twenty federal agents are surrounding the Biograph Theater. Each exit is secured. For the next two long hours on this brutally hot night, the agents await the final act of *Manhattan Melodrama*, in which Blackie Gallagher is executed—hoping all the while to do the same to John Dillinger.

---

* That sum would be worth $561,000 in modern dollars.

✦

Federal agent Melvin Purvis can't wait for the movie to end.

"Nervous Purvis," as his fellow DOI agents call him behind his back, stands outside the Biograph in front of the ticket booth. The special agent in charge (SAC) of the Division of Investigation's Chicago bureau carries a cigar and box of matches in his suit pocket. Purvis will light the cigar once he spots Public Enemy Number One leaving the theater. This will be the signal for his agents to move in and arrest John Dillinger.

Purvis nervously scans the sidewalk in front of the theater. He can see the lighted cigarettes of his agents as they pass time in nearby alleys, sidewalks, and paired up at the exits of the Biograph. Since the fiasco at Little Bohemia, the search for John Dillinger has been a series of blunders. Stakeouts and surveillance of Dillinger's known accomplices have yielded no results. Even worse are the number of eyewitnesses who falsely claim to have witnessed the bank robber as far away as London. The transatlantic steamship *Duchess of York* was recently searched three times in one day because of rumors that Dillinger might be on board.

As a result of his failure to capture Dillinger, Purvis's relationship with his boss has gotten increasingly worse. The agent has not been completely relieved of his duties as head of the Chicago bureau but J. Edgar Hoover has sent another agent, Samuel Cowley, from Washington to lead the forty-man "Dillinger Squad." The thirty-four-year-old Cowley is a terse bureaucrat with a pencil-thin mustache, pasty skin, and a gift for organization. The teetotaling Idaho native is the polar opposite of the hard-drinking southern-born Purvis. Yet while the two men are vastly different, they unite in their desire to capture John Dillinger. Earlier in the evening, when the location of the cinema where Dillinger planned to see a movie was unclear, Cowley and several agents staked out the downtown Marbro Theatre, seven miles away. But once Dillinger was pinpointed, Cowley's team joined Purvis's at the Biograph.

Both men are well aware that should tonight result in the successful capture or killing of John Dillinger, they are by no means allowed to take personal credit.

That belongs solely to J. Edgar Hoover. The cardinal sin of a DOI career is deflecting the spotlight away from the director. One of the agents, Charlie Winstead, standing guard around the Biograph, will note of his time in the Washington bureau: "Everyone at headquarters knows Hoover is an egomaniac and they flatter him constantly."

The truth is that Hoover is pondering a run for the presidency in 1936 but is careful to keep these thoughts private. He continues to seek the approval of current president Franklin Delano Roosevelt, knowing that FDR's new crime bills give the DOI—and Hoover—more power and publicity. The director sees no need to threaten that relationship.

In addition to placing Agent Cowley in charge of the Dillinger investigation, Hoover has also gone to the extraordinary measure of adding a posse of sharpshooters to the Dillinger Squad. The shoot-out at Little Bohemia proved that lawyers and accountants—occupations comprising the majority of DOI agents—are not up to the task of shooting it out with hardened criminals. Thus, a small band of detectives and police from Texas and Oklahoma have been recruited solely for their prowess with firearms—as well as having no problem with the moral ambiguity of shooting first and asking questions later. The posse trained for a month in Washington before traveling to Chicago. In stark contrast to the typical buttoned-down DOI agents, Hoover's "hired guns," as they are known, prefer to wear Stetson hats, cowboy boots, and diamond pinky rings. They are also allowed to choose their own weapons.

Two of these sharpshooters now stand just south of the Biograph's main entrance. Charles Hurt was formerly Oklahoma City's chief of detectives. Charles Winstead, known to be "notoriously insubordinate" within the division, spent the early part of 1934 chasing Bonnie and Clyde through Texas before being reassigned by Hoover. Though the owner of several handguns, Winstead has chosen a standard DOI-issue .45 automatic pistol this evening.

Just prior to tonight's movie, Winstead and Hurt easily could have arrested John Dillinger, for he was just inches away as he walked past them into the theater.

But the agents did not recognize the face-altered Dillinger, who lived to see one final film.

✦

The clock ticks slowly on this muggy evening. *Manhattan Melodrama* is ninety-four minutes long. Finally, at 10:20, the movie ends.

Agent Purvis was made aware of Dillinger's presence at the film by none other than the bank robber's landlady, Ana Akalieva. The former madam is facing deportation charges as "an alien of low moral character." In an effort to remain in the United States, she contacted Purvis through her boyfriend, East Chicago, Indiana, policeman Martin Zarkovich, stating she could hand over John Dillinger. Purvis quickly made a deal with Ana that led him and his agents to the theater.*

Earlier this evening, as Dillinger played pinochle with Polly Hamilton in Ana's apartment, the madam slipped out under the pretense of needing more butter to cook the fried chicken dinner she had planned for the three of them. Ana then called Purvis from a pay phone. Once the call came in a few minutes past seven, the federal agents quickly took their places around the theater. Per J. Edgar Hoover's directive, the Chicago police were *not* informed of the operation.

Now, as patrons begin exiting the theater, Ana, wearing a bright orange skirt, walks next to Dillinger and Hamilton. This is the signal that the man at her side is Dillinger. Purvis had instructed Ana to wear red. Indeed, she will go down in history as "the lady in red." But orange is the closest color she has.

Purvis strikes a match. The agent's hands are shaking, but he manages to light the cigar.

Dillinger walks south on Lincoln Avenue, once again right past agents Winstead and Hurt. Both men have seen Purvis's signal and now fall in behind Dillinger. Hamilton hangs on the robber's left arm. Ana is to the left of Hamilton.

---

* Ana was deported anyway. Though she received a $5,000 reward for her part in Dillinger's demise, J. Edgar Hoover ignored the deal she made with Purvis and supervised her return to Romania. Some believe the Dillinger killing was staged, using an innocent stranger instead of the bank robber, and that Ana's deportation was an attempt to keep her silent about her role in the cover-up. In June 2019, descendants of Dillinger filed a request to exhume his body to ascertain the truth about the corpse's identity. An Indiana judge refused to sign the permit. The authors of this book do not believe the conspiracy theory.

A third DOI agent, young Herman "Ed" Hollis, falls in alongside Winstead and Hurt.

Sensing danger, Dillinger suddenly wheels and sees the three men in suits. Suspecting they are agents, the bank robber shakes loose of Hamilton and Ana. He lunges toward a nearby alley. Simultaneously, Dillinger reaches in his pocket for a gun and lowers his body into a crouch.

"He whirled around and reached for his right front pocket," Winstead will remember in the official DOI version of events. Purvis will claim that he cried out for Dillinger to halt.

Then all three agents open fire.

To this day, there is considerable debate about which agent's bullets actually killed John Dillinger. The majority opinion believes it to be Charles Winstead, the Texan known for insubordination. Regardless, Public Enemy Number One is now dead.

Six shots were fired—none by Dillinger. Two miss completely. Two others nick the bank robber but otherwise do no harm. Another penetrates the left side of his body. But the sixth shot shatters the vertebra in Dillinger's neck, destroying his spinal cord, passing through his brain, and exiting just beneath the right eye.

Dillinger slams into the ground face-first, landing just shy of the alley entrance. His last words are gibberish as the agents descend.

A crowd forms around the dead man. Hearing it is Dillinger, citizens dip their handkerchiefs into his pool of blood as a keepsake. DOI agents push them back, but the throng presses forward once again, everyone straining for a look. As one, men and women begin saying the same word over and over: "Dillinger."

✦

J. Edgar Hoover is put on notice.

The thirty-nine-year-old director has been waiting at home in Washington with his mother for word from Chicago. It is Agent Purvis who delivers the news, calling from the telephone in the theater office.

"We got him," says Purvis.

"Dead or alive?" asks Hoover.

"Dead."

Hoover races to the Justice Department. There, he holds a midnight press conference to announce the shooting. "The only good criminal," Hoover says, "is a dead criminal." The director expresses no remorse to the media about his agents shooting first.

Meanwhile, at the Cook County Morgue on West Polk Street in Chicago, "every politician and his friend in Chicago crowded into the morgue for the morbid purpose of viewing John Dillinger's remains," in the words of an official DOI report. In the midst of this chaos, a young chemist from a local embalming college convinces authorities to allow him to place wet plaster over Dillinger's face to mold a death mask. As a sign of his victory over John Dillinger—a moment some still consider the greatest day in Division of Investigation history—J. Edgar Hoover will place this mask on display outside his office, where it will remain for decades to come.

✦

So it is that John Dillinger is dead at age thirty-one. His criminal career lasted more than a decade, but it is the last year of his life for which the bank robber is infamous. In the period from September 1933 to his death in July 1934, the Dillinger Gang killed ten men, wounded seven more, staged three jailbreaks, and robbed eleven banks of more than $300,000.*

Years from now, when J. Edgar Hoover is asked about his "greatest thrill" as a crime fighter, the answer will come immediately: "The night we got Dillinger."

✦

In the dramatic midnight press conference, Hoover seizes a moment to shift America's eyes away from the deceased Dillinger. He promises re-porters that he will soon name a new Public Enemy Number One—the next day, Charles Arthur "Pretty Boy" Floyd receives that designation. A bounty of $23,000 is placed on Floyd's handsome, well-coiffed head.

The new Number One is already a legend in the bank-robbing

---

* Roughly $5.7 million in modern currency.

world. Bonnie and Clyde were so enamored of his skills that they once contacted him about joining forces—a request Floyd rejected, considering the young lovers to be more trouble than he could handle.

Floyd is a thirty-year-old Georgia native who moved to Oklahoma at the age of seven. He is divorced from his wife, Ruby, and never sees his nine-year-old son, Dempsey, named for the legendary prizefighter, Jack, whom Floyd idolizes. In addition to bank jobs, Floyd is thought to be responsible for almost a dozen murders, including the notorious Kansas City Massacre, where four law enforcement officers were shot to death. Floyd is also suspected of being part of John Dillinger's gang for his final robbery, that of the Merchants National Bank in South Bend. Floyd has not been seen publicly since that heist.

Although Charley Floyd is a media hero to some, he is actually a hardened criminal. He carries automatic weapons wherever he goes and thinks nothing of opening fire on any man or woman who crosses him.

✦

Agent Melvin Purvis is not directing the search for Pretty Boy. He has violated the Division of Investigation's number one rule. Director Hoover bristles as Purvis receives public accolades and celebrity for the Dillinger takedown. Hoover is publicly unwilling to state which agents killed the fugitive, not wanting the press and public to know he had hired a posse of violent men to do the division's dirty work. And though Purvis never claims to have fired a single round on the night of Dillinger's death, the absence of information about who actually pulled the trigger has led the press to make a hero of Melvin Purvis, giving him credit for the bank robber's demise.

Hoover responds by nitpicking the agent's behavior, demanding a strict accounting of Purvis's time and activities. The chasm between director and special agent grows day by day. On September 6, 1934, just six weeks after Melvin Purvis oversees the most successful event in DOI history, he is officially demoted. Sam Cowley, the jowly bureaucrat who attended the same law school as Hoover, now takes charge of the Chicago bureau.

A humiliated Purvis retains his job and office but is forbidden from venturing out into the streets to investigate leads. The agent is devastated by the demotion. Single and childless, Purvis lives for the division. But mundane paperwork now occupies his office hours, even as Cowley turns the screws on Chicago's DOI agents, desperate to fulfill Hoover's order that Pretty Boy Floyd be captured within "the next thirty to forty-five days." Melvin Purvis drinks to console himself, though in secret, knowing J. Edgar Hoover would not approve.

✦

To his friends, Pretty Boy Floyd is called "Choc," after a brand of beer known as Choctaw. The legend of his more famous nickname is unclear. Some say it was an old girlfriend who called him "Pretty Boy," while others claim the name came from a prostitute. But the career criminal hates the Pretty Boy moniker. He prefers to go by Charley. Floyd comes from a long line of dirt-poor sharecroppers who farm cotton on rented land. Though his father eventually runs a small grocery store, Floyd grows up in poverty, living with his parents in what is known as a "boxcar house"—a low, flat building with a tar-paper roof. There are just two rooms, a kitchen and bedroom. Newspapers are glued over cracks in the walls to keep out the wind. There is no heat or running water.

The Floyds are a religious family, active in the Hanson Baptist Church. But upon leaving school after the sixth grade, young Charley begins working the harvests in Kansas and Oklahoma. There he falls in with a tough crowd, becoming known for brawling, drinking, and chasing girls. At age twenty, he tries his hand at farming after getting married to seventeen-year-old Ruby Hardgraves but soon grows bored.

One year later, in 1925, Charley Floyd commits his first robbery, a Kroger grocery store. Floyd is soon arrested and sent to the Missouri State Penitentiary, where he serves four years, enduring an incarceration of floggings and brutal twelve-hour workdays. Ruby divorces him before his release in 1929.

But even after getting out of the penitentiary, Floyd is not really a free man. He takes up residence in Kansas City, where local police regularly arrest him for crimes he does not commit, knowing he is an ex-convict. Finally, in November 1929, eight months after earning his freedom, the man now nicknamed "Pretty Boy" learns that his father has been gunned down in the grocery store.

Walter Floyd was tough and sometimes overbearing, but his son deeply respects his father. When Walter's killer is exonerated on charges of self-defense, Pretty Boy's immersion into the criminal world becomes complete. His father's assailant soon vanishes, never to be seen again.

Pretty Boy Floyd has taken his revenge. He will kill nine more times over the course of his life. Using a blade, he will carve a notch into his pocket watch for each murder.

✦

As the summer of 1934 turns to autumn, the post-Dillinger hunt for other top bank robbers becomes intense. In addition to Public Enemy Number One Floyd, police and DOI agents across the nation are looking for criminals like Baby Face Nelson and the equally notorious Karpis-Barker Gang. Robbing banks has been part of the national culture for a hundred years, a get rich quick crime with its own unique romance originating during the nation's western expansion. But the publicity and glory of bank robbing has never been so great as it is now.

The Great Depression, which began in 1929, has embittered millions of Americans to the financial industry. Banks foreclose on desperate farmers and workers. The poor have no power, and the financiers have a lot of power. Bank robbers and other grifters become accepted avengers.

Pretty Boy Floyd has even been nicknamed the "Sagebrush Robin Hood" for his prairie roots and has inspired devotion throughout the Midwest for his habit of buying groceries for poor families and tearing up mortgages in the course of robberies. Floyd is renowned for being courteous and impeccably groomed during those stickups. He never wears a mask to conceal his identity. His four front teeth are capped in gold, and he flashes a tattoo of a rose on his left forearm. Such is Floyd's popularity in rural areas that total strangers often prepare him meals and hide him from the authorities. In return, he always leaves money as a way of saying thanks.

Charley Floyd's former wife and son are even capitalizing on the bank robber's notoriety, earning their living by performing a stage show titled *Crime Doesn't Pay*.

Yet crime does pay. America's most wanted criminals are flush with cash and spend it easily, often paying for purchases with thick rolls of bills from their armed heists. But the robbers are hardly carefree. Now that Hoover and his federal agents have nationwide control of the manhunt, the robbers feel pressure no matter where they go. Baby Face Nelson is currently camping in Nevada and California, unable to stay in a proper hotel because his face is so well known. Compatriots in the underworld who once sheltered Nelson now refuse to hide him, describing his current state as "too hot."

Pretty Boy Floyd is in a similar fix. Like John Dillinger before him, Charley Floyd is rumored to be everywhere at once. Some say he's in Mexico, while others even insist he has joined the Chinese army. In reality, Floyd's cut from the South Bend robbery is running out and he can almost feel the federal noose tightening. He is hiding in Buffalo, New York, but after Dillinger's death, Floyd decides the time has come to return home to Oklahoma.

En route, on October 19, 1934, Charley Floyd and two other men rob the Peoples Bank in Tiltonsville, Ohio. The take is a paltry $500. A four-year-old girl bursts into tears during the robbery. "Don't cry, little girl," Floyd soothes her. "We ain't going to hurt you."

The child's terrified mother holds out the small deposit of three dollars she is about to make. Floyd refuses to take the money.

The subsequent getaway is unremarkable. By nightfall Floyd is forty miles away. But the following morning, a Saturday, just outside the Ohio town of Wellsville, Pretty Boy Floyd loses control of his Ford sedan on a rain-slicked road. The car slides into a telephone pole. Floyd is traveling with a partner in crime, Adam Richetti, along with their girlfriends, Beulah and Rose Baird. As always, Floyd is armed with a machine gun. Believing that two sisters would be less conspicuous than two men, Floyd instructs the ladies to drive into town and have the car repaired. Floyd and Richetti will hide on a nearby hillside until they return.

The breakdown was an ominous reminder of past events for Floyd. One year ago, while driving through Missouri with Richetti, their vehicle suffered mechanical issues. Upon taking the car to a local shop for repairs, the pair are surprised to see the local sheriff walk into the garage. Immediately, Floyd and Richetti kidnap the lawman at gun-point, steal a vehicle from the garage, and drive him fifty miles north before setting the sheriff free.

Floyd and Richetti escape into Kansas, arriving in Kansas City at 10:00 p.m. Floyd has previously spent a great deal of time there and has a number of contacts. The two criminals choose to hide out in the home of an assassin named Vernon Miller, a South Dakota native and World War I army veteran whose wartime specialty was operating a machine gun.

By sheer coincidence, Miller has been contracted by a Chicago crime syndicate to commit a murder the following day. He tells his house-guests of an elaborate plan to free a career criminal named Frank Nash from federal custody. Nash, who recently escaped from the Leaven-worth Penitentiary in Kansas, has been recaptured and is being escorted by two Division of Investigation agents back to Leavenworth. Miller's job is to intercept the agents as they alight from a morning train. But a solo job is risky. Prior to the arrival of Floyd and Richetti, Miller has spent hours trying to recruit cohorts. He has been unsuccessful. But Floyd and Richetti instantly agree to help him.

On the morning of June 17, 1933, Miller, Floyd, and Richetti drive to the Kansas City's Union Railway station in a stolen Chevrolet. They observe federal agents and police officers armed with shotguns waiting for the train.

It is shortly after agents escort Frank Nash off the train that a gun-fight begins. The shooting lasts only thirty seconds. When it is over, three Kansas City policemen and federal agent R. J. Caffrey lie dead.

The three gunmen then rush to free Nash, who has also been shot. "They're all dead. Let's get out of here," one of the shooters yells, leaving Frank Nash to bleed out in the street.

The killers are not followed as their Chevrolet speeds from the station. Floyd and Richetti conceal themselves so expertly during the shooting that it will be many months before federal agents can place them at what will be labeled the "Kansas City Massacre."

The same, however, cannot be said of Vernon Miller, though it is not the federal government that will bring him to justice. The assas-sin's failure to successfully extricate Frank Nash alive will prove very unpopular in Chicago. Five months after the massacre, Miller's strangled body is found in a roadside ditch, his head caved in after repeated blows from a claw hammer.

✦

With Kansas City still fresh on his mind, Pretty Boy Floyd knows he cannot risk another encounter with the law. Thus, he sends Beulah and Rose Baird into Wellsville to get their car fixed.

And so begin the last forty-eight hours of Charley Floyd's short life. He and his accomplice are soon spied by locals, who report the presence of suspicious men to local law enforcement. Richetti is quickly arrested. He is just twenty-four and will soon be executed in the Missouri State Penitentiary gas chamber for his role in the Kansas City Massacre.

But Pretty Boy Floyd will never go back to jail. He escapes into nearby woods, where he lives off the land for two days. Finally, starving and exhausted, he knocks on a farmhouse door and asks for a plate of food. The time is just past noon on October 22, 1934.

Unbeknownst to Floyd, the Division of Investigation is on his tail. Floyd's movements have been sighted by several eyewitnesses. By 4:25 p.m., two Chevrolets loaded with DOI agents and local police are blocking the driveway to the farmhouse where Floyd has just finished his last supper of spare ribs, bread, and pumpkin pie.

Leading the agents is none other than Melvin Purvis, sent to Ohio by J. Edgar Hoover as a chance for redemption. As the team of agents prepare to open fire, Floyd runs and takes cover behind a corn crib. It is Purvis who gives the kill order: "Let him have it!"

Purvis fires his service revolver six times but does not hit Charley Floyd, who begins sprinting across a field of clover to the safety of dense woods. All told, more than one hundred other shots are fired simultaneously by the agents and police—pistols, Winchester rifles, and machine guns.

Three bullets do strike Pretty Boy Floyd. His gun hand can longer function due to a round shattering his right arm. Two other bullets tear through his torso, breaking Floyd's ribs, severing major arteries, and destroying his stomach, small intestine, right kidney, and pancreas.

Pretty Boy Floyd falls to the ground, one pistol in his waistband and another clutched in his useless right hand.

He is dying.

Special Agent Purvis walks across the field and leans over the bank robber. "You are Pretty Boy Floyd," he says, seeking confirmation.

"I'm Charles Arthur Floyd."

Moments later, Floyd breathes his last.*

✦

A pleased J. Edgar Hoover immediately names a new Public Enemy Number One. Even as more than twenty thousand people from an estimated twenty states travel to Oklahoma for the funeral of Pretty Boy Floyd, the director tells the world about yet another notorious murderer and bank robber. "He's a crazy killer," says Hoover. "A vicious half-pint yellow killer who shoots without provocation."

Indeed, the handsome young man nicknamed Baby Face Nelson is a psychopath but also a poor shot, which is a bad combination for any man wielding a machine gun.

Born Lester Joseph Gillis, the career criminal was raised in Chicago, the seventh son of Belgian immigrant parents. His mother, Marie, dotes on her youngest boy, even claiming that the blond-haired, blue-eyed Lester is the most attractive of her children. The family lives in an area of southwest Chicago known as The Patch, populated almost entirely by first-generation immigrants. From an early age, the future killer shows enormous compassion for animals, often bringing home stray dogs and kittens. Much to the chagrin of his mother, a former teacher, Lester also develops an aversion to school, preferring to walk the streets instead of attending class.

Since the end of the American Civil War in 1865, two distinct cultures have developed in Chicago. The first is the Union Stockyards, 475

---

* In September 1979, Captain Chester Smith of the East Liverpool Police Department came forth with a different version of the events surrounding the death of Pretty Boy Floyd. Smith, who was present at the time of Floyd's arrest, claimed in *Time* magazine that Purvis ordered fellow agent Herman Hollis to fire a machine-gun burst into Floyd, who had already been captured and disarmed. The FBI disavows this claim.

acres of cattle, hogs, and sheep destined to be slaughtered, butchered, and shipped all around the country. No place in the world processes more meat than Chicago. The brutal manual labor of slaughterhouses and stockyards is the only employment open to many immigrants. Lester's father tans cow hides for a living, enduring sweltering temperatures in the summer, subzero gales in the winter, and the pungent smells of animal waste and rotting carcasses all year round. This is the life awaiting young Lester Gillis.

The other culture that has come to define Chicago is the criminal gang. These gangs comprise mainly immigrant men who choose to live a life of crime, believing that being murdered or imprisoned is preferable to a life in the packing houses. Many gangs are divided along ethnic lines, particularly between the Italians and Irish. Their specialties include extortion, bootlegging alcohol, and car theft. The gangs also play a major role in Chicago society. Local politicians and business owners secretly hire young hoodlums to terrorize their rivals. This relationship between the criminal world and Chicago's wealthy elite is gaining the city a reputation for widespread corruption, which will endure for decades.

For young Lester Gillis, so fond of skipping school and wandering through Chicago, it is only a matter of time before he falls in with the criminal element.

His first arrest is a complete accident. The date is July 4, 1921. Lester and a friend come across a revolver belonging to the other boy's father. Thinking it will be fun to shoot a gun on the Fourth of July, they take the pistol to an alley, where Lester's shot ricochets, hitting a nearby child in the jaw. Though the boy survives, twelve-year-old Lester Gillis is sentenced to one year in the Cook County School for Boys.

Soon after his release, Lester is sentenced to eighteen months in the Illinois State School for Boys after stealing a car. He is later returned to the same institution for a second auto theft. Then a third. His beleaguered father commits suicide during this time, leaving Lester's mother penniless. A devoted son, Lester promises to support his mother upon his release from prison.

For a short time, Lester Gillis keeps his promise. He marries a store clerk named Helen Wawzynak, takes care of his mother, and keeps his criminal behavior to a minimum. Lester likes cars and works at a Standard Oil station. He and Helen have a son, Ronald. But when Helen becomes pregnant for a second time, a strapped Lester Gillis—believing the only way to make ends meet is a return to his criminal past—forms a gang.

Between January 6 and November 23, 1930, Lester Gillis breaks into the homes of two prominent Chicago families, stealing $300,000 in jewelry.* He also robs the Itasca State Bank, kills his first man when he fatally shoots a Chicago stockbroker during a botched robbery, and takes part in a gun battle outside an Illinois roadhouse resulting in the deaths of three patrons. Lester's handsome personal appearance and short stature are easily remembered by eyewitnesses: "He had a baby face," one woman will recall. "Good-looking. Hardly more than a boy."

Lester Gillis had previously used the last name "Nelson" as one of many aliases. Thus, "Baby Face" Nelson is born.

✦

One year later, in 1931, police arrest Nelson and his gang. He is sentenced to a term of one to ten years in the Illinois State Penitentiary at Joliet. While in prison, Nelson is charged with another crime and must travel to Wheaton, Illinois, to stand trial. There he receives a term of one year to life. Helen is in the courtroom to witness the verdict.

So it is, at just twenty-three years old, that Baby Face Nelson's criminal career seems to be over. The date is February 17, 1933. He is allowed to say goodbye in the courtroom to Helen, who then follows her husband and his guard to the Wheaton train depot to see him off. Baby Face looks anything but tough, shivering as light snow flurries buffet the depot on a cold gray Wednesday. He wears leg irons, and his right wrist is handcuffed to prison guard R. N. Martin. For good measure, deputies frisk the prisoner before he is bundled aboard the train back to Joliet.

Helen watches the train leave the station. To this day, it is not known how she smuggled a gun to her husband. Some believe she hid it in a train station restroom, where Lester was allowed to go unshack-

---

* $5,600,000 in modern currency.

led. Others speculate that perhaps Baby Face's sister Leona, who had also come to watch the trial, had delivered the weapon. What is known is that upon arriving in Joliet, guard R. N. Martin hails a cab to drive Baby Face Nelson back to the penitentiary. The two men get into the back seat. The ride begins quietly, with Baby Face staring out the window in deep thought.

Suddenly, as the car comes within sight of the prison's enormous stone walls, Baby Face Nelson pokes a pistol in Martin's ribs. "Don't give me a reason to kill you," he tells the guard. Forcing Martin to unlock his shackles, Baby Face orders the driver to continue driving straight past the prison gates and back to Chicago. Four miles outside the town of Cicero, Baby Face directs driver Joe Candic to pull off onto a side road. After stealing ten dollars from Martin's wallet, Nelson lets his prisoners go outside the Resurrection Cemetery. Then he drives to Chicago, a free man.

The twenty-three-year-old is now a national fugitive—one of the most hunted criminals in America.

And Baby Face Nelson could not be happier—he likes the action.

✦

Nelson spends the next two years driving back and forth across the country. Sometimes he travels with Helen and his two children, but other times they stay with family.

Nelson's habit is to hide for a time in the growing cities of San Francisco and Reno, where he is less known. When he needs money, he drives back to the Midwest to rob a bank. But Baby Face Nelson is becoming more erratic, fond of squeezing off machine-gun bursts as he flees, unconcerned about striking innocent bystanders.

Yet compared to John Dillinger, Baby Face is still a small-time hoodlum. On December 28, 1933, when the State of Illinois issues its list of most wanted criminals, Dillinger is at the top and Nelson at the bottom, ranked number twenty-one.

In March 1934, word reaches Baby Face through mutual friends that the infamous Dillinger would like his assistance. Though the two men have never met, associates of Dillinger ask him to help fund the bribes that will make the bank robber's escape from the Crown Point

---

46 ◆ BILL O'REILLY and MARTIN DUGARD

County Jail a reality. A strapped Dillinger promises to pay back Nelson through the proceeds of future heists.

Thus, both are present at Little Bohemia when federal agents surround the travel lodge in April 1934. Helen is arrested and taken into custody on that night. Baby Face, making his escape, confronts and kills DOI special agent W. Carter Baum at point-blank range. In time, Baby Face Nelson will kill more federal agents than any other Public Enemy Number One, a total of three.

The murder of Agent Baum elevates Nelson's profile within the division—and the criminal underworld. He befriends not only John Dillinger but also Pretty Boy Floyd and another highly wanted felon named Alvin Karpis, thus becoming the common thread among the four men who will all eventually be named Public Enemy Number One.

On June 30, 1934, Baby Face works with Dillinger and Pretty Boy Floyd to rob the Merchants National Bank in South Bend, Indiana. The action publicly humiliates the Division of Investigation by showing that the three most wanted men in America can rob banks at will.

Yet South Bend is also nearly a catastrophe. While Dillinger, Floyd, and the rest of the gang work smoothly and professionally, executing a carefully prepared plan, Baby Face appears rattled and anxious. He is nearly killed, shot in the chest by a local jeweler. Amazingly, an iron vest stops the bullet, saving Nelson's life. He looses a burst from his machine gun in retaliation, missing the jeweler but wounding a bystander. Then, as the gang races from the bank toward their waiting getaway car, a local teenager leaps on Nelson's back and tries to tackle him. The tussle ends when Nelson brings the butt of his gun down hard on the boy's head.

In the end, Nelson escapes. He then drives across the country and disappears into the anonymity of the American west. Helen, recently paroled after her Little Bohemia conviction, joins him. The couple take care not to commit crimes that might give them away. Incredibly, Baby Face and Helen are taken into custody by small-town police in Utah for speeding. But, after paying a five-dollar fine, Nelson is let go. His car, filled with its usual cargo of machine guns and ammunition, is not searched.

Baby Face Nelson knows he is lucky.

But that luck will soon run out.

✦

John Dillinger is dead, shot by federal agents in Chicago on July 22, 1934.

Pretty Boy Floyd is dead, shot by federal agents outside Chicago on October 22, 1934.

Two days later, Baby Face Nelson decides to drive from Nevada to Chicago. Money is running low and he hears rumors that DOI agents have been seen searching local campgrounds, knowing that is his preferred hideout.

On Monday, November 26, Baby Face and Helen drive into Chicago with a criminal named John Paul Chase. Helen is dropped on the North Side to see a movie. Nelson then steals a brand-new Ford V-8. That night, Baby Face and Helen sleep in the car, but the cold weather makes it obvious that they need to move indoors. Baby Face knows of a resort just above the Illinois-Wisconsin border called the Lake Como Inn. He's stayed there before and is confident that once the hotel closes for the winter they can hide there without fear of discovery.

On the morning of November 27, Baby Face and Helen drive north from Chicago in the stolen Ford. John Paul Chase rides with them. At 2:00 p.m., the three arrive at the home of Hobart Hermanson, owner of the Lake Como Inn. Hermanson is a former bootlegger with connections to the Chicago underworld and can be depended upon to remain silent about suspicious guests—or so Nelson thinks.

Baby Face pulls into the driveway and notices a young man squinting at the car. The bank robber doesn't recognize the man, which he finds odd, having spent considerable time at the inn and getting to know the staff. Without shutting off the engine, Baby Face rolls down the window and makes pleasantries, inquiring about Hermanson.

The scene is calm, and the man on the porch has no clue that the legendary Baby Face Nelson is clutching a .38-caliber pistol, ready to shoot him dead should anything go wrong.

After being told that Hermanson is on vacation, Baby Face backs out and drives away. Much to Helen's surprise, he is in a panic.

"That was a G-man," says Baby Face, using underworld terminology for government agents. "And we caught him with his pants down."

✦

"That's Baby Face Nelson," Special Agent James Metcalfe anxiously tells himself.

Metcalfe, a veteran of the Dillinger Squad, has been on a stakeout in the home of Hobart Hermanson for three weeks. Two other agents are also living in the house, tipped off that Nelson planned to spend the winter there. By a stroke of luck, they captured the girlfriend of John Paul Chase in San Francisco, who gave them explicit details about the Lake Como Inn and Nelson's plans. Hermanson was then questioned about Nelson's previous visit. He feigned surprise at the true identity of his former guest but offered to help the Division of Investigation in any way possible. Thus, three DOI agents moved into Hermanson's home.

It is 2:30 p.m. when Agent Metcalfe uses a local pay phone to call the Chicago office. Sam Cowley takes the call. Preparing to leave immediately for Lake Como, he stops in the office of Agent Purvis to tell him of the Baby Face sighting.

"Let's get going," says Purvis.

But Cowley reminds Purvis that Baby Face has already driven away from the inn. And although Agent Metcalfe called in a license plate number, finding Nelson on the highway might be difficult. Cowley scrambles Special Agents W. C. Ryan and T. M. McDade, pulling them away from a separate investigation with orders to proceed immediately up Highway 12 toward Wisconsin.

Purvis phones Washington to apprise Hoover of the situation. The director still thinks unfavorably of Agent Purvis, so it is an aide who receives the briefing about Nelson's new location.

✦

The action happens very quickly.

The time is 4:00 p.m. as the black Ford V-8 travels southeast on Highway 12 toward Chicago. Baby Face and Helen ride up front, with Chase in the back. The road is divided by a grass median. A half mile north of Fox River Grove, Illinois, Special Agents McDade and Ryan spot the stolen Ford, Illinois license plate 639-578. They travel two hundred yards up the road to a bend, then prepare to make a U-turn and give chase. McDade is fresh out of training school and seeing his first action, but Ryan is a veteran of the Little Bohemia and Biograph Theater shootings. As McDade drives, Ryan unholsters his .38 Super pistol.

Nelson suspects he is being followed. So he makes a U-turn of his own and drives straight toward the agents.

Minutes pass, and Baby Face Nelson pulls alongside Agents McDade and Ryan. Without warning, John Paul Chase leans over from the back seat and aims a Browning rifle at the agents. He lets loose a burst but misses the men.

The situation seems hopeless for the G-men. In the reverse of almost any normal situation, it is the criminals who control the highway. McDade and Ryan lack firepower compared to the gangsters, carrying only sidearms.

Agent McDade does not pull over. Instead, he steps on the gas, swerving to miss a milk truck while pulling away from Nelson. John Paul Chase opens fire again, hitting the back of the federal vehicle from close range but not striking either agent. McDade and Ryan drive with their heads low for three hundred yards, before Ryan turns and fires seven shots at Nelson's car. One bullet pierces the Ford's radiator.

Baby Face nurses the Ford down the highway. McDade and Ryan pull ahead, then stop near a field, anticipating the gangster's car. They will wait in vain, for Baby Face Nelson exits the highway to avoid this confrontation.

Simultaneously, Agents Sam Cowley and Ed Hollis arrive on the scene. Hollis was one of the three DOI agents who shot John Dillinger and now prepares to take aim at Baby Face as well. They watch as Nelson's car leaves the highway at a place known as Park Road. Cowley and Hollis give chase. The disabled Ford comes to a stop as the two agents close in.

But before Cowley and Hollis can stop their Hudson sedan, Nelson and Chase are standing on the Ford's running boards, shooting at the agents as Helen presses herself into a ditch to take cover. Nelson fires a machine gun as Chase takes aim with his semiautomatic BAR.* Cowley and Hollis are not hit as they swerve to a stop, then use their vehicle as a shield to return fire from a distance of forty yards.

In the ten-minute gun battle that ensues, Special Agents Sam Cowley and Herman Hollis are shot dead. Hollis dies instantly, a bullet from Nelson's machine gun piercing his forehead and exploding out the back of his skull. Cowley, shot several times in the stomach, hangs on for ten hours before dying at a local hospital. Agent Melvin Purvis, along with Cowley's wife and young son, are at his bedside.

In the meantime, Baby Face steals the Hudson sedan that the agents were driving. There are bullet holes in the rear of the vehicle and back window. Baby Face, Helen, and John Paul Chase drive to the home of a local priest whom they have met several times before. But Father Phillip Coughlan refuses to provide them shelter for fear of implicating his sister, who owns the house. So Baby Face travels on, arriving at a known safe house in the nearby town of Niles Center. Baby Face, Helen, and Chase leave their car shortly after 5:00 p.m. It is already dark. They enter the small gray stucco home at 1627 Walnut Street without being spotted.

Baby Face Nelson has gotten away again—or so the Division of Investigation believes. A massive federal manhunt begins immediately.

The first break is when the Hudson belonging to Agents Cowley and Hollis is found abandoned in Winnetka, Illinois, its front seat covered in blood.

✦

Immediately after arriving at the safe house, Helen cuts off Nelson's blood-soaked clothing to treat his wounds, but she is too late. The gangster dies at 7:35 p.m. By then Chase had fled with the stolen Hud-

---

* The Browning Automatic Rifle, or BAR, was originally designed by John Browning in 1917 for use by American troops in World War I. The weapon would go on to see widespread use in World War II and the Korean War.

son, leaving the couple to their fates. It is 1:30 a.m. when the owner of the safe house insists they dump the body. Baby Face Nelson's naked corpse is wrapped in a red, green, and black Navajo Indian blanket, loaded into an Oldsmobile, and driven to the edge of town by Helen and the owner of the safe house. It is then dropped outside St. Paul's Cemetery. Helen insists he be laid upon the grass near the gate instead of on pavement. Before leaving, she tucks the blanket tightly around her husband to keep him warm. "I wanted Les to be comfortable," Helen will later testify. "He always hated the cold."

That morning, an undertaker at the Sadowski Funeral Home in the town of Niles Center receives an anonymous phone call, directing him to a corpse dumped outside St. Paul's Cemetery.

The body is naked. Buckshot wounds speckle both legs, and a machine-gun round has torn open the abdomen. It is a gruesome sight.

The corpse is that of Baby Face Nelson.

✦

Helen is then driven to the North Side of Chicago, where she wanders the streets for two days. The newspaper headlines scream that she is America's first female public enemy, and J. Edgar Hoover issues an order to "find the woman and give no quarter." In the end, she turns herself in. Helen is later convicted of violating her parole agreement from the Little Bohemia shootings. She serves one year and a day at the Women's Correctional Farm in Milan, Michigan, but faces no other legal charges. When asked why she went along with her husband's wicked ways, Helen answers: "I loved Les. When you love a guy, you love him. That's all there is to it."

Helen Gillis never remarries. Later in life, she goes by the name Helen Nelson.

✦

After the anonymous phone call concerning the location of Baby Face's corpse, the body is transported to the Cook County Medical Examiner's Office in Chicago—the same place John Dillinger was taken. The public is allowed to file past during a public viewing. On December 1, 1934, the twenty-six-year-old Lester Gillis is laid to rest at the St.

Joseph Cemetery in River Grove, where he is buried next to his father. Two hundred people attend the funeral. The six pallbearers are all men with known connections to the Chicago underworld.

There is no eulogy, no priest, and no music.

The only sound is that of Baby Face Nelson's crying mother.*

✦

Almost immediately, J. Edgar Hoover sets up another confrontation. The new Public Enemy Number One is a kidnapper, bank robber, and murderer named Alvin Karpis. The twenty-seven-year-old "Creepy" Karpis is Canadian-born and possesses a photographic memory. He describes his profession as "robbing banks, knocking off payrolls, and kidnapping rich men." Karpis has aligned himself with a family of criminals known as the Barkers, consisting of the brothers "Doc" and Fred, and their mother, Kate, simply known as Ma. Together the Karpis-Barker Gang have terrorized much of the Midwest. Karpis's whereabouts are currently unknown, but Hoover feels that his capture or killing should not take long. Karpis had plastic surgery in March 1934, along with a procedure to burn off his fingerprints. Both operations were unsuccessful, meaning that his appearance is not only easily recognizable but also portrayed on wanted posters splashed across the United States.

But if the pursuit of Alvin Karpis feels different to Hoover from that of previous Public Enemy Number Ones, it is because none other than President Franklin D. Roosevelt has begun a personal involvement in the case. On January 17, 1934, Edward George Bremer of St. Paul, Minnesota, is kidnapped at gunpoint by the Karpis-Barker gang. The ransom is set at $200,000.†

Bremer is a prominent local financier, chairman of the American National Bank and also manager of the Home Owners' Loan Corporation. In the eyes of the public, the dark-haired Bremer is a villain, the sort of banker embodying the foreclosures and repossessions so common in America during the Great Depression. The gangsters who

---

* Helen Gillis and Mary Gillis would later be buried alongside Baby Face.
† $3,826,776 in modern money.

slid inside the banker's Lincoln Continental at a crosswalk, guns drawn, just seconds after he dropped his nine-year-old daughter Hertzy off at her private school, are making such men know the same pain countless families across the country now feel. In fact, Bremer is known to be selfish and possess a volatile temper. A DOI report on his character will state that "he is very much disliked, not only by his family, but generally."

Bremer fights back ferociously, and almost manages to escape while being abducted, but is struck repeatedly over the head with a handgun after his car is hijacked, then pushed to the floor. Goggles are placed over his eyes. Bremer leaves behind so much blood from his pistol whipping that investigators will doubt his survival.

If Edward Bremer were just another banker, the crime might not have made national headlines. But Bremer is also the son of Adolph Bremer, owner of the Jacob Schmidt Brewing Company. The older Bremer is a major campaign contributor to President Roosevelt's upcoming 1936 reelection campaign and is considered such a valuable supporter that his company will soon receive an exclusive contract to provide beer to the United States Army.

Upon receiving word of the kidnapping, a sympathetic Roosevelt speaks publicly about Bremer's abduction, calling it "an attack on all we hold dear."

Hoover's agents are unable to find a single clue to Bremer's whereabouts, and the family soon pays the ransom, using marked bills provided by the DOI. On February 7, three weeks after the kidnapping, Edward Bremer is released.

Of course, the manhunt continues. Using details provided by Bremer, as well as discovering key fingerprints that place the Karpis-Barker gang at the scene of the crime, the DOI arrests "Doc" Barker, who is eventually sentenced to life in prison. On January 8, 1935, Fred Barker and the notorious Ma Barker, whom many consider the logistical mastermind of the robberies and kidnappings, are shot dead by the DOI at their hideout in Lake Weir, Florida.*

---

* Arthur "Doc" Barker spent four years in Alcatraz but tried to escape and was shot dead by guards.

But Public Enemy Number One, Alvin Karpis, remains at large. And J. Edgar Hoover has absolutely no idea where to find him.

✦

"Did you ever make an arrest?" the Tennessee senator asks J. Edgar Hoover. The date is April 11, 1936. The last year has been a success for the director, who forced the resignation of Agent Melvin Purvis by falsely accusing him of public drunkenness. And at Hoover's insistence, on July 1, 1935, the Division of Investigation was renamed the Federal Bureau of Investigation in hopes that the public will find the name easier to remember. But fifteen months have passed since the Bremer kidnapping, and Alvin Karpis is still nowhere to be found.

The director is now appearing before the Senate Appropriations Committee, boldly asking that the FBI's annual budget be doubled to $5 million. Hoover has come prepared, armed with charts, graphs, and a deep pile of statistics to buttress his request. But Senator Kenneth McKellar has a deep dislike for Hoover, founded by the director's refusal to hire more men from Tennessee as special agents. In fact, Hoover does quite the opposite by firing three special agents with Tennessee roots shortly after McKellar's request.

Now the senator is getting his revenge. As chairman of the Senate Appropriations Committee, the bellicose McKellar, who wears wire-rimmed glasses and a dark suit, is within his rights to question Hoover in detail. But rather than focus on money, the senator has belittled the director publicly, making Hoover squirm so much that Missouri freshman senator Harry Truman has even intervened on his behalf, hoping to lighten the line of questioning.

But McKellar presses on, demanding to know Hoover's qualifications to lead the FBI.

"No, sir," Hoover responds to McKellar's question about making arrests. "I have made investigations."

"How many arrests have you made, and who were they?"

Hoover deflects, describing the many cases he has managed.

"Did you make the arrests?" McKellar demands.

"The arrests were made by . . . officers under my supervision."

"I am talking about the actual arrests . . . you never arrested them, actually?"

The director does not answer the question.

"Here is a man who never captured a criminal in his life, never solved a case in his life," McKellar concludes, his destruction of Hoover complete.

The director will remember this day for the rest of his life, though not because the Senate turned down his request for additional appropriation. Instead, it is the public humiliation that remains with him, which Hoover compares with being publicly castrated.

And for J. Edgar Hoover, for whom a positive public impression is vital, nothing is more important than his image.

So Hoover swings into action.

✦

No one can find the handcuffs.

Just two weeks after J. Edgar's debacle before the Senate, Alvin Karpis has been spotted in New Orleans. Local residents have tipped off the FBI about the gangster's location. Agents confirm this, but rather than make an immediate arrest, the agents place a call to Hoover in Washington. Upon being notified, the director immediately flies south to apprehend the suspect himself. Shortly after 5:00 p.m. on May 1, Karpis and an accomplice leave their apartment on Canal Street and step into a Plymouth Coupe. Just as Karpis settles into his seat, five special agents surround the car, guns drawn.

Hoover steps through the crowd. "Put the cuffs on him, boys," the director says grandly.

But no one thought to *bring* handcuffs. Instead, Alvin Karpis is bound with the necktie of Special Agent Clarence Hurt.

The fourth and final federal Public Enemy Number One is now in custody and Director Hoover finally has an arrest.

✦

Alvin Karpis is flown to St. Paul, where he stands trial for kidnapping and is sentenced to life in prison. Karpis is incarcerated at the new Alcatraz federal penitentiary in the middle of San Francisco Bay. There, he does his time alongside another Public Enemy Number One—Al Capone.

The term *Public Enemy* was made famous by J. Edgar Hoover, but it was not his idea at all. It was 1930 when the Chicago Crime Commission named Capone the city's Public Enemy Number One. His type of crime was not the robbing of a bank but a far more complex web of misdeeds ranging from bootlegging to extortion to murder for hire. And unlike bank robbers, Capone does not operate informally. He is part of a larger body of felons seeking to control the criminal enterprises of entire cities.

These men go by several names: Mafia, Cosa Nostra, Black Hand, the Organization.

Or simply: the Mob.

And while J. Edgar Hoover believes the demise of Bonnie and Clyde, John Dillinger, Pretty Boy Floyd, and Baby Face Nelson signal that he has triumphed in the war on crime, the truth is that the "Mob" is far more dangerous than individual gangsters.

Which J. Edgar Hoover will soon learn the hard way.

CHAPTER FIVE

Al Capone lets down his guard.

It is shortly after breakfast as the man nicknamed Scarface works his shift, mopping the prison shower room. He once wore expensive suits and diamonds but now displays the standard Alcatraz uniform of blue chambray shirt, trousers, belt, and shoes. Capone is thirty-seven, the former head of a notorious Chicago crime syndicate that earned profits of more than $100 million annually.* He lived without fear of arrest—paying off judges, police, and politicians to ensure his freedom. But the mental acuity necessary to oversee a criminal enterprise is now beyond Capone because of a chronic syphilitic infection that is eroding his mind. And while Alphonse Gabriel Capone was once the most feared Mob boss in America, reputed to have killed more than thirty human beings, he is now just another inmate at this escape-proof prison on a windy island in the middle of San Francisco Bay.

Capone knows he has enemies here at Alcatraz. He has a reputation among the inmates for seeking special treatment from Warden James A. Johnston, who has famously declared that his prisoners are

---

* Worth more than $18 billion in modern currency.

A candid photo of Al Capone; his wife, Mae;
his son, Albert Francis "Sonny" Capone; and Sonny's wife, Ruth,
outside his Florida home.

"entitled to food, clothing, shelter, and medical attention. Anything else you get is a privilege." This dictum, also known as Rule Number Five in the inmate regulation handbook, is the reason Warden Johnston constantly denies Capone favors.

But that doesn't stop the Mob boss from trying. In one instance, he attempts to avoid the wait at the prison barbershop. "Get to the back of the line, you bum," says fellow inmate James Lucas, a twenty-two-year-old Texan known as a chronic hothead.

"Do you know who I am, punk?" snarls the thickset Capone.

Lucas grabs a pair of barber shears and presses a blade into Capone's jugular vein. "Yeah, I know who you are, grease ball. And if you don't get back to the end of the line, I'm going to know who you *were.*"

The two men—one, a bank robber and car thief; the other, America's most famous mobster—become mortal enemies after the incident. Capone puts out the word that anyone who kills Lucas will be handsomely rewarded.

But it is Lucas who takes action. As Al Capone mops the shower room, the young Texan attacks from behind, slashing at the gangster with scissors. Capone wheels and throws up his hands to defend himself, but blood flows onto the floor as Lucas plunges the scissors into his fellow inmate's back, chest, and palms.

Sounds of the fight bring guard Thomas J. Sanders on the run. Beating Lucas severely with his billy club, Sanders puts an end to the murder attempt. James Lucas is quickly sent to D-Block and placed in solitary confinement. Al Capone is hustled off to the prison infirmary for treatment of his wounds. He survives, though with a new set of scars to go with the three others cascading so dramatically down his left cheek. Four years into an eleven-year sentence for tax evasion, Capone quickly returns to life as an Alcatraz inmate. At night, like the other prisoners, he is tormented by laughter and partying in the city of San Francisco—the sounds carried across the cold waters of the bay, as if the nightlife was right next door.

But it is not. San Francisco is over one mile away from this island the inmates call "The Rock."

✦

For Al Capone, it has always been about not keeping his mouth shut.

He is eighteen and working as a bartender and bouncer at a cabaret in Brooklyn's Coney Island called the Harvard Inn. The young man can be charming, but one evening as he takes a shine to a beautiful patron, he prefers to be crass. "Honey," Capone whispers to a dark-haired woman sitting at a table with another man, "you have a nice ass and I mean that as a compliment. Believe me."

The beauty's name is Lena Galluccio. The other man is her brother. A drunken Frank Galluccio lunges at Capone after hearing the lewd comments. Capone fights back. Galluccio draws a pocket knife and slashes at the young bartender, slicing open the left side of his face. As Frank and Lena hustle from the dance hall to escape further conflict, a dazed and bleeding Capone is rushed to the hospital. Soon after his release, face still covered in stitches, the future mobster goes looking for Galluccio, seeking revenge.

As it turns out, both men work for crime families. A meeting is arranged to broker a truce. It is a hoodlum named Charles "Lucky" Luciano who arranges the sit down at the Harvard Inn with both men.

Al Capone is ordered to apologize for insulting Lena. He is also told not to seek revenge. Capone does not argue the ruling, understanding that he must obey or die.

Capone also understands his new nickname: Scarface.

This is the way of life within the world of organized crime. The syndicates consider themselves family units, and leaders are sought out for their wisdom in times of conflict. Capone enters this world after dropping out of school at the age of fourteen. He first belongs to a Brooklyn street gang named the Rippers, who mainly steal cigarettes. But soon a twenty-five-year-old mobster named Francesco Ioele—a.k.a. Frankie Yale—takes young Capone under his wing.

Yale is a criminal visionary, the first gangster to use the term *family* to describe Italian immigrants who perform acts of racketeering, extortion, and murder. He is not averse to working with local Irish gangs, knowing both will profit despite their ethnic differences. Frankie Yale, who adopted the last name to coincide with the collegiate theme of the Harvard Inn, becomes the main influence in Al Capone's life.

In 1920, knowing that he must leave Brooklyn if he is to prosper on his own, a newly married Capone moves to Chicago with Frankie Yale's blessing.* There he joins the Colosimo family, along with fellow New York transplant Johnny "the Fox" Torrio. The Fox is the nephew of "Big Jim" Colosimo, who controls more than one hundred brothels staffed by sex slaves. But Big Jim has a problem.

A gang known as the Black Hand, imported from Italy, is making extravagant extortion demands against Colosimo. Big Jim assigns the Fox, known as a brutal enforcer, to put that to an end.

At thirty-eight, Giovanni Torrio is older than Al Capone by seventeen years. Born in Southern Italy, he changed his name as a young man to sound more American. Torrio is a natural leader, known for being strategic and cunning. However, within weeks of moving to Chicago,

---

* Al Capone married Mae Coughlin, an Irish girl from a middle-class family, in 1918. Although he frequently consorted with mistresses and prostitutes, the couple remained married the remainder of Capone's life. They had one child, Albert Francis Capone, who went by the nickname Sonny.

the Fox is clashing with his uncle, Big Jim. Torrio believes that Colosimo's focus on prostitution is limiting.

On January 17, 1920, a new law known as the Volstead Act goes into effect. This prohibits the sale or possession of alcohol. Prohibition, as it becomes known, does not at first seem like a new revenue stream for the criminal families—or at least not to Big Jim Colosimo. But the Fox sees it differently. Secretly providing a thirsty American public with alcohol has the potential to reap an enormous amount of wealth. Torrio believes that the crime syndicates are making a grave mistake if they do not participate in the new pastime of "bootlegging," in which alcohol is smuggled into the country and made available for sale at highly inflated prices.*

So it is that Johnny "the Fox" Torrio resorts to extreme measures. He arranges a business meeting with the Genna crime family, on the surface an ally of Big Jim. Torrio boldly informs the Gennas of his plans to expand into bootlegging and seeks their permission to murder his uncle. The gangsters, led by six brothers known as the Terrible Gennas, control the Little Italy section of Chicago. Sicilian by birth, they own a federal license to manufacture industrial alcohol. Along with communion wine, this is one of the few types of spirits allowed to be sold legally in the United States. Torrio's plan will expand those legal sales into the bootlegging market, and the Genna brothers quickly agree to placing a hit on Big Jim.

This is not a decision made lightly. Colosimo is one of the most famous men in Chicago, well connected with politicians and celebrities. Colosimo's, his South Side restaurant, is routinely packed with the city's wealthiest and most famous denizens.

On May 11, 1920, Big Jim Colosimo enters his restaurant and is shot dead by an assailant hiding in the cloakroom. There is evidence that the gunman might have been Al Capone. But to this day, no one knows his identity.

What is known is that Johnny Torrio then becomes leader of Colosimo's crime syndicate. Al Capone becomes his number two. Acting

---

* *Bootlegging* is a nineteenth-century term based upon the smugglers' trick of concealing bottles in their boots.

as an understudy to the Fox, he is given free rein to open brothels, gambling dens, and speakeasies—the secret establishments where Americans now go to drink.*

In a strange turn of events, Johnny Torrio is shot four times on January 12, 1925. Torrio is sitting in his car as the murder is carried out by members of a rival Irish gang. The Fox is shot in the chest, neck, right arm, and groin, but when the shooter approaches the car and places a pistol to Torrio's temple to finish the job, there is no bullet in the chamber. The gunman flees, sure that he has completed the hit, but the Fox lives up to his reputation and survives the assassination attempt. However, Johnny Torrio knows his death is near. So, a few weeks later he chooses to retire from organized crime and moves back to New York City.

Before Torrio leaves, he anoints Al Capone as his successor.

✦

It's good to be Scarface. Now twenty-six years old, the new head of what is known as the Chicago Outfit controls an empire that consists of prostitution, speakeasies, illegal breweries, and racetracks, bringing in hundreds of thousands of dollars a week.

The new boss quickly gains weight, beefing up to 250 pounds on his five-foot, ten-inch frame. He becomes a Chicago celebrity, dominating the city's criminal subculture. Capone also attracts the media by issuing provocative quotes like "You can get much farther with a kind word and a gun than you can with a kind word alone." Despite the violent imagery, many Chicagoans laugh.

To the public, Capone is the mobster who travels around town in a bulletproof car, wears outlandish suits, and sports a broad fedora hat. The Mob boss is also generous when it suits his purpose, giving outlandish tips to waiters and providing clothing to the city's poor on cold winter nights.

Of course, Capone's power is not built on charity. It is stark brutal-

---

* The term refers to the practice of not speaking at all about the establishment, for fear of alerting the police.

ity that really defines him. Soon, he clashes with Chicago's North Side Gang and shoots their leader, Earl "Hymie" Weiss, dead.

As a result of his aggression, Al Capone lives in constant fear of his own assassination, so anyone suspected of treachery is harshly punished. At one dinner in 1929, Capone invites three men he believes are planning an act of betrayal. It is only after the unsuspecting trio eat and drink their fill that they are set upon. Their hands and legs are tied to their chairs, and they quickly realize their lives are in danger.

Al Capone approaches John Scalise, Albert Anselmi, and Joseph "Hop Toad" Giunta clutching a baseball bat. Then he starts swinging.

The mobster brutally slams the bat into the heads of each man. Then he works on the fingers and forearms. The bat is brought down hard on the groins of the alleged Judases. The air is rent with screams and the sound of breaking bones. But Al Capone refuses to let the men die. The violence only stops when he becomes too tired to swing the bat anymore.

The bodies of the three gangsters are found outside Hammond, Indiana, shortly thereafter.* The local coroner will state for the record that he has never seen human beings so utterly destroyed.

But that is only the beginning.

✦

In February 1929, Al Capone sits agitated in his Florida compound. He has just been told that a gang under the leadership of Capone's greatest rival, George "Bugs" Moran, has been plotting to kill him.

So under a bright Florida sun, Capone decides to strike first. Hiring four assassins from outside Chicago, so their identities will be unknown, Capone hatches a plan to lure the Moran gang to a local garage under the ruse of selling them top-grade Old Log Cabin whiskey for a low price. Bugs Moran himself is also supposed to arrive at the SMC Cartage Company at 10:30 a.m. to assist the seven other gang members

---

* John Scalise, Albert Anselmi, and Joseph Giunta did indeed plan to betray Al Capone. Because of Capone's paranoia, he was able to pick up on the plot against him.

in collecting the liquor. But Moran is running late, perhaps because it is Valentine's Day.

His tardiness will save his life.

The assassins drive up to the garage in a stolen police car. Two wear law enforcement uniforms. At first, the Moran gangsters believe this to be a normal police raid.

But it is not.

The men are herded inside the garage and lined up against a wall. They cannot fight back as their weapons have been confiscated. Then, using tommy guns and a sawed-off shotgun, the assassins shoot each man at least fifteen times.

Knowing neighbors may have heard the loud thunder of machine-gun fire, the two killers dressed in police uniforms escort the other two assassins out of the garage, as if arresting them. All four step inside the stolen police car and drive away.

No one will call the police.

The brutal killings become legend in Chicago and will go down in history as the St. Valentine's Day Massacre.

Al Capone is thousands of miles away as the murders take place, but no one doubts that he is responsible. Because of massive press coverage, the massacre makes Capone more famous than ever.

It also marks the beginning of his downfall.

✦

It is August 22, 1934, when Inmate #85 arrives at Alcatraz. Unable to convict Al Capone of the St. Valentine's Day Massacre or other crimes, federal officials seek any means possible of putting him behind bars. In 1931, the Treasury Department under Agent Eliot Ness finally gets a Capone conviction for tax evasion. The mobster is sentenced to eleven years in prison. The first portion of his sentence is spent in the Atlanta federal penitentiary, where his opulent wealth makes it possible for him to bribe prison authorities and receive any pleasure he wants. But things are different at Alcatraz.

In addition to being assaulted by James Lucas, Al Capone is subject to an extremely hard daily regimen. His mind soon begins to rapidly deteriorate. Finally, five years after his arrival at Alcatraz, Capone is released with time off for good behavior on November 16, 1939. He has the mental capacity of a twelve-year-old.*

✦

With the gangsters of the 1930s almost completely wiped out, J. Edgar Hoover is convinced that his new FBI has crime under control in America. Hoover now turns to a completely different set of law enforcement problems.

As the Second World War breaks out in Europe, the FBI is mandated to keep track of possible spies from America's enemies abroad. The director takes to his new task with relish.

What he doesn't know is that the war mandate will soon actually help a new breed of criminal organization that will spread terror and corruption throughout America.

The Mafia is on its way.

---

* An interesting sidebar to Capone's Alcatraz incarceration is that he shared space with Alvin Karpis, the public enemy arrested by J. Edgar Hoover. Karpis is Inmate #325 and will go on to serve the longest term of any convict in the prison's history—twenty-seven years. Alcatraz will close for good on March 21, 1963, and Karpis will be relocated to another penitentiary. He will be released on parole in 1969 and die from an accidental overdose of pills and alcohol in 1979.

PART II

THE CORRUPTORS

CHAPTER SIX

Field Marshal Erwin Rommel is on the run.

The long day of combat has been devastating. As night falls, desert winds carry the smell of death and burning German tanks. Rommel is fifty-one, a career soldier whose face is sunburned from years of desert warfare. His lips are chapped from the heat and his eyes lined from goggles that keep out the dust. The Desert Fox, as British journalists have nicknamed the Allied army's most wily adversary, is also Nazi Germany's top field general.[*]

Rommel has known defeat before, but not like today. His army, known as the Afrika Korps, has not just been defeated—it has been decimated. So, rather than watch the total annihilation, Rommel now makes a calculation that could alter the course of World War II. His new plan is centered around a military reality.

Today was supposed to be a huge victory—with Rommel boldly striking at Allied troops under British general Bernard Law Montgomery.

That did not happen.

Unbeknownst to the Desert Fox, British code breakers intercepted his battle plans. At 5:36 a.m., just twenty-four minutes before

---

[*] Rommel made his name in the Nazi blitzkrieg assault on France in 1940.

Rommel's troops were to launch their first bombardment, British forces were alerted to his strategy. Thus, the surprise became a debacle. Through fourteen hours of fighting, the British were always one step ahead. More than thirty thousand shells rained down on German positions. Rommel began the day with 140 tanks—he now has just 52. His veteran Panzer crews lie dead and burned on the sands of North Africa. In addition, more than three hundred German infantry have been killed, wounded, or taken prisoner by the British.

Montgomery's forces did not lose a single tank.

Now, as night falls over the desert, a weary Rommel orders retreat. He knows that the time to flee has come. German Panzer tanks and infantry-carrying trucks turn north, fleeing to the coastal Mediterranean city of Gabès.

"The battle was lost," Rommel will later write. "A great gloom settled over us."

For two years, Erwin Rommel has controlled the war in North Africa. The Desert Fox utilized an aggressive style of tank warfare to win territory ranging from Tunisia in the west to Egypt in the east—a distance as wide as all of Western Europe. But then, just shy of taking the Egyptian capital of Cairo in July 1942, Rommel's Afrika Korps was first defeated by Montgomery and the British at El Alamein. Two more defeats at the hands of the British soon followed. To save the lives of his men, Rommel ordered a retreat. The Afrika Korps pulled back hundreds of miles to Tunisia, hoping to make another stand against the British.

That stand was today.

All this time, the British and their Commonwealth Allies have been Rommel's only opponent. But now the Americans have arrived. Rommel easily overwhelmed and defeated a U.S. force two weeks ago at the Kasserine Pass, but he knows that their best general was not in command for that battle. That will not happen again. General George S. Patton, a brilliant tactician and America's most aggressive combat general, has just arrived in Africa to take charge of U.S. forces. It is said that his relentless style of warfare borrows heavily from Rommel.*

---

* Patton and Rommel, the two preeminent tank commanders in World War II, never fought opposite each other in battle.

It is just a matter of time until Germany loses control of North Africa. The Desert Fox is sure of that. "For the *Panzerarmee* to remain in Africa was plain suicide," he will recall in the aftermath of the Medenine defeat.

✦

At 7:50 a.m. on March 9, fewer than forty-eight hours after ordering his tanks to pull back, General Erwin Rommel flies to Eastern Europe to meet with German leader Adolf Hitler. American commander Dwight Eisenhower will later write of this transitory moment, accusing Rommel of "foreseeing the inevitable and desiring to save his own skin." But to Rommel, this departure is not permanent. He is the führer's favorite general. No other man can deliver the hard news that the war in North Africa is irretrievably lost. He plans to return to Africa, but not until his message is delivered in person.

Hitler and Rommel meet at the *Werwolf*, Hitler's command post in the Ukraine where the Russian front is the scene of bitter and unrelenting fighting. The führer's forest compound is built of thick reinforced concrete. Snow still covers the ground. Coming directly from the dry heat of Africa, Rommel's sunburn looks dramatically out of place. He shivers despite his greatcoat. Before the strategic discussion can begin, Hitler presents Rommel with a diamond-studded Knight's Cross, making the general only the sixth man in the history of the Third Reich to receive such an honor.

Despite the lavish award, Rommel does not forget why he has made this journey to a cold, remote Ukrainian woods. As the two men sit down to tea, the Desert Fox outlines the hopeless situation in Africa. The tactically brilliant Rommel argues that rather than lose valuable veteran troops to death or imprisonment, they should be moved from Africa to Fortress Europe. Sicily is their most logical destination. That island off the south coast of Italy is the closest portion of Europe to the African mainland. It is just a few hundred miles from Tunis to the Sicilian capital of Palermo. Logistically, such an evacuation is daunting but vital to the future success of the German Army. Rommel plans to begin immediate troop transport, leaving tanks and other vehicles behind.

Adolf Hitler will not hear of it.

"He was not receptive to any of my arguments about Tunisia and seemed to dismiss them by saying I had become a pessimist," Rommel will write to his wife, Lucia. "He simply could not see what was happening in Tunisia."

Rommel never returns to Africa but his predictions soon turn all too true. Just two weeks after his meeting with Hitler, U.S. forces under General George S. Patton rout German tank units at the Battle of El Guettar. This marks the first time American forces defeat the Afrika Korps, but for Patton this is not enough. He longs to defeat the famous Desert Fox and is severely disappointed to learn that Rommel is not present on the field of battle.*

As Rommel has predicted, El Guettar is the death knell for German forces in Africa. They surrender to the Allies on May 13, 1943. The Third Reich has lost thousands of men forever.

✦

As operations in North Africa come to an end, Allied war planners shift their focus to the next step in the Allied fight to end the Nazi stranglehold in Europe: Sicily. The invasion is code-named Operation Husky.

Sicily is the largest island in the Mediterranean Sea, occupied over the centuries by Greeks, Romans, Arabs, Normans, and Vandals. Sicilian locals have survived this history of intrusion and subjugation by forming an extremely tight-knit society. Outsiders are not welcome. The warm climate and simple agricultural lifestyle of the island hides the fact that little about daily life in Sicily is known to anyone but those who actually live there.

Thus, Allied war planners don't have a grasp of the situation in Sicily, which is just ten miles off Italy's southern coast. They *do* know that Sicily has been occupied by the Italian fascist military regime for almost twenty years. A handful of units from the German Afrika Korps have successfully managed to escape from Tunisia, meaning that more

---

* Rommel was granted home leave and then assigned to protect Northern France against Allied invasion.

than two hundred thousand German and Italian troops now await an Allied attack. They are entrenched in mountainous volcanic terrain that favors a defensive strategy.

For Operation Husky to succeed, British and American troops must have help on the ground. They require individuals with insider knowledge, capable of sharing not only possible invasion routes but also the most efficient local roads, size of enemy troop strength, and location of gun emplacements.

They need the Mafia.

✦

But the feared Italian gangsters have largely moved to New York City.

The exodus began shortly after May 1924, spurred on by Italy's fascist prime minister, Benito Mussolini. Il Duce (*the leader*) is a small, rotund, balding man with a penchant for histrionics. Mussolini is determined to control Italy by using totalitarian methods and brutally stamps out all opposition. On the island of Sicily, this means getting rid of the Mafia.*

The etymology of Mafia is unknown, with some believing the term has its roots in an 1863 play known as *I Mafiusi della Vicaria*, about a group of prisoners demanding respect. Others believe it to be an acronym for *Morte Alla Francia Italia Anela* ("Death to the French is Italy's Cry") after the French invasion of Sicily in 1282. Still others believe it stems from the Sicilian adjective *Mafiusu*, a term for bold behavior.

"Mafiosi," in Italian, means someone who asks for favors. But through the centuries those favors often evolved into criminal acts. On the island of Sicily, gangs coerced poor people in a variety of ways. For example, the simple act of seeing a doctor might involve a small payment to the local Mafia chieftain. If a Sicilian wanted a job, wanted his daughter to be married, or wanted a new mule for the fields, the Mafia often got a "taste."

Sicilian businesses were forced to pay *pizzo*, or protection money, to ensure that customers could visit their shops. Those who do not

---

* Sicily was under French rule until 1860. A local revolt drove them out at that time, and the island came under Italian rule. In 1946, Sicily became an autonomous region for the first time in three thousand years. However, its foreign and financial interests are allied with those of Rome.

pay are beaten, sometimes killed. But a strict rule of silence known as omertà means the people of Sicily do not speak out against this predatory behavior. Anyone who defied omertà was in grave danger, subject to immediate execution.

The dictator Mussolini vows to stop the Mafia oppression. But Sicily defies him, and Mussolini backs off. That does not sit well with some fascist leaders. "If we want to save Sicily we must destroy the Mafia," one top fascist militant writes to Il Duce in April 1923.

The following year, Mussolini demonstrates a show of force to remind the Mafia that he is in charge. He travels to Sicily aboard the battleship *Dante Alighieri*. In the skies above, Italian fighter aircraft circle. Submarines prowl the dark blue Mediterranean waters all around the *Alighieri*. Benito Mussolini steps ashore guarded by an intimidating phalanx of bodyguards. He visits the small town of Piana del Greci, where its mayor, Don Francesco Cuccia, actually sneers at Il Duce's men. In addition to running the town, Cuccia is a member of the Mafia. He says to Mussolini: "You are with me. You are under my protection. What do you need those guys for?"

The dictator is taken aback but says nothing. However, he will never forget the incident and begins referring to Cuccia as "that unspeakable mayor."

Don Cuccia is certainly disrespectful. Using his power to great advantage, the Mafioso chief ensures that the village square is all but empty when Mussolini finally stands to speak. The only citizens of Piana del Greci in attendance are twenty derelicts and fools, all handpicked by Cuccia to express disdain for Mussolini.

A few days later, as the dictator continues his tour of Sicily, he is once again reminded of the lack of respect when the Mafia conspires to steal his hat.*

So it is that Benito Mussolini declares war on the Sicilian Mafia. Upon his return to Rome, the furious and humiliated prime minister grants sweeping powers to a special police force led by Cesare Mori, a thickset Northern Italian known for his active disdain for organized crime. Working with his own team of special agents, Mori rounds up

---

* The hat was stolen and never returned.

Mafia by the hundreds. His tactics are simple: surround a village, block off all roads, and then his police move in to arrest the gangsters. Should the suspects flee, Mori's men begin shooting Mafia-owned cattle, one by one. Threatened with this loss of income, many Mafioso eventually come out and surrender. Once in Mori's custody, suspects are tortured in a most medieval fashion, their bodies shocked by electrical wires, burned with flames, flayed with cattle whips, and their bones pulled from the socket while being stretched on the rack—all in an effort for the prosecutor to obtain names and information to further his manhunt.

The collapse of the Sicilian Mafia is almost immediate. Mayor Cuccia and more than twelve hundred men are arrested. The city of Palermo, the scene of 224 murders in 1923, is pacified. Within five years murders drop to just thirty-five.

Quickly, many Mafia chieftains sail to America seeking asylum. They declare themselves refugees from fascism. This plea allows Mafiosi to circumvent the Immigration Act of 1924, which caps the number of foreign nationals into America at 150,000 per year. As the immigrants are refugees, U.S. officials do not inquire about the backgrounds of the Sicilians or their intended line of work.

America has seventy ports of entry in the 1920s, but the Sicilians are not interested in places like Galveston or New Orleans. Instead, they alight in New York City. There, after processing on Ellis Island, in the shadow of the Statue of Liberty, they are free to enter the city without restriction.

New York City's population of almost seven million people is nearly twice that of the entire island of Sicily, and it offers an exponential increase in ways of making money illegally. To extortion, protection, and other forms of racketeering, the Sicilian Mafia now adds bootlegging, prostitution, and control of the waterfront unions.

And always, there is omertà, that code of silence meaning certain death for anyone speaking out against the Mafia, thus ensuring its ability to grow and corrupt their environment.

✦

As Allied war strategists, including General George Patton and Field Marshal Bernard Montgomery, prepare to invade Europe, contact is made with the few criminals left on the island of Sicily. They will be helpful in defeating the fascist Italian Army and their German allies. They will carry messages. They will destroy installations. And they will even kill on behalf of the Allies. For the Mafia, Benito Mussolini and Adolf Hitler are far worse than the Americans or the British. And for their help, the gangsters of Sicily will soon reap a huge reward.

CHAPTER SEVEN

July 10, 1943
Great Meadow Correctional Facility
Comstock, New York
Dawn

As British and American troops storm the beaches forty-five hundred miles away in Sicily, Charles "Lucky" Luciano impatiently awaits his release from prison. It has been seven years since the Mob boss received his sentence of thirty years to life. Luciano's conviction is for running a prostitution ring, but his litany of crimes is endless, ranging from extortion to murder to bribery. Luciano's most recent payoff, however, has allegedly taken place since he has been behind bars: a $25,000 "contribution" to Manhattan district attorney Thomas Dewey that will ensure the commutation of Luciano's sentence. The money will be paid as a donation to Dewey's gubernatorial campaign. Luciano will owe Dewey another $65,000 upon his release.*

That day will come. The conditions of Luciano's release have already been agreed upon. In order to avoid negative media attention by appearing to let a known mobster go free, Thomas Dewey's terms are that Luciano—who is still a Sicilian, never having obtained American

---

* In 1948, Thomas Dewey ran against Harry Truman for the presidency. Many experts picked Dewey to win, but he lost to Truman by an electoral vote tally of 303 to 189. Throughout his life, Thomas Dewey always denied taking bribes from Lucky Luciano.

Charles "Lucky" Luciano, convicted former New York vice lord who was pardoned by Governor Thomas E. Dewey and deported to his native Sicily, sits at a table during a visit to the home of relatives in Naples, Italy, March 1, 1946.

citizenship—will be deported immediately after getting out of prison. However, the German Army still occupies Sicily and the Italian mainland. So Dewey has arranged the mobster's transfer from a maximum security penitentiary to the "country club" here at Great Meadow. Until the Allies win victory in Europe, Luciano must remain behind bars. "They couldn't send me to Italy while we was still at war and it was an enemy country," the Mob boss will later explain to a biographer.

Charles "Lucky" Luciano is determined to help America and its Allies win the Second World War. One wall of his cell is covered with an enormous map of the European theater, on which he has marked the location of Axis front lines in anticipation of an Allied invasion. Luciano has become a voracious reader during his time in prison, and he has immersed himself in military strategy and tactics. His favorite American commander is General George S. Patton. Luciano regales visitors with commentary on the shortcomings of Supreme Allied Commander Dwight Eisenhower, and he has come to the conclusion that a Mafia-style hit on German dictator Adolf Hitler is all that lies between himself and his freedom. "If somebody could knock off that son of a bitch the war would be over in five minutes," he laments to visiting mobsters Joe Adonis and Tommy Lucchese.

When Luciano's suggestion is greeted with laughter, his response is immediate: "What the hell you laughing at? We've got the best hit man in the world over there—Vito Genovese. That dirty little pig owes his life to me and now it's time to make good on it."

But Lucky Luciano's role in World War II goes far beyond schemes and theories. Even as Luciano enjoys a leisurely Saturday, knowing it might just be possible for prison warden Vernon Morhaus to once again set him free for a few hours to enjoy a steak and a conjugal visit in Albany tonight, he is also buoyed by the news coming out of Europe that Patton himself is leading today's Allied invasion of Sicily.[*]

As a budding military strategist, Luciano takes great pride in knowing that he personally has helped make this invasion possible. For General George Patton's Seventh Army's landings on beaches at Gela, Scoglitti, and Licata could not have happened without the intervention of Lucky Luciano. Using his contacts in New York City, Luciano ordered his crime gang to compile information that would assist Patton in the invasion. Luciano even provided names of Sicilian Mafiosi who could be counted upon to help the Allies.

Luciano's motive is simple: get out of jail. But the saga of how one brutal convict saved lives in World War II is far more complicated.

✦

It is 1936 when Lucky Luciano is first sent to the penitentiary.

The powerful mobster begins serving his thirty-year sentence behind the towering gray walls of the maximum security Clinton Correctional Facility, a remote prison hundreds of miles from Manhattan in the town of Dannemora, New York. Conditions are so harsh that the penitentiary owns the nickname Siberia. Before his incarcera-

---

[*] More than 160,000 American, Canadian, and British troops went ashore during the invasion of Sicily, suffering 5,500 men killed and 14,000 wounded.

tion, Luciano reigned over his own crime family, with a personal net income of several million dollars per year. Now he is a ward of the state.*

Lucky Luciano is Sicilian by birth, given the first name of Salvatore. But upon immigrating to America with his parents at the age of nine he was renamed Charles. The name Lucky comes from surviving otherwise fatal beatings as a young hoodlum.

Like Al Capone, Luciano got his start with the Five Points Gang, an Italian outfit on Manhattan's Lower East Side. Over time, Luciano learned the power of cooperating with other ethnic groups. To avoid bloodshed and increase profits with underworld organizations, he masterminded the National Crime Syndicate, bringing together Italian, Irish, and Jewish crime families. To ensure the cohesiveness of the syndicate, Luciano created a dedicated enforcement arm known as Murder, Incorporated, to assassinate enemies and informers. No matter where they try to hide, the victims are never out of danger. Some say that Albert Anastasia, a former longshoreman who became Luciano's top hit man, personally murdered more than a thousand men.

Others say that number is far too small.

Lucky Luciano enjoys certain luxuries befitting an inmate of his criminal stature, such as a special cook to prepare his favorite meals. The Clinton Correctional Facility is about three hundred miles north of Manhattan, making it difficult for Luciano to run his organization from within its walls.†

However, Luciano still exerts influence. His top lieutenants regularly make the long drive from New York to Dannemora. Visiting hours are 8:30 a.m. to 3:00 p.m. each day, and Luciano is allowed to meet with four visitors per session. Among those who come to see the

---

* Luciano grossed more than $12 million in 1925, with a net of $4 million. This is $57 million in modern currency.

† First built in 1845, the maximum security Clinton Correctional Facility is still in operation. Notable inmates include the rapper Tupac Shakur. The Clinton facility most recently made headlines in 2015, when convicted murderers Richard Matt and David Sweat escaped and led police on a widespread manhunt that resulted in the shooting death of Matt.

Albert Anastasia (left) leaves Federal District Court with his attorney
Anthony Colendra. He pleaded not guilty to charges of evading payment of $11,742
in income taxes in 1947 and 1948. Camden, New Jersey, May 23, 1955.

handsome, olive-skinned gangster on a regular basis are Jewish crime
boss Meyer Lansky and the acting ruler of the Luciano crime family,
Frank Costello.

Luciano enjoys these visits, but he is "going nuts" in prison and
longs to be a free man again. The first two years of his incarceration are
spent in a futile attempt to appeal his conviction. But when the U.S.
Supreme Court refuses to hear Lucky's plea in 1938, the gangster is
forced to find more ingenious methods of gaining his freedom.

Soon after, when the U.S. government takes possession of the
French luxury liner SS *Normandie*, Lucky Luciano recognizes that this
majestic vessel represents an enormous personal opportunity.

Normandie is the pride of France, larger by a third than the legendary *Titanic* and owner of the Blue Riband, the award given to the vessel holding the record for fastest Atlantic crossing. But France has fallen to the Nazis, and the U.S. Navy now controls *Normandie*.

With the world swept by war, luxury cruise ships have no place on the oceans, particularly in the hostile waters between New York and England, now controlled by Nazi U-boat submarines. In the past month alone, thirteen Allied cargo vessels have been torpedoed. So like the British luxury liners *Queen Mary* and *Queen Elizabeth*, the speedy *Normandie* is being retrofitted to ferry soldiers into combat. The three mighty vessels each have a top speed of more than thirty knots, which many believe makes them capable of outrunning any U-boat.

The *Normandie* is berthed in Manhattan alongside the *Queen Mary* and *Queen Elizabeth*. Despite their enormous size, those vessels hardly dominate the waterfront. The dimensions of New York City's port are huge: eighteen hundred piers, 750 miles of shoreline, ten thousand ships coming in and out every year—all manned by thirty-five thousand longshoremen workers.

And the Mafia controls those workers.

Utilizing the same practices that worked so well in Sicily, only now played out on a much larger scale, nothing happens on the waterfront without Mafia approval. This system depends on regulating the harbor's labor unions.

The term *longshoreman* refers to an individual whose job is to load and unload ships, then put the cargo onto trucks, trains, and planes. By controlling these men, the Mafia has complete dominance over every act of commerce going in and out of New York City.

The process works from the bottom up and begins with the simple act of getting a job: all longshoremen must join a union as a prerequisite for employment. Yet membership is not enough to begin working. A special payment to the Mob for the privilege of being granted work is also required. And once a longshoreman starts receiving a salary, a portion of his income is then kicked back to union bosses. Since it is the Mafia that decides which men receive the most powerful union titles, the supervisors pay a larger stipend to the local crime families as a prerequisite of keeping their privileged positions.

Also, union leaders can steal or delay any shipment. A typical example is New York's Fulton Fish Market, America's largest wholesale seafood distribution center. The boss there is Joseph "Socks" Lanza, a.k.a. Joe Zox, who owes his power and allegiance to Luciano's outfit. It is mandatory that Fulton merchants pay a stiff bribe for doing business at the market, as well as another gratuity for the rapid loading and unloading of ships and trucks. A total of one hundred dollars for every fishing boat entering the port and fifty dollars for every truck transporting fish to market makes its way to Joe Zox, who then passes along a cut to Lucky Luciano. Should fishmongers choose not to pay up, the fresh catch rots in a ship's hold.

New York City police, politicians, and judges know better than to interfere. Those who meddle simply disappear, shot in the head and buried in the New Jersey woods under a pile of quicklime, or taken out to sea and dropped overboard, the corpse weighted down to ensure a quick descent into the depths.

So it is that Lucky Luciano concocts a "sabotage incident" scenario. Should something happen to *Normandie*, the U.S. government will surely realize it needs help controlling the docks of New York. Therein lies Luciano's opportunity.

Clearly, it would be in the best interests of federal officials to align with the Mafia to ensure the safety of the port. Should the government actually make this request, Luciano will certainly cooperate—but only if given a full pardon and release from prison.

That's Lucky's vision. But nothing happens.

Then comes Pearl Harbor.

As America declares war on Japan and Germany, New York City is a logical target for a similar attack by the Nazi regime.

Less than one week after the Pearl Harbor attack, on December 13, 1941, thirty-three German members of what is known as the Duquesne Spy Ring are convicted of espionage in a Brooklyn federal court. During the trial it is revealed that their primary goal was acquiring information that could lead to acts of sabotage. J. Edgar Hoover, having switched the FBI's focus from chasing bank robbers to tracking foreign spies, declares that the bureau's agents "have guarded the secrets that give the army and navy their striking force in the field."

But not even the FBI can guard the New York waterfront. And

therein lies the crux of Lucky Luciano's elaborate plan to get out of prison. It is well known that pro-Nazi elements are active in Brooklyn and that many German immigrants are employed on the docks. It is also feared that some Italian immigrants working as longshoremen may be sympathetic to Hitler's ally, Benito Mussolini.

In the weeks after Pearl Harbor, U.S. Naval Intelligence inadvertently plays into Luciano's hands when a special unit code-named B-3 assigns one hundred agents to canvas the docks for information. But they are frustrated to learn that longshoremen, knowing the code of omertà, refuse to talk.

The U.S. Navy, having no other choice, publicly admits its concerns about Germans and Italians committing sabotage in New York harbor.

In January 1942, one month after Pearl Harbor, Lucky Luciano sends word for Frank Costello to visit him in Dannemora. Anxiety about attacks on American soil is at an all-time high. The situation is ideal for reminding America's federal government that the Mafia has power unlike any other organization in the country.

The nattily dressed Costello, who just turned forty-one, arrives bearing the news that a leading figure in the International Longshoremen's Association named "Tough Tony" Anastasio has agreed to allow an act of sabotage on one of the three large cruise ships in New York harbor. The man carrying out this scheme will be his brother, Albert, the infamous hit man from Murder, Inc.

"Albert figures that if something could happen to the *Normandie*, that would really make everyone crap in their pants," Luciano will later remember.

Lucky Luciano gives his blessing.

"It was a great idea and I didn't really see how it was gonna hurt the war effort because the ship was nowhere near ready and, besides, no American soldiers or sailors would be involved because they wasn't sending them no place yet," recalled Luciano.

Normandie is due to sail with her first group of U.S. fighting men in mid-February 1942.

That journey will never take place.

✦

A faint trace of a smile appears on gambler Frank Costello's face as he poses in the anteroom of the Federal Courthouse in New York, on April 8, 1952, after being sentenced to eighteen months in federal prison and fined $5,000 for contempt of the U.S. Senate.

The SS *Normandie* is burning.

"That Anastasia," Luciano marvels from prison. "He really done a job."

Flames billow from the burning luxury liner as New York City firemen race to put out the blaze. Belowdecks, crews scramble to pour water on the flames, even as thick black puffs of smoke seep from every opening of her superstructure.

The blaze is fought from the shore and the sea, with New York City firemen and fireboats pouring as much water as possible on the flames. Fears that the fire will spread to the city itself fuel their determined efforts. Gallon after gallon from the hoses attacks the fire, filtering down in torrents from the upper decks to the very bottom of the hull's interior. In all, six thousand tons of water cascade into *Normandie*. The ship's architect, Vladimir Yourkevitch, is in New York City to advise on the retrofit and rushes to the port to insist that sea cocks belowdecks be opened to save the vessel. Her hull will settle immediately into the harbor sediment and be stabilized. But harbor police bar the frantic designer from getting anywhere near the ship.

By nightfall, the flames are extinguished. But the water belowdecks has made *Normandie* unsteady. She now lists hard to port. The ship is abandoned. Shortly after midnight, *Normandie* capsizes. She will be salvaged and later sold for scrap, never to ply the Atlantic again.

To many in the United States Navy, still reeling from the attack on Pearl Harbor just five weeks ago, the *Normandie* sinking is an obvious act of sabotage. Now that America is at war, the construction and maintenance of military vessels in New York's busy ports will be paramount. But it is becoming apparent to Naval Intelligence that many of the longshoremen owe their loyalty to the union instead of America. In addition to deliberate acts of sabotage, there is every chance the workers could go on strike or delay cargo desperately needed for the war effort. One of Naval Intelligence's greatest fears is Nazi agents coming ashore by submarine, and it is not difficult to surmise that such an event could occur if the longshoremen's union allows it.

So, much to Lucky Luciano's delight, the United States government reluctantly forms an alliance with the very men it once diligently tried to prosecute and send to prison.

Operation Underworld has begun.

✦

On March 7, 1942, working in conjunction with the office of Manhattan district attorney Thomas Dewey, Lieutenant Commander Charles R. Haffenden of United States Naval Intelligence meets with Joseph "Socks" Lanza, the gangster who runs the Fulton Fish Market. The hour is midnight. The location is Grant's Tomb on Riverside Drive on the West Side of Manhattan. In a carefully scripted discussion, Lanza says he will help the navy place agents on the docks and aboard commercial fishing boats.

Then Lanza goes on to tell Commander Haffenden that the true power over the docklands is Lucky Luciano. He suggests that the imprisoned mobster might be willing to help the government in exchange for release from the penitentiary.

In moments, a deal is struck.

On May 12, 1942, Lucky Luciano is moved south to the Great

Meadow Correctional Facility to await the end of the war. Some believe his initial "contribution" of $25,000 has helped elect Thomas Dewey as governor of New York. Almost immediately, Luciano arranges a network of informants and spies to monitor all suspicious activities on the waterfront. Even bartenders and hatcheck girls are enlisted to eavesdrop on suspicious conversations. The result is no further acts of sabotage in New York for the remainder of the war. Simultaneously, longshoremen of Sicilian heritage are ordered to provide names and details that could be of use to the Allies.

On August 17, 1943, five weeks after the first amphibious landings, the Allies drive the German and Italian defenders from Sicily.

✦

Almost three and a half years later, on January 3, 1946, New York governor Thomas Dewey commutes the sentence of Lucky Luciano to time already served. "Lucky Luciano Walks" reads the headline in the *New York Daily News Mirror*.

On a windy and bitterly cold day five weeks afterward, Luciano boards the SS *Laura Keene*, an aging cargo ship bound for Genoa, Italy.

Lucky Luciano's last act on American soil is paying the remainder of his bribe to Thomas Dewey.

"We did pay it," Lucky would later recall of the $65,000 still owed the Dewey campaign as part of the deal. "In cash, in small bills, the minute I set foot on the boat that was gonna take me to Italy."*

✦

The early release is highly controversial and damaging to the governor as well as to the navy. Both sides immediately seek to downplay the gangster's role in the war effort.

Subsequently, an eight-month investigation is launched into the Luciano affair. In a confidential 1954 report commissioned by Thomas Dewey himself in order to clarify the early release of Luciano, New

---

* "Later on, I made a check about that ninety grand," Luciano would later write about the bribe to Dewey that freed him from prison. "It never showed on none of our books for tax returns, naturally; but it never showed up on any of Dewey's campaign returns either." As stated, Thomas Dewey denied any impropriety.

York State commissioner of investigation William B. Herlands concludes that "as a result of the activities of Luciano and his intermediaries, a network of contacts and informants was made available to Naval Intelligence.

"They performed such services as obtaining information about and reporting suspicious activities on the waterfront; keeping an eye out for sabotage and espionage; obtaining union books and union cards so that Naval Intelligence agents could be placed (ostensibly as employees) in hotels, restaurants, bars and grills, piers, docks, trucks, factories, and elsewhere."

✦

On November 22, 1954, six weeks after the release of the Luciano report, acting director of naval intelligence Rear Admiral Carl F. Espe requests that the 2,984-page document be withheld from the public. In doing so, he acknowledges the findings are "admirably" documented and "thorough."

The report will not see the light of day for twenty-three years.

✦

Lucky Luciano is free. No sooner does the *Laura Keene* drop him in Genoa than the mobster makes plans to consolidate his personal power in the underworld. But New York City is too hot, and he faces a certain return to prison should he go back to the United States.

Thus, Luciano decides to get as close to America as he can without actually setting foot on U.S. soil.

The time is Christmas 1946. The location is the Hotel Nacional in Havana, Cuba, ninety miles away from Florida. The entertainer singing in the showroom is named Frank Sinatra.

But the real star is Lucky Luciano, who now brings together America's most lethal crime families to discuss a new way of doing business.

Over the next few days, organized crime will plan a stealth war to gain power in America and all over the world.

Lucky Luciano's corrupt dream is about to come true. And he knows it.

CHAPTER EIGHT

L ucky Luciano wants total control.

More than twenty of the most powerful men in organized crime have been summoned to this island paradise. It is ten months since Luciano was released from prison in New York. He has established a presence in Italy and is now moving to consolidate his underworld power. Each gangster present has already given Luciano a thick envelope filled with cash to show respect. It is money Luciano will use to buy an ownership stake in the Hotel Nacional, the stately waterfront casino and hotel in which the gangsters now gather. His ownership in the hotel will allow him to make a new home in Cuba.

This weeklong "Havana Conference" is the first meeting of America's top crime bosses since 1932. A single well-placed explosive device could radically alter the leadership of organized crime, so security is tight. Armed guards prowl the hallway outside the conference room doors. The Hotel Nacional was built for tourists, not locals, and the people of Cuba are forbidden from even entering its grounds. But during the conference those restrictions are even more stringent. The entire mezzanine floor is off-limits to other hotel guests, allowing the bosses to meet, drink rum, and dine without threat of interruption. In addition, the top four floors of this six-story establishment are allocated for the gangsters and their subordinates.

The Havana Conference is top secret, and decades later the actual number of attendees will still be open to debate. But it is known for certain that Mafia leaders from New York, Chicago, New Orleans, and Tampa are in attendance. Wives and girlfriends are not allowed to arrive until Christmas Eve.

Officially, the gangsters have all come to see the young Italian crooner from New Jersey, Frank Sinatra, perform downstairs in the showroom. Lucky Luciano himself has personally funded Sinatra's rise to celebrity. The young singer's ancestors lived in the same Sicilian town in which Luciano was born, and Lucky is eager to meet the thin, thirty-one-year-old singer for the first time.*

✦

The powerful Luciano sits at the head of a highly polished wooden conference table. Despite the tropical setting, he wears a dark suit and tie. Luciano is hardly an anonymous figure in Havana but now goes by his given name of Salvatore in order to help maintain a low profile. Each man at this meeting has specific orders not to call him Charles or Lucky. Luciano is now forty-nine but remains trim and powerful, with a full head of black wavy hair.

Ideally, the Havana Conference would have taken place in New York, but Luciano is forbidden from entering the United States. The gangster believes that stipulation is temporary, and it will be just a matter of time before he can arrange a bribe with New York governor Thomas Dewey to make possible his return. Luciano knows that the ambitious Dewey is planning to run again for president, having been

---

* Frank Sinatra's alleged ties to organized crime have been the subject of discussion for many years. Lucky Luciano was very specific in stating that the entertainer's early career was funded by the Mafia. "He had a job working for Tommy Dorsey's band," Luciano will later recall about the young Sinatra. "He was getting about a hundred and fifty bucks a week. But he needed publicity, clothes, different kinds of special music things, and they all cost quite a bit of money. I think it was about fifty or sixty grand. I okayed the money and it come out of the fund, even though some guys put up a little extra on a personal basis. It all helped him become a big star."

beaten by Franklin Roosevelt in 1944. A hefty contribution to the governor's campaign fund should be enough to get him back into America.

Until then, Luciano must be patient, conducting his business in places like Cuba without interference from the FBI or Internal Revenue Service.

The Mafia is always welcome on this island nation. And where the Mafia is welcome, it soon finds a way to make money. Sugar is Cuba's main product, but Havana is also home to hundreds of brothels, making the sex trade a source of Mob income. Cubans are also so fond of narcotics that one local writer has noted that "as a consumer nation of hard drugs, Cuba occupies first place." So far, the Mafia has not entered the business of drug trafficking, but it is just a matter of time before it does so.

The gangsters know that the Cuban people do not have much money. Their real source of income comes from Americans. U.S. citizens view Cuba as an island of "prostitutes, cigars, abortions, resort life, and pornographic movies," in the words of one journalist.

Prominent American playwright Arthur Miller describes Cuba as "hopelessly corrupt, a Mafia playground, a bordello for Americans and other foreigners."

Americans flocked to Cuba during Prohibition, eager to enjoy the mojito and Cuba libre—rum cocktails specially created for U.S. tourists by Havana bartenders. But Prohibition ended more than a decade ago, and the Mafia knows that prostitution and drugs are not enough to consistently lure Americans back.

The future is resort casino gambling. Done properly, gambling is lucrative, consistent, and more glamorous than the sordid pursuits of prostitution and drugs. And unlike in America, gambling is legal in Cuba.

The Cuban government would certainly welcome a steady stream of Americans, bringing with them the money and the loose morals that lubricate the island's tourist economy.

Cuba is currently run by President Ramón Grau San Martin, who entered office in 1944. His predecessor, Fulgencio Batista, considered by many to be a gangster himself, looted the national treasury just before stepping down. This puts the San Martin regime in the unlikely position of needing unconventional sources of revenue to fund the economy. The Mafia is happy to oblige with hefty bribes and a piece of the action.

At the time of his election, President San Martin was viewed as an idealistic savior "chosen to effect the moral liberation of our youth." But his two years in office has shown the president to be only slightly less corrupt than the ruthless Batista. The Cuban president well knows that allowing gangsters to meet so freely in Havana could one day lead to a lucrative partnership between the island nation and the Mafia.*

✦

As the gangsters settle into their seats around the long table, Lucky Luciano smokes a cigarette.

Seated just six feet away from him is the one man standing in the way of Luciano being named *Capo Di Tutti I Capi*—Boss of All Bosses. Vito Genovese is a longtime rival whom Luciano often refers to as the "fat pig."

Genovese, a brutal psychotic, is notorious for favoring violence over diplomacy. Once, after falling in love with a woman already married to another man, he solved the problem by strangling the husband on a Manhattan rooftop. The widow married Genovese twelve days later.

Though born just three days before Luciano, Vito Genovese has the strained face and receding hairline of a much older man. He is shorter by three inches, with a broad waistline and thick black eyebrows. His suit is wrinkled and coated with a fine layer of ash from the cigar he now smokes.

What Vito Genovese lacks in physical presence, however, he more than compensates for with conniving and guile. He has been through the same New York Mob wars as Luciano, whom he once considered a friend. In fact, the recent history of the New York Mafia can be traced through the actions of both men.

---

* This came to pass. As a result of the Havana Conference, an alliance was formed between the Cuban government and the Mafia, which resulted in the building of several posh Mob-run casinos in Havana and a powerful Mafia presence on the island nation. This did not diminish until dictator Fidel Castro kicked the American Mafia out of Cuba in 1959.

*In this handout photo
provided by the New York
City Police Department,
reputed mobster Vito
Genovese is shown in a
police mugshot in New York
City, July 1946.*

In 1931, Genovese and Luciano took part in the legendary murder of "Joe the Boss" Masseria at an Italian restaurant in Brooklyn. At the time, Luciano served as Masseria's top lieutenant but it was Genovese who engineered the complex hit that ensured he would personally take over Masseria's crime family.

Normally surrounded by four bodyguards, the burly Masseria was mysteriously left alone at the table in Nuova Villa Tammaro, even as Lucky Luciano excused himself to use the restroom. Suddenly, a hit team consisting of Genovese, Bugsy Siegel, and Joe Adonis burst into the restaurant and gunned down Masseria, shooting him four times in the back and once in the head.

The assassination brought Luciano and Genovese to leadership roles in the New York underworld, but their friendship ended when Lucky was sent to prison in 1936. In Luciano's absence, Vito Genovese became acting boss of the Luciano family. But Genovese saw the role as a lifetime position rather than a temporary one. Lucky Luciano never forgave him. In 1937, Genovese was forced to flee to

Italy to escape murder charges, whereupon Luciano appointed his protégé Frank Costello to run the family until his release.

Vito Genovese prospered in exile, successfully creating black market operations during World War II. The totally amoral Genovese actually pilfered money and goods from British and American forces and then funneled them into Nazi Germany. After the Allies took control of the Italian mainland, Genovese was appointed a liaison officer at the U.S. Army headquarters in Naples. The move so emboldened Genovese that he returned to America once the war ended to face the 1937 murder charges.

Things worked out well for Vito. The two leading witnesses were found murdered before they could testify. The case was dismissed.

✦

Yesterday, for the first time in ten years, Luciano and Genovese met face-to-face in Lucky's villa a couple of blocks from the Hotel Nacional.

"You been away a long time," Genovese says after lunch. "You don't realize how much things are changing."

"You've been away a long time, too, Vito. What are you getting at?"

"I think you ought to quit—I mean, retire," Genovese proposes. He has come to Havana to retake control, confident in the secret knowledge that his rival will never be allowed to return to the United States—and that all power, eventually, will be his and his alone.

Luciano fumes. "Right now you work for me and I ain't in no mood to retire. Don't you ever let me hear this again, or I'll lose my temper."

Genovese knows better than to force the issue. He remains silent. Moments later he asks for a lift back to the hotel.

"I had a car with a driver and I sent him back," Luciano will recall. "Naturally, I realized that he went away unhappy, but I didn't give a fuck. I knew there were enough guys on my side to keep him in line. So all that fat little bastard could do was dream.

"I'll tell you one thing, though: it wasn't easy to keep my hands off his fat throat. He'll never know how close he came to it."

✦

Lucky Luciano opens the Havana Conference with a few jokes and words of greeting. He alludes to the fact that there has not been a Boss of All Bosses in the American Mafia for more than fifteen years. The job was once his for the taking, he reminds those in attendance, but in the name of a more united Mafia family he has long chosen not to accept the title.

Times *have* changed. With the war now over, and the days of Prohibition and bootlegging long gone, the Cosa Nostra ("our thing")—as the alliance of Mafia families is also known—needs a single leader to guide its business.

The members listen quietly, allowing Luciano his say. The selection of a Boss of All Bosses and the decision about whether or not to become more active in the narcotics trade are two of the most important topics of these meetings.

To Lucky Luciano's right sits his top lieutenant, the dapper Frank Costello. He has run the Luciano crime family during Lucky's time in prison but has no intention of making that a permanent arrangement. Costello has been part of organized crime his entire life, working not just with Italian families but also Jewish and Irish mobs. In addition to being handy with a gun, he has also worked closely with organized crime syndicates in New York, New Orleans, and Los Angeles on a number of illegal ventures focused around gambling, such as slot machines and horse racing. Costello's decade as head of the Luciano crime family during Lucky's imprisonment was a time of prosperity, and he was a popular leader. But Costello is not reluctant in the slightest to hand the reins of the family back to his boss. The Italian-born Francesco Costello is utterly loyal to Lucky Luciano. He is more than content to bear the trusted title of consigliere—that of counselor and adviser.

✦

To Luciano's left sits Meyer Lansky, the forty-four-year-old Russian-born Jewish mobster who also showed loyalty to Luciano throughout his many years in prison. It was Lansky who arranged the Havana Conference and who dictates the business agenda.

Based in Miami, and known as "the little man" and "the Mob's accountant," the five-foot-tall Lansky is the brains behind the National

Meyer Lansky (1902–83), American gangster, on the steps
of the Federal Courthouse in Miami, Florida, February 28, 1973.

Crime Syndicate's cash flow. His specialty is managing the gambling operations, both legal and illegal, which have become such a huge source of revenue.

Lansky has a particular fascination with Cuba. He not only enjoys the island's lifestyle and climate but is intent on bringing a different sort of casino gaming to the island. Currently, gambling in Cuba often relies on sleight of hand by the dealer. Lansky knows that casual tourists might put their money down for such trickery, but big money

Benjamin "Bugsy" Siegel poses after apprehension in Los Angeles on April 17, 1941, in connection with an indictment returned in New York charging him with harboring Louis "Lepke" Buchalter.

gamblers who put thousands of dollars on a single bet will stay away. The players are looking for an honest game. Once Mafia casinos are built, the mobster envisions a school here in Havana to train card dealers to be straight.

Unlike the Italian bosses seated around the table, Lansky and the Jewish representative from New Orleans, "Dandy Phil" Kastel, will not be allowed to vote on any issues presented this week because they are not members of the *Unione Siciliana*. But out of respect, they are allowed to speak their mind.

Lansky, in particular, has something very urgent that needs to be discussed. The problem is his trusted childhood friend and fellow associate Jewish mobster, Benjamin "Bugsy" Siegel.

Meyer Lansky has long supported Siegel's attempt to turn a dusty truck stop in southern Nevada into a destination resort focused around casinos. Nevada formally legalized gambling in 1931 as a budgetary remedy against the financial hardships of the Great Depression. Other states have forms of legalized betting such as horse races and even bingo, but Nevada's decision to allow statewide gaming makes it the only state to mimic Cuba in its embrace of casinos.

Thus far, Nevada has not seen enormous returns on this law due to its remote desert location. But the growth of air travel means potential gamblers no longer have to drive for days to roll the dice. That has caught the attention of Meyer Lansky.

"Las Vegas," as Bugsy Siegel's proposed gambling mecca is now known, is close to Los Angeles and is accessible to the glamorous Hollywood crowd.

Using money borrowed from the Mafia, Siegel is building a new resort-casino known as the Flamingo. There, guests will be treated to the very best in entertainment and luxury at rock-bottom prices, knowing that gambling revenue will drive the profit margin.

But Siegel has managed the construction poorly and the Mob's patience is being tested. Cost overruns have been enormous, inflating the original price from just over $1 million to almost $6 million. Siegel has gone outside the Mafia to seek loans, effectively taking his business into the public realm.

There are also disturbing rumors that Siegel is skimming money for his own enrichment. Siegel's mistress, Virginia Hill, has been seen flying to Switzerland to deposit enormous sums in bank accounts. She also recently leased a Swiss apartment, leading some to speculate that Hill and Siegel are scheming to flee America.

"There was one thing everybody was sure of," Lucky Luciano will later recall. "On them nights that Bugsy spent on the pillow with her, he spilled enough into her pink ear about the outfit and the top guys that could cause plenty of trouble. The logical thing was to get rid of her."

The same holds true for Bugsy Siegel.

Though most rooms at the Flamingo are unfinished, the casino is due to open in just six days. The Mafia is growing impatient for a return on its investment, and though the day after Christmas is considered the worst possible time to open a new hotel or restaurant, Bugsy Siegel is eager to prove his brainchild a success. A late-night phone call from

Mink-bedecked Virginia Hill Hauser, onetime girlfriend of slain mobster Bugsy Siegel, listens to a question from the Senate crime probers in New York, March 15, 1951, and provides an answer with an expressive wave of her hand.

Las Vegas to Cuba after the opening will inform the conference about his progress.

If the Flamingo is successful, every man in this room will cheer.

If it is not, Bugsy Siegel will be killed.

✦

Next to Meyer Lansky sits Giuseppe Antonio Doto, a.k.a. Joey Adonis. The seating choice is a display of power, reminding all in the room that Adonis is yet another intensely loyal follower of Lucky Luciano. In their teenage years, Luciano, Bugsy Siegel, Meyer Lansky, and Adonis ran their own bootlegging operation in Brooklyn. Like Luciano and Al Capone, Adonis once worked for mobster Frankie Yale. After Yale was assassinated in 1928, it was Adonis who took over the dead man's operation.

*Former casino operator Santo Trafficante Jr. (left) of Tampa, Florida,
was detained by police in Havana, Cuba, June 10, 1959. He is in the custody
of police captains Sergio Martin Vidal (center) and Ignacio Barbon (right).*

Vain and fixated by mirrors, Adonis was once offered the chance
to murder Lucky Luciano by a rival gang. Instead, he warned his boss
about the hit. That display of loyalty has never been forgotten.

✦

The list of high-level mobsters continues down the length of the meeting room table: Joe Bonanno and Tommy Lucchese of New York; the

up-and-coming thirty-seven-year-old Sam Giancana from Chicago; Carlos Marcello from New Orleans; Santo Trafficante from Tampa; and many others.

But all eyes are on Lucky Luciano and Vito Genovese, who is seated next to Joey Adonis.

"Charlie, pardon me if I interrupt," says hit man and alleged saboteur of the SS *Normandie*, Albert Anastasia, as Luciano is about to conclude his opening remarks. The trigger-happy mobster sits directly across from Vito Genovese—a man who wants him dead. Genovese has quietly been sounding out other Mob leaders about a hit on Anastasia.

But "Mad Albert" is unafraid and now takes it upon himself to crown Luciano as the Boss of All Bosses.

"I want to say this in front, before the meeting goes any further. For me, you are the big boss, whether you like it or not. That's the way I look at it, and I would like to hear from anybody who don't feel the same way."

Anastasia glares at Genovese, daring him to make a claim to the top spot. Silence fills the room.

Luciano speaks up. "When I was in Italy, I heard about the trouble between Vito and Albert. I also heard some news about other guys who was trying to move in."

The gangster then continues to speak for another hour, reminding everyone that their greatest enemy is jealousy. "In our kind of business there's so much money to be made that nobody has the right to be jealous of anybody else."

As planned, Luciano veers away from the rivalry, instead focusing on the Mafia's future under his control. Many in this room are in favor of adding narcotics trafficking as a revenue source. Foremost among them is Vito Genovese, who has argued vigorously for a Mafia business expansion into drugs. Heroin, for instance, is much easier to transport and has a much higher profit margin than the alcohol the Mafia once smuggled during Prohibition. Another advantage to hard drugs is that they can be used to enslave and blackmail people.

But Luciano is adamantly opposed to the narcotics traffic. "It had become clear to me that there was so much dough to be made in everythin' else we had, why ruin it with the dangers of playin' around with junk that would only bring the federal guys down on us?" he asked.

"People wanted to gamble, we helped 'em gamble; they needed booze, cigarettes and meat durin' the war, we took care of that. Sure, here and there we would squeeze some guys, but on the other hand, look at all the money we was puttin' in circulation just from other good businessmen buyin' our protection. . . . There wasn't a politician or a cop who could hold on to none of the money we paid him off with . . . they spent it as soon as they got it, and that was very good for the American economy."

Luciano looks to his left, directly into the eyes of Meyer Lansky.

Both men burst out laughing, followed by everyone else in the room. But as the tension deflates, Lucky Luciano knows that he has lost the argument against drugs—and all because Vito Genovese quietly went from delegate to delegate before the meeting, lining up votes in favor of narcotics trafficking.

Advantage Genovese.

Luciano knows better than to go against the majority and quietly accepts the loss.

Ironically, he well knows that his name will become associated with narcotics once the Mafia begins selling "junk." As Boss of All Bosses, federal authorities will treat Luciano as the instigator of the drug trade.

Thus, Luciano's attempt to return to America will be made even more difficult. Vito Genovese has engineered the whole drug thing to defeat the Boss of All Bosses.

Knowing he has been defeated, Luciano sits back down. Frank Costello leans over. "Charlie, don't hit your head against the wall. Vito rigged it before the meet started."

"Frank was right," Luciano will later remember. "Vito won that round."

But Vito Genovese is not finished.

✦

The time is 4:00 a.m. Lucky Luciano is going to bed after a long evening. The Flamingo has finally opened in Las Vegas on a cold and rainy night. Despite the presence of heavyweight entertainers Jimmy

Durante, Xavier Cugat, and George Jessel, few guests made the journey across the desert from Hollywood for the grand opening. Bugsy Siegel only made matters worse, verbally threatening customers and even evicting one group.

Siegel's fate is all but sealed.

Meyer Lansky, in a desperate attempt to recoup the monies lost by the Mafia and hoping to save the life of his good friend Bugsy, has persuaded Luciano and the other delegates to allow him a bit more time to come up with a last-ditch plan for saving the Flamingo. But the assassination clock is ticking.

✦

As the Mob meeting in Havana comes to a close, Lucky Luciano is depressed. An old friend might soon be killed and his organization might be out millions of dollars in Las Vegas. Luciano begins walking slowly from the gathering.

But Vito Genovese intercepts him, asking if they might talk. He invites Luciano to his penthouse suite. The two men ride the elevator in silence. Immediately upon entering his room, Genovese bluntly informs Luciano: "I want half of Italy."

"What are you talking about?"

"I set up the whole thing in Europe," Genovese tells Luciano. "The black market. The truck routes to Germany, everything. It's waiting for you when you get back."

"You're nuts, Vito. I ain't going back. I'm staying in Cuba."

"I understand different," Genovese responds. "I heard that Washington knows you're in Havana and they're putting the screws on those jerks in Cuba to get you thrown out. There's gonna be so much heat that nobody can do nothing to help you. Charlie, you're gonna have to get out of here and go back to Italy. By rights, everything over there is half mine—and I want it."

Luciano's worst fears are confirmed. He is all but certain that Genovese has tipped off the U.S. government about his stay in Havana. "The dirty cock was trying to take me," Luciano will remember. "Vito figured he could muscle me out and finally get the last step up the ladder and be the Boss of Bosses."

Luciano has a personal code of nonviolence toward other members of the family. Such an honor violation could lead to a hit being called on him. But Lucky Luciano can't help himself. He now breaks his own rules.

"I done something I've never done before," Luciano will recall. "I pushed him up against the wall and beat the living daylights out of him.

"He was a tough little prick, but I was bigger and a helluva lot tougher. Besides, I was damn mad. I started to knock him around the room like he was a rubber ball. I didn't hit him in the face—I didn't want to mark him up. I just belted him in the guts and the kidneys, and when he fell down I just started to kick him in the belly, and every shot I took with my fists and foot I told him he was only a shit and a son of a bitch and a dirty rotten Neapolitan louse—even worse, he was a fink American who turned on his own country like a fucking traitor.

"I beat him up so bad he couldn't get out of his room for three days."

Vito Genovese is diagnosed with three broken ribs and a fractured left arm. Under penalty of death, the hotel doctor is ordered by Luciano to say that Genovese slipped in the shower.

The Havana Conference has come to an end.

But things have not ended for Genovese and Luciano.

✦

The date is February 23, 1947. Lucky Luciano is enjoying Saturday lunch in the Vedado section of Havana, just around the corner from the Hotel Nacional. Tipped off by Genovese, the American government is angered by Lucky's presence in Havana. Syndicated columnist Walter Winchell has published the mobster's whereabouts in the swank Havana suburb of Miramar, leading to magazines like *Time* and *Newsweek* publishing their own stories about the famous gangster.

Soon, the United States demands that Luciano be deported from Cuba. However, the Cuban government ignores the command. Benito Herrera, head of Cuba's Secret Police, argues in favor of the island's sovereignty and refuses to arrest Luciano. Alfredo Pequeño, the Cuban minister of the Interior, has even formally reminded the American embassy in Havana that Luciano is not currently doing anything illegal.

But Lucky is nervous, unable to forget his recent confrontation with Vito Genovese. "I couldn't shake the feelin' I had about Vito blowin' the whistle on me in Washington," he will later recall.

Lucky Luciano's feeling is correct.

✦

It has been two months since the Havana Convention. Since its decision to enter the world of narcotics, the Mafia has moved quickly to import more heroin and other hard drugs into the United States.

The director of the Federal Bureau of Narcotics, Harry Anslinger, believes Luciano's presence in Havana is the reason for the drug flow. The fifty-four-year-old law enforcement official has held his job since 1930 and has waged a ferocious war on alcohol and cannabis—both seen as societal evils. Now he turns his focus to heroin.

But Anslinger does not pursue suspects on an equal basis. He is openly racist, believing that drugs wrongfully encourage relations between blacks and whites. Even worse, it encourages racial parity. "Reefer makes darkies think they're as good as white men," he has written.

Anslinger also believes jazz musicians "reek of filth" and has arrested prominent stars like Louis Armstrong and Billie Holiday for alleged drug use, knowing the busts increase the prominence of his bureau, which competes with J. Edgar Hoover and the FBI for prestige. Like Hoover, the heavyset Anslinger has enjoyed close relationships with several presidents, allowing him to pursue a highly personal law enforcement agenda.*

Director Anslinger's disdain for jazz musicians and minorities is closely matched by his hatred for Italians and the Mafia—in particular for Lucky Luciano.

"Lucky," Anslinger will tell *True* magazine, "is the largest single figure in the traffic of this (drug) contraband in America today."

In fact, Harry Anslinger is *obsessed* with Lucky Luciano, seeing

---

* More than forty years after Anslinger's death, that competition between the FBI and FBN is still evident. The website of the Drug Enforcement Agency, as Anslinger's FBN is now known, boasts that Anslinger was tracking the Mafia's drug activities "long before the FBI even acknowledged that the Mob existed in the United States."

the mobster as the most high-profile suspect in his bureau's history. Anslinger is so consumed by Luciano that he will soon write a book about "The Boss," as he titles the unpublished work.*

So despite Cuba's protection of the mobster, Anslinger refuses to back down. He meets personally with President Harry Truman, stating that the flow of drugs from Havana to the United States has profoundly increased in the last two months because of Lucky Luciano.

Truman gives Anslinger the approval to do whatever necessary to remove Lucky Luciano from Cuba. The response is an embargo of all medicines from America. This means that patients in Havana hospitals will suffer and die.

The Cuban government postures, announcing publicly that Lucky Luciano has nothing to do with the illicit flow of drugs into America. But the corrupt politicians can only hold out for so long.

Finally, Cuba buckles to Anslinger and Truman. Cuban secret police arrest the gangster for drug trafficking. He is deported back to Italy, where he is thrown in prison upon landing in Genoa. Eventually he is released, but Lucky Luciano will never again be a force in organized crime.†

Yet Vito Genovese is still not the boss. It is Frank Costello who once again takes control of the Luciano crime family.

But being a Mafioso is a lifetime commitment. So Genovese is content to bide his time, awaiting the moment to strike. And when that moment comes, it will be vicious.

---

* Anslinger's works remain unpublished. His papers are today held at the Harry Truman Library in Independence, Missouri.

† Lucky Luciano settled in Naples. He did not resume his life of crime and eventually ran low on money. He petitioned his old friends in New York for financial help, but they refused.

CHAPTER NINE

JUNE 20, 1947
BEVERLY HILLS, CALIFORNIA
10:45 P.M.

B ugsy Siegel is finally able to relax.
It has been a grueling Friday and the charismatic Jewish mobster is looking forward to a weekend of peace and quiet. "Ben," as he likes to be called by his friends, flew in from Las Vegas just after midnight—then spent the day in meetings. He had dinner with film producer Allen Smiley at a fish restaurant south of Santa Monica. Now the married Siegel, whose wife has just filed for divorce in Nevada, sits on the couch in his mistress's rented Beverly Hills mansion, reading the *Los Angeles Times*' early edition. That mistress, the volatile redheaded Virginia "Ginny" Hill, flew to Paris several days ago. A few months back Siegel hit the thirty-year-old Alabama native so hard she required plastic surgery. Their relationship has not been the same since.

Siegel believes Virginia Hill has traveled to France to select wines for his new casino. But that is not the case. For years, Ginny Hill has played the role of a courtesan for the Chicago Mob, unbeknownst to Siegel. A couple of weeks ago, a Chicago mobster "suggested" she get out of Los Angeles for a while.

Hill left immediately.

Also in the house with Bugsy Siegel and Allen Smiley are Ginny's brother, Chuck, and his girlfriend, Jerri Mason. The two later testify that Bugsy seemed to be in "good spirits" while enjoying the rented pink, seven-bedroom, Moorish-style mansion.

Troubles with his mistress and wife notwithstanding, life is finally settling down for the forty-one-year-old Siegel. His tremendous wealth and fondness for publicity have made the handsome, blue-eyed, nattily attired mobster a regular fixture in New York and Los Angeles gossip columns. Taking the bold risk of developing the high-class Flamingo Hotel has only heightened Siegel's image as a charismatic gangster playboy. His appearance and mannerisms have become so recognizable to the American public that the Warner Bros. movie studio recently released a *Looney Tunes* cartoon in which Bugs Bunny briefly impersonates a mobster who looks and acts like Siegel.*

But the truth about Bugsy Siegel is much darker than a cartoon. He is prone to arrogance and streaks of rage. Born of poor Austro-Hungarian immigrants, Siegel began roaming the streets of New York as a child. He made his reputation in the youth gangs of Brooklyn, forming an alliance with Meyer Lansky at the age of twelve. A hair-trigger temper and penchant for violence earned young Benjamin Siegel the name he would carry the rest of his life, that of Bugs—as in "crazy as a bedbug."

It is a name Siegel loathes, thus ensuring that no one calls him Bugs to his face.

Together, Siegel and Lansky became the Bugs and Meyer Gang, extorting pushcart vendors for protection money and otherwise competing with the Italian and Irish gangs for control of the street action. But those rivalries subsided as the two men grew older, and by their mid-twenties both were working in alliance with Lucky Luciano and the more powerful Italian families.

In time, Bugsy Siegel establishes himself as a hit man, engaging in several famous murders. Although Siegel's actual number of hits is in question, it is known that he worked alongside killers like Albert Anastasia, Vito Genovese, and Luciano himself in the brutal world of Murder, Incorporated. While developing the Flamingo, he even startles his construction supervisor by making a joke about Mafia killings. When

---

* *Racketeer Rabbit* was released on September 14, 1946.

Del Webb blanches at the comment, Siegel calms him by stating, "Relax. We only murder our own."

Though the Bugs and Meyer Gang prospers enough for Siegel to own an apartment in Manhattan's Waldorf Astoria hotel, his notoriety soon brings FBI scrutiny. So, in 1936, at the suggestion of Meyer Lansky, Siegel moves to Los Angeles. The Mob is expanding from its traditional bases in New York, Chicago, and Cleveland, and Siegel quickly acts to take control of West Coast Mafia activity.

Working in conjunction with Mickey Cohen, a five-foot, five-inch former featherweight boxer and onetime enforcer for Al Capone in Chicago, Siegel oversees gambling, prostitution, off-track betting, and narcotics in California. A close friendship with famous actor George Raft, a fellow son of Jewish immigrant parents, allows Siegel to cultivate Hollywood. He soon pals around with actors Clark Gable, Gary Cooper, and Cary Grant.

Siegel's fondness for excitement leads him to a number of ill-fated schemes—including one that would have sold arms to Italian dictator Benito Mussolini.

But now, far-fetched scenarios are put aside. Bugsy Siegel's entire fortune hangs on the Flamingo Hotel.

✦

Casinos and hotels already existed in Las Vegas, beginning soon after the state legalized gaming in 1931. Among the first was a gambling-only joint called the Pair-O-Dice Club. This was soon followed by accommodations like El Rancho Vegas and Last Frontier Hotel. Soon, the roadway connecting them became known as the Las Vegas Strip. And it was here that Bugsy Siegel envisioned his gambling mecca. He soon begins spending time in Las Vegas, dining with local politicians in order to curry favor.

But Siegel's criminal past is too well known. His attempt to purchase a ramshackle casino named the El Cortez is denied by city officials. Then Bugsy hears that a casino development led by Billy Wilkerson, founder of the *Hollywood Reporter* magazine, is just outside the city limits but running short of funds. Masquerading as a potential investor, Siegel purchases a two-thirds stake in what will eventually become the Flamingo. Within a short period of time, he takes complete control.

Bugsy Siegel names his newly acquired resort after girlfriend Virginia Hill, whose shapely legs remind him of those pink, long-limbed Florida birds.

But be careful what you wish for. Years of construction woes take a heavy toll on Siegel, straining his relationship with longtime allies Lucky Luciano and Meyer Lansky, with whom he often becomes irritable and short-tempered. Siegel does not know about the Havana Conference or how close he is to losing his life because of the Flamingo's cost overruns. He is also unaware that Meyer Lansky has temporarily saved him—buying time for Siegel to pay back the Mafia investment.

Lansky's plan does indeed save his friend's life. The Flamingo reopens in mid-March. By June, it is turning a profit, bringing in millions each month. Siegel has begun paying back the Mafia loans, instantly cashing out anyone who requests immediate reimbursement. The casino is packed each night, the spa is getting rave reviews, and most of the 105 rooms are booked. In addition, the showroom has become a Las Vegas entertainment centerpiece.

So Bugsy Siegel is now comfortable spending time away from the resort, enjoying a quiet evening of dinner and light reading. He knows the FBI is watching him and that his international narcotics empire with dealers in Mexico is attracting the attention of Harry Anslinger and the Federal Bureau of Narcotics. Yet he seems unconcerned because success is what Bugsy Siegel is all about.

In his whole life, Siegel has never been convicted of a major crime or been held accountable in any way for his violent behavior. He is wealthier and more famous than John Dillinger, Pretty Boy Floyd, and Baby Face Nelson combined. In fact, if any mobster's life can be considered charmed, it is that of Bugsy Siegel.

Or so he thinks.

✦

A man needs to be careful around Virginia Hill.

Beautiful, voluptuous, and bipolar, the daughter of a backcountry southern mule trader first learned the power of her body when she became sexually active at the young age of twelve. By fourteen the future "Queen of the Mob" is married to a man named George Rogers, whose fate is lost to history. By seventeen she is living in Chicago, working as a waitress at the San Carlo Italian Village during the World's Fair. There, she catches the eye of mobster Joe Epstein. The bookmaker is gay but sees Hill's good looks and southern drawl as a potential asset to the Outfit. "Once that girl is under your skin it's like a cancer. It's incurable," Epstein later confides to Meyer Lansky.

Virginia Hill quickly becomes the sexual plaything of the Chicago Mob, passed from Mafioso to Mafioso. At a Christmas party in 1936, she shocks onlookers by performing oral sex on at least a half dozen gangsters.

By age twenty, Virginia Hill is Joe Epstein's personal spy. Dressed in jewels and furs, she flies back and forth from Chicago to New York to gather information about the East Coast crime business. She sleeps with Joey Adonis during that period but is soon distracted by the man with whom she will have a torrid decade-long romance: Bugsy Siegel.

Ginny Hill is not completely faithful to Siegel during their time together, at one point marrying and divorcing Mexican rumba dancer Carlos Gonzalez and then nineteen-year-old college football player Ossie Griffith, all the while funding her lavish lifestyle by accepting money from Epstein. She dabbles in running her own Mexican narcotics outfit, but her specialty continues to be performing sexual favors to gain privileged information.

And silence. Chicago mobster Jack Dragna once comments that Hill is "the only woman who can be trusted to keep her mouth shut."

Virginia Hill considers Bugsy Siegel her main lover, even though the gangster often beats her so hard she bruises. During one fight in 1944 he punches, then rapes her when she refuses sex. Hill later attempts suicide, swallowing a bottle of sleeping pills, her life barely saved when Siegel rushes her to a Las Vegas hospital to have her stomach pumped.

Siegel and Hill often argue violently, dreadful bouts of screaming and swearing easily overheard by neighbors during otherwise quiet Beverly Hills nights. Yet she loves Siegel enough to risk her life for him, flying to Switzerland with the money he has skimmed from the Flamingo, then depositing the hundreds of thousands of dollars in cash into a private, unmarked Swiss bank account. Siegel talks to her about one day leaving the United States to enjoy all of the money in Europe—and she believes him.

Still, Ginny breaks up with Bugsy time and again and swears that she despises Las Vegas—even punching a Flamingo cigarette girl in the face when she catches Siegel flirting, sending blond Betty Dexter to Clark County Hospital with two broken vertebra. All the while, Hill listens carefully to each word Siegel says, then reports back to Joe Epstein.

On June 8, 1947, Epstein orders Virginia Hill to immediately catch a plane to Chicago. She will later tell authorities she left Los Angeles due to "a lover's quarrel." From Chicago, Hill flies to Paris, leaving the seven-thousand-square-foot rented home at 810 North Linden Drive in Beverly Hills available should Bugsy Siegel wish to take a weekend break from Las Vegas and the Flamingo.

Twelve days later, Siegel takes her up on the offer.

✦

Now, the living-room window just four feet to his right, Siegel throws his left arm over the back of the couch as he reads the *Times*. A terracotta statue of Bacchus, the Roman god of intoxication, stands atop a nearby grand piano. An oil portrait of a nude woman holding a wineglass hangs on the wall.

The curtains are open. A reading lamp illuminates Bugsy Siegel's face.

At that very moment, mobsters Moe Sedway and Gus Greenbaum of the New York Mafia have just arrived in Las Vegas. They have orders from Meyer Lansky and the Luciano Family to enter the Flamingo's offices and take control of the operation.

In Chicago, Virginia Hill's puppet master, Joe Epstein, is just hours away from catching a morning flight to Las Vegas to assist in the Flamingo's "reorganization."

In Paris, Virginia Hill has plans to party into the morning hours on board a luxury houseboat on the river Seine.

✦

Back in Beverly Hills, the night is almost pitch-black, illuminated by the thinnest of crescent moons. Outside the living-room window, a shooter stands on the neighbor's driveway, steadying his .30-caliber military-style M1 carbine against a latticework fence covered in roses. The nearest streetlight is a hundred yards away, ensuring the assassin works in complete concealment.

The gunman is fewer than ten feet from Bugsy Siegel as he pulls the trigger.

Nine times.

✦

Siegel is dead before he can feel the agony of steel-jacketed bullets tearing into his skull.

Of the nine shots fired, one goes through the fabric of Allen Smiley's suit jacket. Instantly, the producer drops to the floor and cowers.

Four other shots miss, destroying the statue of Bacchus and piercing the nude portrait on the wall. These shots are intentionally errant, keeping Smiley pinned to the floor long after the assassin makes his getaway.

Two bullets strike Siegel in the torso. These are not fatal.

Nor is the round that enters Bugsy's right cheek and exits through the left side of his neck.

However, the slug penetrating Siegel's face at the base of his nose then entering his brain with such force that his left eye is popped from its socket immediately kills the gangster.

The bullet casings found outside are two inches long. Given that the shots are taken from such close range, there is little chance the assassin could have missed. Los Angeles police will later conclude that the killer is a marksman, leading some to believe that Virginia Hill's brother, a marine based an hour south at Camp Pendleton, is the shooter.

Others will say the New York Mafia is tired of Siegel's behavior and is finally completing the hit Meyer Lansky successfully argued against in Havana six months ago.

To this day, no one knows who exactly killed Bugsy Siegel. However, shortly after the assassination, Meyer Lansky expanded his operations, eventually becoming the most powerful force in the Vegas gambling world.

As for Virginia Hill, she soon married a ski instructor and moved to Sun Valley, Idaho. However, that didn't last long and Miss Hill eventually returned to Europe.

But even though she was trying to escape the Mafia world, Virginia Hill could not bring herself to separate from the Mob.

And the consequences would be staggering.

CHAPTER TEN

Virginia Hill pleads her innocence.

Television viewers all across America look on in fascination as the gangster moll testifies before a U.S. Senate Committee investigating organized crime. The testimony is a welcome break for a nation that has been consumed by paranoia over Communism and the atom bomb since the end of World War II six years ago. American troops are now waging war against the "Red menace" in Korea, and a Wisconsin senator named Joseph McCarthy is alleging that the U.S. government is rife with Communist sympathizers.

So just as the nation did in the 1930s, when celebrity gangsters allowed the public to temporarily forget the woes of the Great Depression, these "Kefauver hearings" now veil America's fears of nuclear obliteration.

And no witness is more provocative than Virginia Hill.

Four years after the death of Bugsy Siegel, his mistress sits before the cameras in a cramped hearing room at the federal courthouse here in Foley Square. Now thirty-four and the mother of a newborn son, Hill is unafraid of lead counsel Rudolf Halley, a young attorney from Queens. Dressed in a $5,000 silver mink stole, silk gloves, and black dress with a plunging neckline, she feigns complete ignorance while deflecting his questions with ease.

"The men that I was around that gave me things were not gangsters or racketeers. The only time I ever got anything from them was going out and having fun and maybe a few presents," she insists under oath. At stake is her very freedom. Investigators have concluded that Virginia Hill has never worked an honest day in her life, nor paid much in taxes. Yet her net worth is estimated to be hundreds of thousands of dollars. IRS investigators know that between 1942 and 1947, Hill spent more than $250,000 but showed earnings of just $16,000 per year. So, unless Hill can explain where this money came from, she could face a long prison sentence for tax evasion, as Al Capone once did.

"I never knew anything about their business," Hill adds, speaking of her Mafia friends. "They didn't tell me about their business. Why would they tell me? I didn't care anything about their business in the first place. I don't even understand it."

"The reason I ask," Halley parries, "is that you seem to have a great ability to handle financial affairs."

"Who, me?"

"It just seems impossible," the attorney continues, "that you did not know about Siegel's associates at the Flamingo."

"I didn't ever go out," Hill responds. "In the first place, I had hay fever. I was allergic to the cactus. Every time I went there I was sick."

Hill then adds that she spent most of her time in Las Vegas relaxing in her hotel room. "Ben's friends: I never even met them or was around them."

The courtroom is packed with senators, investigators, and reporters. These hearings—named for Senator Estes Kefauver, the bookish, womanizing Tennessee legislator who leads the committee—have become America's first national television phenomenon. Organized crime is no longer exclusively in big cities but has infiltrated small towns to such an extent that a group known as the American Municipal Association has petitioned the federal government to investigate the scourge.

Ironically, J. Edgar Hoover of the FBI is opposed to the Senate proceedings. He sees no need, claiming that organized crime is a "myth." The director believes that independent racketeers are being mistaken for a national alliance of criminals. For this reason, he posits that local police departments are responsible for prosecuting such crimes. Instead of the Mafia, Hoover would prefer that America's Senate investigations focus on combating the rising Communist threat. The bureau's New York field office has four hundred agents assigned to finding "subversives," as Communist sympathizers are known. But just four agents are assigned to organized crime. Similarly, Hoover keeps files containing detailed personal information about America's most influential individuals but does not believe it necessary to authorize such investigations of Mafia leaders.

Joseph Nellis, assistant legal counsel for the Kefauver hearings, would later relate Hoover's disavowal of organized crime. "We had a long series of meetings with him off the record, at which he told us, 'We don't know anything about the Mafia or the families in New York. We haven't followed this.' He told us what we were learning about the Mafia wasn't true."

Unable to rely on Hoover for assistance, the Kefauver Committee instead turns to the director's rival, Harry Anslinger of the Federal Bureau of Narcotics, for insight into the criminal underworld. Yet when two key Mafia witnesses are found murdered on the eve of giving testimony, Senator Kefauver reaches out to Hoover once more, desperately asking that the FBI provide security for future witnesses. "I regret to advise that the Federal Bureau of Investigation is not empowered to perform guard duties," Hoover responds icily, further distancing himself from the landmark proceedings.

✦

Yet within the FBI, there are some who question Hoover's true motives. Some find it odd that the man who once pursued criminals with relentless ferocity, building the FBI's reputation by arresting or killing America's most notorious gangsters, now refuses to play even a small role in this very public investigation of organized crime.

A handful of agents suspect that the Mafia actually controls J. Edgar Hoover. When he takes the train north for a weekend in New York, the director regularly frequents the Stork Club, a Mafia haven. In Miami, Hoover prefers a seafood restaurant favored by Meyer Lansky and Frank Costello.

FBI director J. Edgar Hoover and assistant Clive Tolson,
circa 1939.

It is whispered by a few agents that Lansky and other underworld leaders have photographs of Hoover in compromising situations with Clyde Tolson, a top man at the FBI who has been the director's constant companion for almost twenty years. The two are so close that they allegedly have been seen surreptitiously holding hands when they believe no one is looking. It is customary for Hoover's limousine to pick up Tolson at his apartment each morning so the two men can ride to work together. The lifelong bachelors also vacation with each other and eat dinner together five nights a week. All the while, Hoover is prosecuting homosexuals on morals charges, as well as keeping those secret personal files on the lives of powerful politicians and even presidents— among them Senator Kefauver. The man from Tennessee is known for his heavy drinking, eager acceptance of bribes, and a habit of using House and Senate committee furniture as spontaneous sex locations.*

---

* The allegations about Hoover and Tolson had followed the two men since 1931, when Tolson first began working at what would become the FBI. There is still debate as to whether the two men were lovers or simply bachelor coworkers. Upon his death, J. Edgar Hoover left his home and almost all his $551,000 estate to Tolson.

FBI agents also know that J. Edgar Hoover surreptitiously meets with Frank Costello in Central Park during visits to Manhattan. The subjects of the conversations are unknown, but it is common knowledge that Hoover has a fondness for gambling on horse races—albeit in small dollar amounts. Sports betting is illegal in Washington, D.C., meaning that the nation's chief law enforcement officer breaks the law to fuel this passion. Some agents believe the Mafia uses this vice of the director's to keep him from investigating their activities. "Hoover will never know how many races I had to fix for those lousy ten-dollar bets," Costello will later admit.

✦

To be fair, J. Edgar Hoover's interactions with Mafia figures are not all that unusual for law enforcement officials. Before his death, Bugsy Siegel secretly met with federal agents in Los Angeles to share details about the criminal activities of his enemies. But due to Hoover's denials about organized crime, the FBI field office in L.A. is not allowed to take action. Instead, agents pass information about the Mafia to local police. And unlike the FBI, the Los Angeles Police Department has no doubt that organized crime exists—so much so that the LAPD has formed a small, elite unit dedicated to destroying the city's Mob element.

The Gangster Squad, as it is called, was originally formed in 1946 as a response to criminals from back East coming west to shake down local restaurants. The owners of famous L.A. eateries like Mocambo and Brown Derby were being forced to pay 25 percent of their income to these "tourists"—or else.

Carrying tommy guns, smoking cigars, and prowling Los Angeles in old Ford automobiles with holes in the floorboards, squad members are all physically powerful men who played sports and/or fought in World War II. Their specialty is cornering a suspected gangster and "strongly suggesting" he leave and never come back.

The Squad is effective, using wiretaps, break-ins, and physical beatings to intimidate the "bad guys."

Officer Jack O'Mara, one of the original eight men chosen for this duty, remembers a typical tactic. "We would have a little heart to heart talk with them. Emphasize the fact that this wasn't New York, this wasn't Chicago, this wasn't Cleveland. And we leaned on them a little, you know what I mean? Up in the Hollywood Hills, off Coldwater Canyon, anywhere up there. And it's dark at night."

O'Mara continued: "We would kind of put a gun to their ear and say, 'you want to sneeze? Do you feel a sneeze coming on? A loud sneeze?'"

✦

Like the Los Angeles Police Department, the American public is completely convinced that organized crime *is* real, but the public is entertained by the spectacle.

"The week of March 12, 1951, will occupy a special place in history," reports a cover story in *Life* magazine. "People had suddenly gone indoors into living rooms, taverns, and clubrooms, auditoriums, and back offices. There, in eerie half-light, looking at millions of small frosty screens, people sat as if charmed. Never before had the attention of the nation been riveted so completely on a single matter . . .

"Dishes stood in sinks, babies went unfed, business sagged and department stores emptied while the hearings were on."

Public fascination with the covert workings of the Mafia has never been more intense: schools across the country are dismissing students from class to watch the televised proceedings, and here in New York, Broadway shows are playing to near-empty theaters. As they have been for decades, Americans are fascinated with the underworld, eager to make celebrities and even heroes of men who steal and kill for a living. Now, the movie newsreels that once highlighted criminal escapades are being replaced by live broadcasts on television.

The hearings are so popular that Senator Kefauver will win an Emmy Award from the Academy of Television Arts and Sciences. He will also choose to run for president in 1952. It will be Kefauver's defeat of President Harry Truman in the New Hampshire primary that convinces Truman to pull out of the race.

But the hearings in his name are not a complete triumph for the senator. During the committee's stop in Chicago he meets privately with Mob lawyer Sidney Korshak. Rather than agree to offer testimony,

*Sidney R. Korshak, attorney for the Englander mattress company,
tells Senate investigators that his firm reimbursed management consultant Nathan
Shefferman for $2,800, after Shefferman paid for observing and checking
plant employees. Washington, D.C., October 1957.*

Korshak presents the married forty-seven-year-old Kefauver with photographs showing the senator at the Drake Hotel, sharing a bed with two young women. From this moment on, even as he runs for president, Kefauver is a captive of the Mob.*

✦

Of course, Virginia Hill is not alone in offering testimony. For the past year, the Kefauver Committee has heard evidence in fourteen cities and

---

* Estes Kefauver failed in his 1952 presidential election bid. He remained in the Senate and ran for president once again in 1956. After being defeated by Adlai Stevenson for the Democratic nomination, Kefauver ran on the ticket as the vice presidential nominee. In 1963, Kefauver suffered a heart attack on the floor of the Senate. He put off surgery so that his wife, Nancy, who was vacationing with their daughters in Colorado, could be at his bedside. Kefauver died two days later of a ruptured aortic aneurysm, just as Nancy Kefauver's plane landed in Washington.

called more than six hundred witnesses. In fact, the investigation was supposed to end in February 1951, but the hearings are so popular that the American public inundated Congress with letters demanding that the televised programs continue. Thus the addition of New York City as the final stop.

Other gangsters subpoenaed to speak here at the federal courthouse include Frank Costello, who now runs the Luciano crime family. Despite Lucky Luciano's permanent absence, the mobster shows respect by not changing the family's name to his own. Now, the public not only sees how stylishly a suspected Mafioso dresses and the precision with which he combs his hair, but Americans also hear an Italian-accented speaking voice made raspy by a botched operation for polyps on his vocal cords. Costello adds to the theater by refusing to acknowledge the existence of La Cosa Nostra.

"I am in no condition to testify," Costello tells Kefauver at one point.

"You refuse to testify further?"

"Am I a defendant in this courtroom?" Costello asks.

"No."

"Then I am walking out," Costello replies, then stands and leaves.

However, the hearings will prove damning to Costello. Eventually, he will be sent to prison for contempt of Congress.

Things will go much worse for Willie Moretti, a Mob underboss who chooses not to take the Fifth. Instead, Moretti, who believes he is not doing any harm, tells the Senate panel that certain "made men" socialized at a club named Duke's. At the time it seems innocuous—but seven months later he will be shot in the face and killed while eating lunch in New Jersey.*

As flamboyant as Costello was, it is Virginia Hill who becomes an immediate sensation. Her feigned naïveté, fearless indifference to the maneuvering of the prosecutors, and an Alabama drawl that Kefauver

---

* Moretti was well connected in the confluence of the Mafia and entertainment worlds. He was godfather to Frank Sinatra, as well as good friends with comedians Dean Martin and Jerry Lewis. All three performed at the wedding of Moretti's daughter. Martin and Lewis were supposed to have attended the lunch with Moretti on the day of his murder but canceled that morning when Lewis contracted the mumps.

will describe as a mixture of "southern poor white and Chicago gangster-ese" gives Ms. Hill a raw glamour that Americans find intriguing. She will only add to that spectacle when her testimony ends, covering her face as she pushes through a gauntlet of reporters screaming questions.

"Get your fucking cameras out of my face. Get out of my fucking way," Hill commands.

But Marjorie Farnsworth, a writer for the *New York Journal-American*, does not listen. She blocks Hill's path only to be smacked hard by a right hook to the face. *New York Times* reporter Lee Mortimer also receives a kick in the shins from Hill. That draws loud cheers from the crowd of spectators.

"I hope a fucking atom bomb falls on y'all," she yells over her shoulder before being driven away from the courthouse.

As brazen as that behavior might be, particularly for a woman straining against the conventional gender mores of 1951, it is Virginia Hill's comments in a closed executive session that will truly upend the investigation.

Hill is being questioned by Senator Charles Tobey of New Hampshire, one of the committee's five members. Reporters are present but there are no television cameras. Tobey is fascinated by Hill's relationship with Joe Epstein and the other men who give her so much money.

"Why would they do it?" asks Tobey, trying to set a trap.

Hill dodges the question. Tobey tries again.

"Why would he give you all that money?" the senator asks, speaking about Epstein.

"You really want to know?" asks Hill.

"Yes. I want to know why," Tobey replies.

The committee waits eagerly for Hill's response. They sense a triumph.

"Then I'll tell you why."

Virginia Hill does not give quite the answer they expect.

"Because I'm the best damned cocksucker in town."

✦

Four hundred miles south of New York City, in Charlottesville, Virginia, an aspiring lawyer and his pregnant wife are fascinated by the Mafia hearings.

*Massachusetts senator John F. Kennedy discusses campaign matters with
his brother and campaign manager, Robert Kennedy, on July 10, 1960.
The senator is seeking the Democratic presidential nomination.*

Bobby Kennedy is twenty-five years old, an idealistic Irish-Catholic
from Massachusetts who tends to be conservative in his political and
moral thinking. He stands five feet, nine inches, weighs just 155 pounds,
and has a reputation for ferocious tenacity. Among his powerful friends
is Senator Joseph McCarthy of Wisconsin, now growing famous by
promoting a Communist witch hunt.*

Kennedy rarely drinks and does not smoke, nor does Ethel, his

---

* Robert Kennedy was actually employed by Joseph McCarthy during his time as a
Senate staff member of McCarthy's subcommittee investigating Communist sympathizers.

bride of less than one year. The couple lives in a three-bedroom home while he finishes law school at the University of Virginia. Both come from means, and Ethel laments that "this place could fit into the living room of one of our guest houses," but the Kennedys are content with their temporary circumstance.

The house is usually a scene of chaos. Ethel does not cook and will not clean, so the kitchen and bedroom fall into disarray on those days when a maid is not present. The family pet, an English bulldog named Toby Belch, is not trained. Add those factors to the rigor of finishing school while awaiting the birth of a first child and it can be said that this time of Bobby Kennedy's life is a period of discombobulation.

Kennedy agrees that the fight against organized crime should be "a national crusade, a great debating forum, an arouser of public opinion on the state of the nation's morals," in the words of Senator Kefauver. For Bobby has a puritan belief in right and wrong, and has chosen to become a lawyer so that he may use the law to root out criminal activities. After passing the bar, he expects to begin working for the U.S. Justice Department's Criminal Division.

However, with every passing revelation by the Kefauver Committee, Bobby Kennedy becomes more aware that his own family name might soon be dragged through the mud. In fact, his father is mentioned in passing as being linked to organized crime during the hearings, but no evidence is cited.

The truth is that Bobby Kennedy's own lavish childhood was made possible by a father who chose to dwell in the shadows between right and wrong. The Kefauver hearings may center around Italian American criminal activity, but the Irish Joseph Kennedy is a multimillionaire who wields just as much power as any Mafia don. In his lifetime, the Kennedy family patriarch will found RKO Pictures, serve as U.S. ambassador to Great Britain, and work as chairman of the Securities and Exchange Commission.

Kennedy also has his learning-disabled daughter lobotomized upon the advice of a trusted physician, is deeply anti-Semitic, and even admired the politics of Adolf Hitler. Mobster Frank Costello will state for the record that he and Joseph Kennedy had a business relationship shipping bootlegged whiskey during Prohibition. Once, when a hit was called on Kennedy in Detroit, it is allegedly Costello who intervened and saved his life.*

Despite the exploits of his high-profile father, Bobby Kennedy will choose a different path. Soon, he will become the leader of the anti-Mafia faction in the federal government.

And vicious criminals will hate him for it.

---

* Despite gangster testimony from Costello as well as Meyer Lansky, there is no firm evidence that Joseph Kennedy was a bootlegger. His father was a liquor importer before Prohibition and Kennedy obtained legal import rights for several brands of spirits once the law was repealed. It should be noted that today the Kennedy family denies that the patriarch was involved in any criminal activity.

CHAPTER ELEVEN

AUGUST 18, 1956
ASTOR HOTEL
NEW YORK CITY
6:00 P.M.

It has been five years since organized crime was exposed on national television. But instead of being cowed, the Mafia has grown even stronger—especially in New York.

Three thousand guests pack the ballroom in this Times Square hotel. Among them are the heads of America's twenty-four major crime families, including Mafia kingpins Vito Genovese, Albert Anastasia, Sam Giancana, and Joe Profaci.* Frank Costello of the Luciano family is currently serving an eleven-month sentence for tax evasion and obviously cannot attend. Longtime kingpin and Costello ally Joe Adonis is also absent, now living in Milan, Italy, after deportation by the U.S. government.

Despite the public awareness brought forth by the Kefauver hearings five years ago, the Mob has thrived, as evidenced by this lavish sit-down dinner reception. Gambling and illegal narcotics are the foundation of the increased affluence, and havens like Las Vegas and Havana allow the Mafia to flourish in settings sympathetic to them.

---

* The character of Vito Corleone in *The Godfather* is based upon Joe Profaci.

Yet America in 1956 is in transition, and criminals are being forced to change right along with the country.

Some historians will later view '56 as the most pivotal year of the decade. The Cold War between the United States and Soviet Union has intensified, and the fear of a nuclear doomsday is very real. Dwight Eisenhower will soon be reelected even though his calm persona and centrist policies are seemingly out of touch with the violent clashes between blacks and whites now ravaging the Deep South. In addition, Congress has passed into law a bill that will construct an interstate highway system, spurring suburban growth and bringing forth new inventions such as the motel and the drive-in movie theater.

But the shift in American culture goes beyond race and roads. Elvis Presley released the breakout smash song "Heartbreak Hotel" in January, ushering in the rock 'n' roll sound that now pushes aside crooners like Mob favorite Frank Sinatra. This new mania is accompanied by a more low-key movement known as the Beat Generation, which turns its back on traditional American values to embrace free sexuality and recreational drugs. And while no Mafioso in the ballroom tonight would ever dream of donning a beret and playing the bongo drum in the manner of some Beat gatherings, they are more than happy to provide the marijuana and heroin that fuel some "beatnik" behavior.

But onstage here at the Astor, rock 'n' roll has no place. Instead, Anthony Dominick Benedetto, who performs under the name Tony Bennett, croons for the mingling crowd. At thirty, Bennett is a singing sensation, but out of respect for the gathering he performs tonight gratis. Another prominent Italian, Eugenio Maria Giovanni Pacelli, sends his best wishes and blessings from Rome. The eighty-year-old Pacelli is known worldwide as Pope Pius XII. The pontiff's motives for involving himself in a Mafia wedding are unclear, but the bride and groom are making plans to stop at the Vatican during their honeymoon to pay their respects.

The occasion at the Astor is the wedding of Rosalie Profaci and Salvatore "Bill" Bonanno, uniting two of New York's most powerful crime families. This is the largest gathering of Mafia notables since the Havana Conference, but the mood is celebration, not business. The groom's father, Joseph Bonanno, a.k.a. Joe Bananas, watches over the proceedings, proud that he has reunited the Mob, if only for one night. He has carefully scrutinized the seating arrangements, making sure that rivals are on the opposite side of the hall from one another.

But no matter where they are, all can easily see the seventeen-foot-tall wedding cake.

"At least they came," Bonanno will later reminisce. "They were making an effort to be nice."

✦

"Nice" does not last long.

The date is May 2, 1957. Frank Costello is temporarily out of "the jug," as he terms it, having been released from prison on bail. Before the Kefauver hearings, Costello's only conviction had been forty years earlier for carrying a gun. But his televised performance changed the mobster's life, making him the focus of intense government scrutiny into his business dealings. In 1954, he was convicted for evading $28,532 in federal taxes. But this past March he was temporarily set free on $25,000 bail to await a ruling on whether his actual sentence should be five years or time served.

New York City has long been divided among what is known as the Five Families, all descended from Sicilian immigrants. The Bonanno, Lucchese, Luciano, Gambino, and Profaci families are also part of the nationwide organized crime consortium known as the Commission. The boss of each family, as well as leaders of the Buffalo, New Orleans, and Tampa mobs, and Chicago's Outfit, hold sway in settling disagreements. To prevent turf wars, each family's territory in the five boroughs and New Jersey is controlled by this collective. Should a leader become unstable and need to be replaced, permission from all the other bosses is required.

Right now, Frank Costello feels safe. It's true that the deportation of Joe Adonis, as well as the three years spent in jail, have weakened the mobster's hold on the Luciano crime family. Yet Costello is sure that his allies will remain loyal. He has a longtime alliance with Albert Anastasia, who now heads his own crime family after murdering former Gambino boss Vincent Mangano in April 1951, even as the Kefauver hearings were still in session. Costello is also close with Tommy Lucchese of the Bronx and New Jersey Mob, a man known for his diplomacy. The three men form a majority within the five families. This should keep Costello in power long after his legal woes pass—or so he hopes.

Unbeknownst to the Prime Minister of the Underworld, as Costello is nicknamed, Vito Genovese is now quietly attempting to pull Lucchese over to his side.

✦

Frank Costello is enjoying his freedom in New York City. He spent several hours on this warm spring day at the Biltmore Hotel, relaxing in a Turkish bath. Then it was on to dinner at the white tablecloth French-Italian restaurant L'Aiglon with his wife, Bobbie, and a few friends. But when the party moves to the bar for drinks, Costello excuses himself and takes a cab to his seven-room Manhattan apartment across the street from Central Park. The time is 10:55 p.m. The mobster does not notice the large black Cadillac that follows the taxi, then slows to a stop in front of the landmark Majestic apartment building.

Costello greets doorman Norvel Keith as he enters the lobby.

Suddenly, a thick Italian voice shouts at the mobster: "This is for you, Frank!"

Costello instinctively turns his head toward the yelling, even as his burly assailant fires a .38-caliber pistol from fifteen feet away. The hit man, Vinny "the Chin" Gigante, is a former boxer who now works as an enforcer for Vito Genovese. Costello recognizes the three-hundred-pound assassin in the split second before a bullet creases the right side of his skull.

Instantly, blood spurts from the wound as Costello falls hard onto a leather lobby couch. Gigante pushes past the doorman and out onto Seventy-Second Street, where the black Cadillac awaits. As the car speeds away, Vinnie the Chin is sure he has conducted a successful hit on the great Frank Costello.

But Costello is alive.

The act of his name being called out before the round left the gun barrel allowed Costello to turn his head just enough to literally dodge the bullet. Though blood flows from the wound, the Mob boss is merely grazed. He is immediately taken by taxi to Roosevelt Hospital, where doctors confirm that the bullet entered near Costello's right ear and traced the curvature of his skull before exiting just above the neck. Incredibly, X-rays show absolutely no damage to his skull.

Meanwhile, as the surgeons do their work, New York police conduct a surreptitious search of Frank Costello's belongings. "Gross casino wins as of 4-26-57," reads one scrap of paper: "$651,284." A subsequent investigation reveals the money to be his "take" from the brand-new Tropicana Hotel in Las Vegas. This is the first confirmed involvement between the New York Mob and the Vegas casinos.

That fluke piece of evidence is enough to have Frank Costello returned to prison.

But it is the near assassination that changes his life. When called upon to name his assailant in court, the boss invokes the code of omertà, claiming he didn't recognize the man who shot him. "I don't have an enemy in the world," Costello tells the NYPD, apparently befuddled as to why anyone would try to kill him. "I must have been mistaken for someone else."

Yet Frank Costello knows that Vito Genovese will not rest until he takes control of the Luciano crime family, which would certainly mean death for Costello. At sixty-six years old, he is financially comfortable and enjoys the love of the former showgirl to whom he has been married for almost forty years.

So rather than endure the threat of another hit, Costello takes the unprecedented step of "retiring" from the Mafia. He will return to prison to complete his sentence, then upon his release live out his days at the Majestic, no longer boss of the Luciano crime family. Costello settles into a daily routine of rising at 9:00 a.m., walking to the Waldorf Astoria for a shave, manicure, and shoeshine, lunch at the Madison Hotel, and then evenings entertaining celebrities at the Majestic's corner apartment 18F. Costello's days of worrying about law enforcement arrest or a surprise Mafia hit are over. He is even on record as seeing a psychologist once a week to discuss his feelings.*

Vito Genovese, who has patiently bided his time since that long-ago attempt to take control at the Havana Conference, wants nothing to do with retirement. His only concerns are power and wealth.

---

* Frank Costello also had a lavish home in Sands Point, Long Island.

Vito Genovese has finally won. The Luciano crime family is no more. The Genovese crime family is born.

✦

Albert Anastasia is also expanding his crime family.

The mobster once nicknamed Il Terremoto—The Earthquake— has matured, and is no longer the impulsive executioner of his younger days. For instance, it was just a few years ago that he ordered the murder of Brooklyn resident Arnold Schuster, a twenty-five-year-old clothing salesman who became a local hero for capturing legendary bank robber Willie Sutton. But when Schuster went on television to boast about the apprehension, Anastasia just happened to be watching. Shouting at the TV, "I can't stand squealers," he then sent his crew to assassinate the amateur detective. Schuster was shot once in each eye and twice in the groin as a message to others who might meddle in the crime world.

But now, Albert is a changed man.

"Anastasia," the *New York Times* will note, "could seem pleasant, genial, and generous." It is 10:18 on this chilly Friday morning. The notorious former hit man for Murder, Incorporated, wears a brown suit and gray hat as he enters the Park Sheraton Hotel here in Manhattan. Anastasia removes his long blue topcoat and takes a seat in Grasso's, the lobby barbershop. The recessed fluorescent lighting accentuates the deep lines on Anastasia's face, brought on by heavy losses at the racetrack.

The mobster takes a seat in Chair Four, facing out the window onto Fifty-Fifth and Seventh. His back is to the door.

The small shop is busy, with two other customers already seated, as well as a staff of five barbers, a manicurist, a valet, two shoeshine men, and owner Arthur Grasso.

"Haircut," Anastasia says brusquely to barber Joseph Bocchino.

Bocchino places a sheet around the gangster's neck. Anastasia's chair is reclined and hot towels are placed over his face to soften his beard for a shave that precedes the barbering.

Anastasia is now fifty-five. The attempted hit on longtime friend Frank Costello has rattled the burly mobster. Fearing he might be next, Anastasia recently increased his number of personal bodyguards from one to three. A ten-foot-high metal fence now surrounds his new mansion in Fort Lee, New Jersey, and the lawn is patrolled by two snarling Doberman pinschers. Anastasia's greatest fear, however, is not his own death but a hit on his wife and twenty-two-year-old son.

In truth, the possibility of such an attack dwindles with every passing day. Anastasia almost went to war with Vito Genovese, but instead the two men sat down to dinner with the leaders of the five families, where they traded accusations before making peace. "Reluctantly, they renounced going to war with one another," boss Joseph Bonanno will recall. "The rest of us raised our glass in a toast for peace. Albert and Vito kissed each other on the cheek."

That peace has allowed Anastasia time to conspire with Meyer Lansky and Tampa Mob boss Santo Trafficante, in hopes of expanding his family's operations into Cuban casinos and drug smuggling. In fact, Anastasia is so confident in the gangland truce that he travels without a bodyguard today. He now relaxes as the towels are removed. The barber spins him around to face the mirror. The time is now 10:30 a.m., as Anastasia reclines with his eyes closed.

Suddenly, two men of below-average height enter the barbershop from the hotel lobby. Both wear fedoras and aviator sunglasses. Scarves cover the lower portion of their faces. Each wears one black glove.

Striding quickly to Chair Four, the two gunmen quietly poke barber Joseph Bocchino with the barrel of their pistols as a "suggestion" to get out of the way immediately. As he flees, they take up positions on either side of Albert Anastasia.

Everyone else in the shop moves quickly for the door.

Hearing the commotion, Anastasia sits up quickly and attempts to protect himself, but it is too late. Ten quick shots are fired. The first two are what coroners call "defensive wounds," shattering Anastasia's left hand and wrist as he throws up his arm in a failed attempt to protect himself.

Moving quickly, Anastasia lunges at the gunmen but in the confusion makes the tragic mistake of attacking their images in the mirror. Now facing the wrong direction, he is hit in the hip, the spine, and, finally, the skull.

As the *New York Times* reports, "Apparently, the bullet at the back of the head had ended Anastasia's life immediately."

As the crime boss crumples to the floor wrapped in white barber towels, the killers exit onto Fifty-Fifth Street and immediately blend into the sidewalk crowds before entering a waiting car. The pistols are already abandoned, one dropped in a doorway and the other in a trash can.*

By midnight, New York police will interview fifty eyewitnesses, with a list of ten more to be interrogated. Vito Genovese had the most to gain from Anastasia's slaying, and despite the truce called by the five families, there is every reason to believe he authorized the hit. Yet to this day, the killers are still unknown.

Curiously, Anastasia was a known crime boss, and the very public murder had all the appearances of a gangland slaying, but in Washington, J. Edgar Hoover of the FBI still insists that organized crime in America is a myth.

That is about to change.

✦

"Is there any organization such as the Mafia," Bobby Kennedy asks Federal Bureau of Narcotics agent Joseph Amato, "or is that just the name given to the Italian underworld?"

The date is November 13, 1957, two weeks to the day since Albert Anastasia was gunned down. The weather outside is wet and dreary. As television cameras broadcast the proceedings nationwide, Kennedy addresses the witness in a caucus room of the Old Senate Office Building in Washington. The thirty-one-year-old Massachusetts native now serves as chief counsel for the committee while the Senate investigates "improper activities in labor and management" as they relate to organized crime.

Since 1946, Agent Amato has been part of a four-man detail of Italian American FBN agents working out of the New York City field office. Their stated purpose is to end the Mafia's narcotics operations. Now, with Kennedy as the chief counsel, Amato appears before a select Senate hearing investigating the Mob. Known as the McClellan Committee, after John Little McClellan, the Southern Baptist senator from Arkansas, the panel more often goes by the nickname Rackets

---

* The site of Albert Anastasia's murder still exists on the corner of Fifty-Fifth and Seventh in Manhattan. However, it is now a Starbucks instead of a barbershop.

Committee. At Kennedy's request, the freshman senator from Massachusetts has acquired a seat. That senator would be his big brother, John, a World War II hero and Democratic presidential hopeful.*

Bobby Kennedy has served as Senate counsel since 1954, taking on his current lead role when the Democrats obtained the Senate majority. Rumors of illicit behavior within America's top labor unions surface in 1955, leading President Dwight Eisenhower to request a federal investigation. Senator McClellan soon asks that Bobby serve as the committee's lead counsel, giving him broad authority to set the agenda and question witnesses.

The bold young attorney takes on his new role with typical zeal, knowing very little about unions or organized crime but determined to end labor corruption. He even travels to New York as part of his research, where he accompanies Joseph Amato and the FBN "Italian Squad" as they make drug busts on the nighttime streets. Washington insider Alice Longworth, daughter of Theodore Roosevelt, describes the earnest Kennedy's moralistic fervor as that of a "revolutionary priest."

This places Bobby squarely at odds with his father and older brother. As the Kennedy clan gathers for Christmas in 1956, he eagerly announces his role in the hearings about organized crime, only to encounter one of the most furious rows in family history. Sister Jean Kennedy Smith will call the fracas "the worst one we ever witnessed."

Joseph Kennedy rages that his young son is naïve, a danger to family ambition.

John F. Kennedy's plans to run for president in 1960 are closely tied to the Mafia-controlled unions, who traditionally vote Democrat. JFK sides with his father, fearing that his brother's investigation might turn the longshoremen and teamsters against his candidacy.

In the end, Bobby gets his way. John Kennedy reluctantly accepts a spot on the committee to block the conservative South Carolinian Strom Thurmond from being part of this high-profile panel.†

In 1956, JFK was passed over for a vice presidential spot on the

---

* Other senators serving on the McClellan Committee were heavyweight Senate legends Barry Goldwater, Sam Ervin, and Frank Church.

† The committee consisted of eight members, composed of Democrats and Republicans.

Democratic Party's ticket in favor of Senator Estes Kefauver. And as Kennedy has been reminded by journalists, Kefauver's national fame derived solely from prosecuting organized crime on national television. Doing the same with these McClellan hearings could go a long way toward propelling John Kennedy to the next political level.

Yet the normally charismatic Massachusetts senator does not seem to care. John Kennedy shows his apathy through poor attendance and a bored demeanor on those days he does sit in committee.

Bobby Kennedy is the exact opposite. His relentless pursuit of organized criminals has led him to this very moment, as Agent Amato sits before the committee and prepares to answer the simple—and dangerous—question: "Is there a Mafia?"

Amato has been a federal agent for seventeen years and well knows the peril associated with the answer he is about to give. Television cameras have been forbidden from showing any part of his image and he sits with his back to the room to hide his face.

"That is a big question to answer," Amato replies. "But we believe that there does exist today in the United States a society, loosely organized, for the specific purpose of smuggling narcotics and committing other crimes in the United States."

Bobby Kennedy launches his follow-up question immediately. "And that is what you consider the Mafia."

"It has its core in Italy and it is nationwide," Amato concludes. "In fact, international."

✦

By sheer coincidence, at the very same moment Bobby Kennedy is grilling Joseph Amato about the existence of the Mob, an international Mafia summit is about to begin.

Three hundred miles north of Washington, in the tiny upstate New York town of Apalachin, Vito Genovese has called a meeting of North America's top Mafia members. With Frank Costello and Albert Anastasia now gone, Genovese considers himself the uncontested Boss of All Bosses, and he has called a meeting to make it official.

As far as the FBI is concerned, this conference is fiction. If there is no such *thing* as organized crime, then mobsters could not possibly gather anywhere. But as Agent Amato is testifying in Washington, this "loosely organized" syndicate is very much a reality.

✦

Upstate New York is a vast rural area that extends from the lower Hudson Valley to Canada. It is here that Mafiosi have traveled from all across America, as well as Cuba, Puerto Rico, and even Sicily. They gather at the fifty-three-acre estate of mobster Joseph Barbara, with its big stone house, guest cottage, and sprawling lawn. The Mafiosi are dressed in fine suits and coats, with the bosses meeting inside the main lodge as their soldiers gather outside around the massive barbecue grill. The smell of thick steaks being cooked mingles with the aroma of cigar and cigarette smoke. This is a business meeting, with all the tension that implies, but it is also a gathering of far-flung friends and associates, with profane jokes and insider conversations about a world all their own.

The neutral site of Chicago was Genovese's first choice for the meeting. There, violent Mob boss Sam Giancana would have been able to host the conference at any number of locations without any fear of police interference.* But Genovese's fellow crime boss, Joe Bonanno, prefers Barbara's wooded property, thinking it far more inconspicuous. Out of respect, Vito Genovese bows to Bonanno's wishes.

There are so many Mafiosi in attendance that there is not enough room in Barbara's home to accommodate them. Reservations have been made for the very best rooms at a number of local hotels. Barbara's spacious lawn is now a parking lot filled with the Cadillacs, Lincoln Continentals, and Lincoln Premieres favored by mobsters. But even amidst this lavish collection of automobiles, the Chrysler Crown Imperial limousine that delivered Vito Genovese to the gathering stands out for its opulence.

The vicious Genovese holds court as the assembled gangsters calmly discuss gambling, narcotics, prostitution, and the division of Albert Anastasia's empire. A radical new idea is also on the agenda, that

---

* Giancana spent millions of dollars to make sure that Chicago and Cook County authorities would allow his criminal enterprise to prosper unimpeded.

New York State Police sergeant Edgar D. Croswell points to a photograph as he tells
the Senate Rackets Committee about a raid he led on an Apalachin, New York,
meeting last November. Police rounded up sixty men, many of them mobsters.
Washington, D.C., June 30, 1958.

of expanding Mob operations that already account for more than $7 billion in illicit revenue annually. The plan is to move beyond traditional core Mob businesses into the very fabric of American government. This scheme would mimic traditional Mafia operations in Sicily by taking control of national unions, interstate trucking, the textile industry, Cuba's sugar trade, and the prison system.

But unbeknownst to the mobsters, Sergeant Edgar Dewitt Croswell of the New York State Police has other plans.

Sergeant Croswell is forty-four, pale, tall, and a thirteen-year veteran of the force—the sort of man so fascinated by his job that he trains his young sons to recognize cars by make and model, should they ever need to identify a vehicle in court. "My hobby is police work," he explains to those wondering about his passion for law enforcement. Croswell is thin to the point of being gaunt, a chain smoker who favors Salem cigarettes.

A stomach ulcer requires that he drink nothing more potent than milk. The detective not only commands the local state trooper barracks at Vestal, seven miles from Apalachin, but the divorced Croswell also sleeps each night in the Spartan concrete structure. With no place else to call home, and nothing else to occupy his time, the lanky trooper makes it his business to know every single criminal happening in his jurisdiction.

Thus, Detective Croswell has spent considerable time scrutinizing the individual he believes to be Apalachin's most sinister resident. Joseph Barbara is a transplant from Pennsylvania who moved to town in 1944, then bought his property and a Canada Dry bottling plant, in that order. By all appearances, Barbara is a solid citizen who now controls the local beer and soft drink dealerships. He is an active community leader and philanthropist, as well. His property is actually a compound: a home made of stone, a stable, garage, and barbecue area—the sort of estate a man of means might rightfully enjoy.

But to Trooper Croswell, something about Joseph Barbara is not quite right.

Croswell has been suspicious for a very long time. The Barbara home has seen dubious comings and goings in the past, so it has become common practice for Croswell to keep the estate under surveillance. In fact, he has been keeping tabs on Barbara since the suspected mobster's arrival in Apalachin thirteen years ago. Croswell has maintained an informal vigil, learning that Barbara's background includes a significant number of arrests. That piques the detective's interest and leads to surveillance.

The Barbara family is not oblivious to Croswell's attention. They do not know his name, simply referring to him as "that state trooper."

One year ago, Croswell's vigilance paid off when state police arrested an underboss of the Bonanno crime family as he left Barbara's home. Surprisingly, once Carmine Galante was in custody, a contingent of police from New Jersey arrived in Apalachin and tried to bribe the troopers in an attempt to arrange Galante's freedom. This unusual—and highly illegal—abuse of police power led to the indictment of those officers. That also served as a lesson to Croswell that the Mafia's tentacles are everywhere.

More recently, while at the local Parkway hotel investigating an individual who paid for his room with a bad check, Sergeant Croswell overheard Joseph Barbara's son making a large number of room reservations. Joseph Barbara Jr. explained to the clerk that he required double rooms for an upcoming beverage convention but would not name the individuals who would occupy them.

Apalachin has a population of just one thousand, so any such convention will have a major impact on the town's economy. Out of curiosity, Croswell starts checking around town to see if there have been any other unusual transactions. He asks the local butcher if the Barbara family had recently placed any large orders.

The answer is yes. Not trusting the quality of the local butcher's fare, Joseph Barbara has ordered 220 pounds of steak, ham, and veal from Armour and Company to be shipped from Chicago and delivered to his home. The cost comes to $432.* Bowing to the Mafia's code of grandiosity, Barbara has pointedly *not* ordered chicken, which isn't considered manly to the Mafia, thus not worth serving to esteemed guests.

In addition, Detective Croswell finds out that Barbara has also been purchasing enormous quantities of sugar, which could indicate the presence of illegal alcohol production on the premises of the Barbara compound.

Suspecting that the Barbara estate has been an organized crime refuge in the past, Sergeant Croswell has every reason to believe that the out-of-town guests might have a similar affiliation. And due to those hotel reservations, Croswell knows the date on which the visitors will be arriving.

✦

McFall Road is the only path leading in and out of Barbara's property. On the morning of November 14, dressed in plain clothes, Trooper Croswell drives his unmarked police car to within fifty yards of the compound, then uses binoculars to surveil the cars parked on the lawn. The air is cold and smells like rain. Croswell is accompanied by his partner, Trooper Vincent Vasisko, as well as two agents from the Treasury Department. Art Ruston and Ken Brown work in the Alcohol

* Almost $4,000 in modern currency.

and Tobacco Tax Division and have agreed to assist this morning based on the remote chance that they will be able to enter Joseph Barbara's property and catch him in the act of illegally distilling alcohol.

Other than that, there is actually little Sergeant Croswell can hope to achieve. He cannot enter the Barbara property to question the guests. No criminal acts have been committed, so his presence might be construed as bigoted toward Italian Americans. He could concoct a reason to make an arrest, but in reality, unless the individual has outstanding warrants, anyone arrested would most likely be set free immediately for lack of cause. Croswell would then be seen as an overzealous small-town policeman and perhaps lose his job.

However, the trooper *does* possess the authority to stop any vehicle once it leaves Barbara's property and request those inside to provide identification. A person who fails to show ID or attempts to run can then be arrested.

✦

After surreptitiously inspecting the line of Lincolns and Cadillacs, Croswell and the other officers begin writing down license numbers. There is no sign of danger, but sensing he might need assistance, Croswell radios for backup help. Seventeen officers respond. As a lead investigator with the state police, Croswell is now the senior officer on the scene. He orders the installation of roadblocks to prevent any departures from the Barbara home and also orders a cordon of officers to surround the house in the local woods to stop any escapes on foot. Now all Croswell can do is wait.

Soon, a local fish vendor drives up to the roadblock after making a delivery. Croswell allows Bartolo Guccia to pass, only to see him turn the truck around and head right back into the Barbara property.

The detective immediately knows what will happen next.

✦

Inside the living room of the main house, the big bosses discuss business. Sam Giancana, Santo Trafficante, Joe Bonanno, Carlo Gambino, Joe Profaci, and Vito Genovese are all engaged. The walls are paneled in wood, the fireplace is twelve feet wide and made of stone, and the windows are covered in thick drapes. A baby grand piano and a china hutch also fill the room.

Ironically, given Genovese's once-passionate belief in the value of the narcotics trade, the big bosses are currently discussing whether to abandon drug trafficking. New laws mean severe prison sentences for dealers. But despite the enormous drop in Mafia earnings should they decide to leave the lucrative drug business, Genovese is really not interested in that. He is more concerned with being named Boss of All Bosses.

Outside, near the barbecue, lower-level Mafia soldiers talk among themselves. The steaks from Chicago are cooking, the smell filling the air in anticipation of an enormous feast once business is concluded. Beer on tap is available in the screened-off summer pavilion. One of the attendees, Carmine Lombardozzi, fears imminent death. As a former fixer for Albert Anastasia, Lombardozzi knows that the big bosses are currently discussing his future. A death sentence has already been passed, but he is hoping they will reconsider. Should they not, there is a very good chance Lombardozzi's steak lunch will be his last.

In the kitchen of the main house, Josephine Barbara and her housekeeper sit at a large round breakfast table. Mrs. Barbara has a view out the window toward McFall Road, where she sees a familiar face just beyond the parked Cadillacs.

"It's that state trooper," she says to Marguerite Russell.

Suddenly comes the sound of shouting.

"State police," fishmonger Bartolo Guccia warns the mobsters in a thick Italian accent. "They're stopping everybody!"

The steaks are left to burn.

The gangsters run.

✦

Sergeant Croswell can't believe it.

Italian men in thick coats and hats swarm into the parking lot, walking at a very fast pace. Unaware that law enforcement has no evidence against them and cannot enter the property, the mobsters are panicking. Despite criminal pasts that have taught them to show nonchalance when encountering law enforcement, the assembled gangsters buckle. The fear of years in prison overcomes reason.

Some flee to their cars; others trudge into the thick woods. "Like vermin scuttling out of burning woodwork," writes the *New York Daily News*, "the underworld chiefs headed for open air."

At first, Chicago mobster Sam Giancana remains in the main house, believing that the police will not enter the estate. But he soon grows weary of the uncertainty and darts into the forest, becoming one of the few escapees. "I had to run like a fucking rabbit through the goddamned woods," he would later complain. "The place was full of briars. I tore up a twelve-hundred-dollar suit on some barbed wire, ruined a new pair of shoes."

On the road, the first vehicle carrying a mobster approaches the barrier manned by Sergeant Croswell. He waves it through.

This is an intentional act. Croswell hopes that this display of nonchalance will encourage other drivers to approach him.

A few moments later, Croswell is rewarded as a line of cars approach his position.

Quickly, he orders the Chrysler Imperial containing Vito Genovese to halt. Five men are packed inside the car. "You've been at Mister Barbara's?" the detective asks.

"He is very sick, the poor man," says Genovese, sitting up front on the passenger side. "We just came to wish him a speedy recovery. But I don't need to answer these questions, do I?"

Croswell requests IDs, then waves the Imperial through. More troopers await farther down the highway, prepared to stop and detain the car's inhabitants. No arrests are being made, but state police have the legal authority to hold suspects without filing charges. New York mandates that this period of time not exceed twelve hours.

With all avenues of exit sealed, the detainments are swift—and numerous. Sixty suspected Mafioso are placed in custody, including leaders of the New York families: Vito Genovese, Joe Profaci, Joe Bonanno, and Carlo Gambino. Tampa mobster Santo Trafficante is also nabbed. Each is taken to the Vestal barracks substation, where they are ordered to take off their shoes and sit on the floor with their hands on their heads for processing—all the while guarded by armed state troopers. With their gold watches, diamond pinkie rings, and expensive suits, these men look drastically out of place in the dusty barracks.

Croswell has instructed the state troopers to make every effort to coerce the mobsters into doing something wrong—so that they can be held in jail longer. But the Mafioso know better than to react. "We gave them a tough time at the station house," Croswell will admit, "but we couldn't even make them commit disorderly conduct."

Each mobster's belongings are searched, but no guns or drugs are found. Sergeant Croswell rushes to beat the twelve-hour deadline for setting the men free but also takes time to personally interrogate each man. "What were you doing at Barbara's?" he asks time and again.

Most respond in similar fashion, stating that they were concerned about Joseph Barbara's health and had come to wish him well. In fact, back at the estate, stress has gotten the better of Joseph Barbara, and he has suffered a second nonfatal heart attack. He will be dead in just two years, having lost his house and business due to the infamy created by Trooper Croswell's aggressive policing on this November day.[*]

As Croswell concludes his questioning just before the twelve-hour deadline expires, he tallies his findings. These men are definitely career criminals—only nine of the detained gangsters have no criminal record. Between the others, Croswell counts 275 prior arrests and one hundred convictions. Their average age is fifty-three. Half of them were born in Sicily or Southern Italy.

The most astonishing new evidence is the breadth of the criminal operations. It has long been suspected that New York, Chicago, and Miami are Mob hotbeds, but the detained delegates also hail from places like Texas, Colorado, Kansas, and Alabama.

"They are the hierarchy of the Eastern Seaboard criminal world," Croswell tells reporters, who first interview the trooper by phone. The press then floods into Apalachin to cover this incendiary story.

✦

---

[*] Joseph Barbara's health slowly deteriorated, due to a series of heart attacks. Several tax liens were placed on his property, forcing him to sell the estate and relocate to a much smaller home. After seventeen months in hiding, he appeared in court to face charges of tax evasion. One month later, Barbara suffered a fatal heart attack and died on June 17, 1959. The former Barbara estate was at first turned into a tourist attraction and is now a horse property.

KILLING THE MOB ✦ 145

In Washington, J. Edgar Hoover rises on the morning of November 15, prepared for the calm of his ritual: poached eggs on toast while reading the morning paper. Just one month ago the Soviet Union launched Sputnik, the first satellite in history. The Russians now have complete control of space, a fact that terrifies the American public. Hoover's anti-Communist campaigns are more concentrated than ever.

But all that changes as Hoover opens the morning *New York Times*.

65 HOODLUMS SEIZED IN A RAID AND RUN OUT OF UPSTATE NEW YORK VILLAGE

That front-page headline infuriates the FBI director. For the past two months, he has very publicly stated that Communism is America's biggest threat and that "there is no such entity as the Mafia." But Apalachin makes Hoover look like a fool. For a quarter century, the director has publicized himself as America's top lawman, his finger on the pulse of all criminal activity. But now he well knows his credibility is shattered.

The director can barely contain his rage as he speaks with Clyde Tolson about the situation during their drive to work. In the end it is decided that Hoover must cling to his story. The Mafia still does not exist. Agents will be instructed to refer to Apalachin as the "so-called" Mafia meeting. Speaking through bureau mouthpiece Louis B. Nichols, Hoover continues to express "strong doubts about the Mafia's existence."

Nichols, the FBI's third in command behind Hoover and Tolson, defines the Mob in Hoover's abstract terms: "The boys involved in these parties in the United States just drift together for a number of reasons, all pretty clear when you think things over. It's like a bunch of Dutchmen getting together, and while hoisting their glass, exclaiming, 'we together are sticking.'"

Incredibly, some members of the media still buy Hoover's version of events.

"No Mafia at Barbara's," begins the headline in the *Binghamton* (NY) *Press*, a city next door to Apalachin. The headline concludes: "None in the US, Says FBI."

✦

Alerted to the news about Apalachin, Bobby Kennedy storms out of his office and drives the ten blocks to the Department of Justice. He takes the elevator up to the office of J. Edgar Hoover. Kennedy requests files on each of the arrested mobsters.

Out of sixty men arrested, America's top law enforcement agency possesses almost no detailed information about them. What files the FBI does have are mostly newspaper clippings instead of intelligence gathered by field agents.

A stunned Kennedy leaves Hoover and crosses the street to the Treasury Building, where he turns to the Federal Bureau of Narcotics for information. Unlike his archrival Hoover, FBN director Anslinger has plenty of documentation on the Mob—and is happy to share.

"The FBI did not know anything," Bobby will later remember, "about these people who were major gangsters in the United States."

As for the FNB, "they had something on every one," Kennedy will note.

✦

On November 27, thirteen days after the Apalachin confrontation, an embarrassed J. Edgar Hoover is finally forced to admit the existence of organized crime. He institutes the Top Hoodlum Program as a modern version of Public Enemy Number One and requires agents in field offices nationwide to draw up a list of the ten most notorious criminals in their cities. The words *Mafia* and *Apalachin* are never referenced.* Yet thanks to the alert investigation of Sergeant Edgar Croswell, America's top crime fighting official is finally acknowledging the Mafia.

But as Hoover well knows, Bobby Kennedy is way ahead of him.

And Kennedy plans to bring down organized crime all by himself.

---

* This top ten list proved impossible for agents in cities truly lacking organized crime, placing them in the predicament of concocting imaginary local syndicates to please Hoover. The Top Hoodlum Program actually began in 1957, but if you read the FBI's official history, it says that Hoover began the list in 1953. Some believe that revisionist history is there to cover for J. Edgar Hoover.

✦

On December 22, 1957, Bobby Kennedy meets behind closed doors with the thirty-three investigators working for the Senate McClellan hearings. He declares his intent to subpoena each arrested gangster from the Apalachin summit, ordering them to appear before the anti-racketeering subcommittee.

Kennedy is sincere in his determination to expose the major crime families. Yet he is equally passionate about his own bloodline. Both elements are slowly emerging into America's consciousness.

Three weeks ago, his brother, Senator John F. Kennedy, was featured in *Time* magazine as "The Democratic Whiz of 1957."

JFK has his sights on the White House, and Bobby Kennedy knows that Apalachin means more viewers of the Senate's televised Mafia investigation, allowing his brother to raise his public profile even higher. That is, if Senator Kennedy actually shows up to the hearings. In many ways, JFK still looks down on his younger brother Bobby, seeing him as a relentless nuisance instead of a resource. The younger Kennedy is determined to change his brother's perception.

But even more than helping to get his brother elected president of the United States, Bobby Kennedy is eager to please his father, Joe. The Kennedy patriarch is sparing in his love for his sons and, as a result, John, Bobby, and little brother Teddy will go to great lengths to make him proud. Bobby also knows that Joseph Kennedy is willing to do whatever it takes to see his son elected to the nation's highest office—including pay $75,000 in "advertising" to get JFK featured in *Time* magazine. "I just bought a horse for $75,000," the patriarch tells the archbishop of New York, Cardinal Francis Spellman, over lunch at the priest's Madison Avenue residence. "And for another $75,000, I put Jack on the cover of *Time*."

Thus begins the symbiotic intertwining of the Kennedy family, J. Edgar Hoover, the Mafia, and the press.

And, in typical gangland style, theirs is a relationship that can only end in mayhem.

CHAPTER TWELVE

JUNE 30, 1958
OLD SENATE OFFICE BUILDING
WASHINGTON, D.C.
9:00 A.M.

Jimmy Hoffa is no longer under pressure—at least not now.

The weather outside is sweltering, but air-conditioning keeps this cramped hearing room comfortable. Chief Counsel Bobby Kennedy is opening a new round of hearings into organized crime, using information gleaned from the Apalachin Summit. The lean attorney is seated at a long table between his brother John and Republican senator Barry Goldwater, facing those who will testify about the Mob.

Last August, it was Hoffa who sat opposite Kennedy, but the president of the Teamsters union is not the subject of today's investigation.

"We intend to focus on the criminal group which held a meeting at the home of Joseph Barbara Sr., in Apalachin, New York, on November 14, 1957," begins committee chairman John McClellan. "The discovery of this meeting by the New York State Police had the effect of revealing the scope of the interrelationships of some of the leaders of the national crime syndicate."

With those words, McClellan publicly refutes decades of federal denial about the existence of the Mob. Millions of Americans are again watching him on television, where they will soon learn that the Mafia is not just a collection of well-dressed hoodlums but a systematic organi-

James R. Hoffa (right), Midwest boss of the Teamsters union, talks with Robert F. Kennedy, counsel for the Senate Rackets Investigating Committee in Washington, D.C., August 21, 1957.

zation that controls many aspects of American life, ranging from entertainment to gambling, politics, and even law enforcement. From this day forward, it will be the policy of the American government not only to acknowledge but to try to destroy the Mob.

McClellan turns the proceedings over to his chief counsel.

So it is that Bobby Kennedy once again takes charge. "The first witness will be Sergeant Edgar Croswell."

The sergeant takes his seat at the witness table and begins answering Kennedy's methodical questions in a slow and deliberate fashion. The trooper has been under intense pressure since the Apalachin incident, with praise and criticism directed at him in equal amounts. He has not managed the pressure well, growing even thinner than before, his peptic ulcer making it almost impossible for him to eat without pain.

But Croswell is an articulate and compliant witness, for which Kennedy is thankful.

The same cannot be said for Bobby Kennedy's confrontation with union boss Jimmy Hoffa, which took place almost one year ago.

✦

Jimmy Hoffa hates Bobby Kennedy, and the feeling is mutual.

The young Kennedy has evolved into a passionate opponent of organized crime. This is due in large part to forty-four-year-old James Riddle Hoffa, lifelong labor advocate and union leader. The two men sparred publicly during the first round of the televised McClellan hearings, with Hoffa very often coming out on top.

And for Bobby Kennedy, a man who hates to lose, this is completely unacceptable.

Hoffa, the five-foot-five, thickly muscled son of an Indiana coal miner, is the well-heeled lawyer's polar opposite. Kennedy's Harvard education alone gives him an advantage over Hoffa, a high school dropout. Both men are more alike than they will ever publicly admit—competitive overachievers who prefer to wear white socks with their dress suits and spontaneously drop to the floor for a quick set of push-ups. Kennedy drinks very little and Hoffa not all. Neither man smokes. Both are married family men. These many shared habits might have led to a friendship but, instead, their hatred for each other runs deep. As long as he lives, Jimmy Hoffa will publicly cheer every Kennedy setback, even as Bobby makes it his personal mission to send Hoffa to prison forever.

To most Americans, knowledge of union business is minimal, gleaned from movies like *On the Waterfront* starring Marlon Brando. But Kennedy's investigation seeks to expose a corrupt union world where bribery of government officials, collusion with known criminals, secret loans from union pension funds, kickbacks, and a plethora of other crimes take place on a daily basis—all while the unions pretend to be benevolent organizations.

Bobby Kennedy and Jimmy Hoffa first meet three weeks after the McClellan hearings begin on January 30, 1957. The occasion is dinner. Kennedy and Hoffa are invited to the home of Teamsters lawyer Eddie Cheyfitz at the behest of union president Dave Beck. Hoffa's job is to convince Kennedy to back off from any investigation of the Teamsters, promising to make internal reforms himself as second in command.

The night does not go well. Kennedy already has evidence that Hoffa is attempting to plant a spy within the McClellan Committee and is planning to have the FBI arrest the teamster.

Also, Bobby Kennedy knows that Hoffa is associated with mobster Johnny Dio, an underboss for the Genovese crime family. Five months ago, it was Dio who ordered that sulfuric acid be thrown into the eyes of *New York Daily Mirror* correspondent Victor Riesel as retaliation for his many articles condemning union corruption. The attack blinded Riesel for life. There is suspicion that Dio engineered the assault at Hoffa's request.

So as Bobby Kennedy sits down for dinner with Jimmy Hoffa, he understands the sort of individual with whom he is dealing. And yet, the union leader is a surprise, bragging continuously about his personal toughness, leading Kennedy to wonder if Hoffa has questions about his own manhood—"a bully hiding behind a façade," Kennedy will later write.

Throughout the meal, RFK questions Hoffa continuously about Johnny Dio. Hoffa is candid. "I do to others what they do to me," the union boss boasts without admitting any connection to the acid attack.

But even as Kennedy sizes up Hoffa, the same thing is being done to him. Despite his lack of formal education, the Teamster leader is an astute judge of character—and he thinks Bobby Kennedy is weak. "I can tell by how he shakes hands what kind of fellow I got," Hoffa later states, referring to Kennedy's soft grip. "I said to myself here's a fella thinks he's doing me a favor talking to me."

And when the dinner finally ends shortly after 9:00 p.m., Hoffa confides to Cheyfitz, "he's a damned spoiled jerk."

Three weeks after the meal, in an FBI sting orchestrated by Kennedy and J. Edgar Hoover, Jimmy Hoffa is arrested for bribery—allegedly passing $2,000 in cash to an attorney as payment for spying on the McClellan hearings' investigators.

"He stared at me for three minutes with complete hatred in his eyes," Kennedy will recall of Hoffa's midnight arraignment.

"Then somehow we got into a discussion about who could do the most push-ups."

Hoffa's recollections of the night are much different. "I said, 'Listen, Bobby, you run your business and I'll run mine. You go on home and go to bed. I'll take care of things. Let's don't have no problems,'" Hoffa will later tell a journalist. The relationship between Kennedy and Hoffa was "like flint and steel" in the union leader's words. "Every time we came together the sparks flew."

The government case against Hoffa was so ironclad that Kennedy boasts he would "jump off the Capitol" if the charges don't stick. But, to RFK's dismay, not only is Jimmy Hoffa acquitted by a jury but he uses the publicity to actually mock Kennedy—who receives a package from the labor leader: a parachute and a one-word note, JUMP!

Hoffa then goes one step further in trumpeting his innocence. After the McClellan Committee's investigation forces Teamster president Dave Beck to step down in disgrace for looting union pension coffers, Hoffa pledges to run for the vacant office.

An angry Bobby Kennedy is certain the union leader is crooked and is determined to prove it. He schemes of ways to put Hoffa behind bars. In August, the union leader is ordered to appear before the McClellan Committee. Kennedy's "Get Hoffa" squad of researchers and attorneys has investigated every aspect of Hoffa's life and is confident he will crack under interrogation.

The drama begins when Hoffa takes the stand. The two men of vastly different backgrounds engage in a verbal duel that comes to fascinate the American public. Kennedy is terse and direct, rattling off questions with a speedy cadence. In the gallery, his wife, Ethel, is heard to exclaim, "Give it to him!"

Hoffa never wavers. He appears relaxed, speaking in fractured grammar with a thick midwestern accent, deflecting questions with ease. He is fond of staring at Kennedy for moments at a time, a very direct reminder to the attorney that the labor leader is unafraid of the committee.

"How many times, approximately, do you think?" Kennedy asks Hoffa about his arrest record.

"Well, I don't know, Bob," Hoffa replies. "I haven't counted them up. I think maybe about seventeen times I have been picked up, took into custody of the police, and out of those seventeen times, three of those times—in many instances were dismissed. But in three of those times I received convictions."

"Now the first one was in 1940, was it?" Kennedy asks, already knowing the answer.

"I believe that was an assault and battery, is that correct?" answers Hoffa, playing dumb.

"That is not the one I was thinking of."

Hoffa responds: "I am talking about the ones where I was simply taken off a picket line because of a disagreement with some so-called policeman."

Hoffa's answers are just as contrived as Kennedy's questions, having spent hours practicing with his attorneys. "I sat down and put on paper everything I could think of they might ask me questions about. Then I got with the lawyers and went over every item. We'd rehearse what we thought Kennedy would do," Hoffa will later write. "And we got it right damned near every time."

Kennedy is relentless in his pursuit of Hoffa. He often eats a sandwich and drinks a glass of milk for lunch at his desk each afternoon and never leaves his office before midnight, even though he has five young children at home, and Ethel is pregnant with a sixth.

Jimmy Hoffa is no less determined. Each night as Bobby drives home, his route takes him past the Marble Palace, as the Teamsters call their Washington headquarters. One evening, traveling with his assistant Pierre Salinger at one in the morning, Kennedy spies the light on in Hoffa's office. He immediately turns the car around. "If he's still at work, we ought to be," Kennedy tells Salinger, and returns to the office.

When Hoffa gets wind of what Kennedy did, he begins the habit of leaving his office light on all night long—whether he is there or not.

To Bobby Kennedy's chagrin, Hoffa emerges from the hearings unscathed. It is Kennedy who looks flustered. Many times, as he launches into an elaborate question, Hoffa winks at him. This annoyance forces Kennedy to finally plead with committee chairman McClellan to "please instruct the witness to stop making faces at me."

Eventually, some of the general public begins sympathizing with Hoffa, believing that Kennedy's attacks are one-sided and unfair. Joseph Kennedy is taken aback by the intensity of his son's questioning, even asking him to back off, lest organized labor fail to support John Kennedy in the next presidential election.

Bobby Kennedy refuses.

Among those inside organized labor, the national hearings make Hoffa a hero. Shortly after his Senate testimony, the International Brotherhood of Teamsters will elect Jimmy Hoffa as their new president. He garners an amazing 75 percent of the vote. Bobby Kennedy has made Jimmy Hoffa a legend.

"The outcome was an almost natural reaction of tough men in a tough industry," the *National Guardian* will note, "who objected to being told how to run their affairs by an anti-labor Senate committee."

Speaking about RFK, Hoffa will gloat: "He's not the brightest fellow in the world, you know," he says. "I . . . love to bug the little bastard."

In the end, Bobby Kennedy fails on the national stage. Despite reams of evidence located by his army of researchers, he is outfoxed. He knows that Jimmy Hoffa has ties to the Mafia, authorizes beatings and murders, and accepts bribes in exchange for favors. While still vice president of the International Brotherhood of Teamsters, he consolidated IBT pension money from across the country into a singular robust fund. Now, as president, he loans the Mob cash to build new casinos in Las Vegas. But Kennedy has been unable to prove any of that. Thus, the corrupt Hoffa dances away.

In truth, the McClellan hearings benefited both Kennedy and Hoffa. Each day, the labor leader waltzes into his walnut-paneled office at the Marble Palace, where a personal chef serves his favorite lunch of cold lobster and crab, and where he sometimes takes a steam bath in the private basement gymnasium. Hoffa's guile is turning into power and he knows it.

Although Bobby Kennedy remains angry, he and his brother John have gained enormous fame from the hearings. The *Saturday Evening Post* runs a story titled "The Amazing Kennedys" and *Look* features "The Rise of the Brothers Kennedy."

One year later, Bobby Kennedy is set to begin the McClellan Committee's second round of hearings. This time Hoffa is absent as the interrogation is aimed at mobsters detained at the Apalachin Summit in New York. Once again, Robert Kennedy will be watched by millions on national television.

This time, he cannot fail.

✦

The criminals will not talk.

Those detained at Apalachin have been ordered to take the Fifth Amendment. Mob lawyers well understanding that their clients cannot be forced to testify against themselves.

So, Bobby Kennedy's excitement about grilling major crime figures like Vito Genovese and Joe Profaci turns to frustration as witness after witness defies him by invoking their right to silence. The Justice Department is of no help to Kennedy, refusing to prosecute those criminals who take the stand, saying there's not enough evidence to build a case.

Bobby Kennedy, whose emotions are always transparent, grows increasingly bellicose during the proceedings. He slowly comes to the realization that this committee is losing ground to "the enemy within," as he refers to the Mafia.

Typical is this conversation between Kennedy and Sam Giancana, the flashy Chicago leader of the Outfit. At fifty, the widower Giancana is known as a playboy Mafioso, fond of the Las Vegas nightlife and palling around with entertainers like Frank Sinatra. He has also been arrested seventy times for acts of violence—including three times for murder. It is thought that he has authorized more than two hundred Mafia hits on his enemies.*

Giancana is listed in the State of Nevada's Las Vegas Black Book, which shows the photographs of eleven suspected Mafioso who are not

---

* Sam Giancana served time for many offenses, including a stretch in the Federal Correctional Complex in Terre Haute, Indiana. However, wiretaps of Giancana speaking with fellow Mob boss Stefano Magaddino of Buffalo, New York, capture him bragging about the number of police chiefs on his payroll. Those bribes, along with the Mob practice of insulating bosses from crimes, are the reasons Giancana is a free man in 1959.

*Singer Phyllis McGuire and Chicago Mob boss Sam Giancana
in a London, England, nightclub in 1962.*

allowed on the premises of any casino. Which does not stop Giancana
in the least. Frank Sinatra is known to hide the mobster in his dressing
room at the Sands when FBI agents visit the casino. The two men often
travel together, and Sinatra not only flies to Chicago to sing for free at
Giancana's Villa Venice club but also closes the shows with "My Kind
of Town Chicago Is," as a tribute to Sam Giancana.

The mobster repays the favor, showing his friendship by always
wearing the sapphire pinkie ring given to him by Frank Sinatra. When
the singer films the movie *Some Came Running* in a town near Chicago, Giancana is a regular visitor to the set, often bringing his Mafia
underlings. Their nightly revelry amazed costar Shirley MacLaine. "I

didn't know who they were," she would remember of the anonymous mobsters. "I only knew that the nightlife of poker, jokes, pasta, and booze went on until 5 a.m."

"Frank wanted to be a hood," singer Eddie Fisher will later marvel at Sinatra's fascination with Giancana. "He once said, 'I'd rather be a Mafia don than President of the United States.'"

The actor Peter Lawford, now married to Bobby Kennedy's sister Patricia, knows Giancana through his friendship with Sinatra. "You better believe that when the word got out around Hollywood that Frank was a pal of Sam Giancana, nobody but nobody ever messed with Frank Sinatra. They were too scared. Concrete boots were no joke with this guy. He was a killer."

Left unsaid in the committee room on this day is that John Kennedy is also a very good friend of Frank Sinatra and his band of fellow entertainers, nicknamed the Rat Pack. Sinatra and his crew often make jokes about their Mafia connections. In doing so, they turn the Mafia from the hoodlums depicted by Sergeant Croswell in his earlier testimony into glamorous mystery men.

The main event of the second McClellan hearing is Bobby Kennedy against Sam Giancana. The encounter does not go well for the government.

Mr. Kennedy: Would you tell us if you have opposition from anybody that you dispose of them by having them stuffed in a trunk? Is that what you do, Mr. Giancana?

Sam Giancana: I decline to answer because I honestly believe my answer might tend to incriminate me.

Mr. Kennedy: Would you tell us anything about any of your operations, or will you just giggle every time I ask you a question?

Sam Giancana: I decline to answer because I honestly believe my answer might tend to incriminate me.

Mr. Kennedy: I thought only little girls giggled, Mr. Giancana.

Sam Giancana will plead the Fifth thirty-four times. The man who privately boasts, "I own Chicago, I own Miami, I own Las Vegas," admits nothing to Bobby Kennedy.

"The Fifth Amendment is for the innocent as well as the guilty. I can think of very few witnesses who availed themselves of it who in my

*John F. Kennedy with Frank Sinatra in front of the Sands Hotel
in Las Vegas, Nevada, circa 1961.*

estimation were free from [wrong]doing," a weary Kennedy will admit.
His frustration grows so great that he often turns off his microphone
during hearings so that his words cannot be recorded. However, after
yet another gangster pleads the Fifth, Kennedy's verbiage is picked up
loud and clear: "You're full of shit."

Over the course of the McClellan hearings, Bobby Kennedy has
authorized 253 investigations, served eight thousand subpoenas, called

1,526 witnesses, and compiled 150,000 pages of testimony. Public awareness about organized crime is at an all-time high—but by the end of 1959, Americans are growing weary of the exposition. It will now be left to law enforcement to complete the task of prosecuting the Mafia.

And in a strange turn of events, it is Bobby Kennedy—not the Mob—who is depicted as the villain. "No one since Joseph McCarthy has done more than Mr. Kennedy to foster the impression that the plea of self-incrimination is tantamount to a confession of guilt," one law professor from Yale will write.

✦

In the summer of 1959, Bobby Kennedy resigns from the McClellan Committee. If there is an upbeat moment for the exhausted chief counsel, it is Vito Genovese's conviction in a New York courtroom on charges of drug trafficking. Prosecutors there succeeded where Kennedy did not, with a jury finding Genovese guilty of conspiring to import and sell narcotics. Never one to forget a grudge, the exiled Lucky Luciano allegedly struck back at Genovese all the way from Italy, arranging for a Puerto Rican drug dealer to implicate Vito Genovese in the sale of narcotics, leading to the fifteen-year sentence. Genovese will continue to run his crime family while serving his time at the Atlanta federal penitentiary, even ordering executions of several of his enemies.

Little else has changed.

The five families still run New York. Sam Giancana and the Outfit have never been more powerful in Chicago. Las Vegas is more firmly than ever in criminal hands.

But in Mob-infested Cuba, there is a new story. In 1959, Communist rebel Fidel Castro seizes control of the corrupt island nation.

On January 1, Castro's rebel band captures Havana. The Mob-run casinos had long been a source of anger to the Cuban people, for the wealth within their walls contrasted so sharply with their poverty. So one of Castro's first orders is the destruction of the casinos. Meyer Lansky's brand-new Riviera Hotel, which the mobster spent millions to construct, is the scene of broken windows, smashed and burned slot machines, and even pigs set free to run loose in the hallways as a symbol of capitalist gluttony. Lansky had sensed that

Castro would be successful in controlling Cuba. So on New Year's Eve, which should have been one of the busiest nights of the year, Lansky made the quick decision to close the Riviera and move all cash on the premises to a safe place. One week later, Meyer Lansky fled Cuba for the safety of the Bahamas, having lost a fortune due to Castro's revolution.

✦

In July 1959, an FBI team led by agent Bill Roemer sneaks into Celano's Custom Tailors on Michigan Avenue under cover of darkness. To their relief, the building is unguarded.

Roemer leads the FBI's organized crime investigation squad here in Chicago. The second-floor office the team soon enters belongs to Jimmy Celano, who makes a substantial portion of his living selling fine suits to members of the Outfit. The room features a large sofa, easy chair, desk, well-stocked bar, and a safe. Roemer has learned that Celano loans out the room to the local Mob each afternoon for private meetings. Agent Roemer hopes to conceal a microphone within the office so that federal investigators can listen in.

The task is not simple. The microphone is the size of a softball and not easily concealed. The agents must also run a wire from the microphone outside the building, then find a way to connect it with their headquarters five miles away on Clark Street. All the while, J. Edgar Hoover has informed Roemer and his team that he will disavow any knowledge of their actions should they engage in gunfire with local Mafioso or be arrested as burglars by the Chicago police.

Working quickly, the agents succeed in concealing the microphone behind a radiator. Connecting the wire is not so simple. The team is forced to return to Celano's office on six different occasions—always a Sunday morning before dawn—before finally running the wire outside and down the building, then connecting it with the local telephone mainframe.

It is July 29—the birthday of Agent Roemer's wife, Jeannie—when the bug becomes active. Code-named Little Al, for the Outfit's connection to Al Capone, the secret microphone is the first wiretap in the history of the Federal Bureau of Investigation. The "bug," as it is known, is illegal, and evidence gained through these transmissions cannot be used as evidence in court.

Yet due to overheard conversations between Sam Giancana and other mobsters in Jimmy Celano's office, the FBI can finally confirm the names of the top bosses of La Cosa Nostra and the fact that a national organized crime body known as the Commission has been in existence since 1931.

With the planting of a single microphone, the FBI learns more about the Mafia in six weeks than Bobby Kennedy's McClellan hearings established in three years.*

✦

Back in Washington, Jimmy Hoffa is not much concerned with Fidel Castro. His obsession remains with Robert Kennedy. He secretly meets with likely Republican presidential nominee Richard Nixon late in 1959 to offer a Teamster endorsement of his candidacy, knowing this could severely impact John Kennedy's hopes of winning the presidency in 1960.

Subsequently, the Hoffa-Nixon relationship will be sorely tested as the presidential campaign unfolds.

Meanwhile, the privately reckless JFK will soon do something that will appall his younger brother.

Senator John Kennedy, relentless in his pursuits of women, will involve himself with a young lady named Judith Campbell—who will soon become the mistress of the very dangerous Sam Giancana.

---

* Little Al will remain in operation until July 11, 1965, when it will go dead after years of continuous use. The Outfit never knew of its existence. On one occasion, the mobsters swept the room for bugs to ensure they were not being overheard. The FBI was listening in on that conversation and successfully broke into the building once again, turned off Little Al to conceal its location, then returned to reactivate the microphone once the sweep was finished. It's worth noting that although the Outfit was unaware that Roemer was recording them, they were well aware that he was the agent assigned to investigate them. Upon learning that Roemer coached his son's Little League team, the mobsters arranged that Mob meetings take place during the team's practices.

CHAPTER THIRTEEN

FEBRUARY 7, 1960
LAS VEGAS, NEVADA
10:00 P.M.

Frank Sinatra sees an old friend in the audience.

A thick haze of cigarette smoke hangs over the packed Copa Room. Near the stage, where Sinatra performs, Antonio Morelli conducts an eighteen-piece orchestra. Each of the 385 audience members is ecstatic, having secured tickets to the hottest show in America.

A little more than a decade after Bugsy Siegel's murder, Las Vegas has become the gambling mecca he once prophesied. More than eight million Americans travel each year to "Sin City," as Las Vegas is becoming known, spending more than $160 million annually on food, drinks, gambling, and lavish stage shows. Of course, the Mob has a big piece, having divided up control of the Sands, Flamingo, Tropicana, Desert Inn, and Riviera casinos between the Chicago, Detroit, and New York families.

Tonight's performance will last precisely one hour. Going just one minute longer will delay the audience's return to the gaming tables, which is where the Sands Hotel and Casino makes its real money. Entertainment is just a diversion to draw gamblers through the door. So the audience sits at closely packed tables draped in white cloths, sipping their two-drink minimum, enthralled by the mellifluous singing of Frank Sinatra.

But they also know that something special is soon to come. The

"Summit at the Sands" is the act's formal title, but almost everyone in the crowd tonight calls it something else: the Rat Pack.

Sinatra, now forty-four years old, is soon to be joined by friends Dean Martin, Joey Bishop, Peter Lawford, and Sammy Davis Jr. for some witty banter and group harmony. Nothing is rehearsed. Nothing is sacred. By day, the group is filming a heist movie called *Ocean's Eleven* on location here in Las Vegas. By night, they perform at the Copa. The grueling schedule includes after-show parties followed by a visit to the steam room to sweat out the booze before a very late bedtime.

Making the act even more unusual is that a different member of the Rat Pack headlines each show, performing his own songs until the others step onstage to interrupt the act, joking and singing along. The audience is never told ahead of time who will come on first—or what outlandish behavior they can expect. One bit has Martin and Bishop walking onstage in their underwear and tuxedo jackets, then launching into song along with Sinatra—all the while maintaining straight faces.

The Pack is so popular that more than eighteen thousand requests have been made for hotel reservations at the Sands during the three-week run from January 26 through February 16. Unfortunately, the resort has just 212 rooms. Many patrons choose to sleep in their cars or even in the hotel lobby. And while the average gambler is unlikely to find lodging at the Sands, Hollywood stars have no such problem. Cary Grant, Kim Novak, Jack Benny, Lucille Ball, and Cole Porter are just a few of the celebrities who make the journey to Las Vegas to see the frenetic Rat Pack.*

But tonight, there is another celebrity in the house.

"Ladies and gentlemen," Sinatra addresses the crowd. A spotlight plays over the room before settling upon a table up front near the stage. "Senator John F. Kennedy, from the great state of Massachusetts."

As the audience erupts into applause, Sinatra continues: "The next President of the United States!"

---

* The Rat Pack was originally founded by actor Humphrey Bogart in the mid-1950s. Its membership included fellow actors David Niven, the hard-living Errol Flynn, and Frank Sinatra. Bogart's wife, actress Lauren Bacall, noted that their drunken escapades reminded her of a pack of rats, thus the name. When Bogart died in 1957, Sinatra transformed the group into a new collection focused around his personal friends.

The perpetually tanned Kennedy rises to his feet and takes a bow as the audience gives him a standing ovation. Sinatra announces to the crowd that JFK is an honorary member of the Rat Pack—later even referring to the group as the "Jack Pack."

The spectators cannot help but notice the young brunette seated next to the senator. Most assume that this is Mrs. Kennedy.

They are wrong.

✦

With his presidential campaign in full swing, JFK *should* be in the Pacific Northwest. That's where the candidate will deliver a speech to the Oregon Chamber of Commerce the day after tomorrow. This afternoon, the forty-two-year-old presidential hopeful delivered an earnest talk about developing the West's natural resources at a conference in Albuquerque, New Mexico. In just one month, voters in New Hampshire will go to the polls to open the electoral primary season, the first step toward winning the presidency.

But as his personal plane, *Caroline*, named for his two-year-old daughter, takes to the air for the journey to Newport, Oregon, Kennedy orders the pilot to alter his flight plan. Frank Sinatra has invited him to Vegas, promising JFK a good time. Rat Pack member Sammy Davis Jr. has made his personal car and chauffeur available to Kennedy. Sinatra will provide the girls. "We all knew he was a swinger," Davis will later say about JFK.

According to Sammy Davis, Sinatra procured an "outside girl" from Los Angeles to entertain Senator Kennedy.

So Oregon can wait.

"There was no goddamn reason for stopping there except fun and games," Blair Clark of CBS News, a college friend of the candidate and one of six journalists on the flight, will long remember.[*]

But John Kennedy is an astute politician and knows better than to

---

[*] Kennedy's Convair 240 was the first private aircraft utilized by a presidential candidate, allowing him freedom to travel without concern for commercial airline schedules. Joseph Kennedy bought the plane from American Airlines in 1959 and had it refitted for his son's personal use. *Caroline* revolutionized campaigning. Since 1960 it has become common for a candidate to travel by private aircraft rather than commercial.

let the public believe he has only landed in Las Vegas to play. So earlier tonight he spoke to six hundred local Democrats at the city's Convention Center, hoping to shore up the organized labor vote, then attended a cocktail party with key local donors—many of whom are connected to the Mafia through their roles in the hotel and casino industry. Only then did JFK slip away to this evening's late show.

The Sands, in the words of one Mafioso, is "*the* hotel for wiseguys."* Kennedy is careful not to spend the night there, avoiding any overt association with organized crime. But there is no stigma in visiting the Copa Room to hear Frank Sinatra. The candidate and the singer have known each other for five years. Behind the scenes, patriarch Joseph Kennedy is trying to leverage this friendship, hoping Sinatra will use his Mafia connections to swing the labor vote toward "Jack," as Kennedy is known by friends and family. The singer was recently invited to the Kennedy family compound in Palm Beach, Florida, where Joe Kennedy also requested that Sinatra sing a few benefit shows for JFK. The elder Kennedy even suggested that Sinatra record a special theme song. This led to the singer reworking the lyrics of "High Hopes," which he had sung in the movie *A Hole in the Head*, into a catchy ditty about Jack Kennedy.

Such behind-the-scenes politicking is a normal part of any presidential campaign, where no detail is too small to overlook.

But there are two glaring weaknesses in the Kennedy machine that must be concealed at all costs. The first is Joseph Kennedy's links to organized crime. The other is JFK's rampant adultery—a habit learned from his father.

One pivotal aspect of JFK's public persona is that of a dedicated family man. With the New Hampshire primary so close, it is imperative that this façade be maintained. But while Kennedy loves his wife, Jackie, and dotes on daughter Caroline, he also looks forward to nights like this, where he will share his bed with another woman.

So, as JFK retakes his seat in the Copa Room following Sinatra's

---

* The quote is by Gianni Russo, a Mafioso in the employ of Frank Costello who also played the role of Carlo Rizzi in *The Godfather*.

introduction, he is mesmerized by the gorgeous Judith Campbell. This is the "outside girl" Sinatra brought from Los Angeles.

Even though JFK's twenty-seven-year-old brother Teddy is closer to Campbell's age, she fights off the younger Kennedy's relentless advances and focuses her attention on the elder brother. The blue-eyed Judith Campbell does all the talking as the senator zeroes in. "It was as if every nerve in his body was poised at attention," she will long remember. "As I was to learn, John Kennedy was the world's greatest listener."

And the twenty-six-year-old Campbell is the world's greatest social climber. She grew up the daughter of a wealthy Los Angeles architect with ties to the entertainment industry. One boyfriend from her teenage years was actor Robert Wagner. At eighteen, she married the actor William Campbell, an alcoholic who appeared in horror films.

Just before that marriage, Campbell met the influential and shadowy "Handsome Johnny" Roselli—an enforcer from Chicago who oversees the Outfit's West Coast and Las Vegas operations for Mob boss Sam Giancana. Despite being almost twenty-five years older, Roselli is smitten. "Beautiful. Looks like Liz Taylor but nicer. A real sweet kid. Comes from a good family. Lots of class," the mobster will tell a friend.

And Roselli has lots of friends, including Joseph Kennedy, with whom he often plays golf and cards.

Now divorced, with no formal education beyond high school, a monthly alimony payment of just $433.33, and with no desire to enter the work force, Judy Campbell uses her wholesome beauty and intellect to cultivate friendships in the most elite Hollywood circles. This means a steady whirl of parties, nightclubs, and relationships with powerful men.

Among these is Roselli. The two have a brief affair, but the mobster chooses to pass Judy along to Frank Sinatra, whose close friendship with Sam Giancana is second only to that of Roselli. Campbell is soon vacationing in Hawaii with Sinatra. Also making that trip is actor Peter Lawford of the Rat Pack and his wife, Patricia Kennedy Lawford—JFK's sister.

Soon, the moody Sinatra and Judy Campbell begin to argue. She decides to fly home early, the relationship seemingly over. But it's not.

June Lang and her husband, John Roselli, at Hopi Point, Grand Canyon, following their elopement. The couple plan a trip to Boulder Dam before returning to their home in Hollywood.

That vacation occurred in November 1959. Yet if Judy Campbell is surprised when Sinatra invites her to spend a weekend in Las Vegas, she does not show it. Nor does she suspect that Frank is using her to ingratiate himself with JFK—at least, not at first. But soon the dynamic becomes quite clear. "They seemed to have a genuine mutual admiration society. Frank was in awe of Jack's background and his power," Campbell will later remember. "And Jack was mesmerized by Sinatra's swinging lifestyle."

Indeed, those who meet JFK in his unguarded private moments are often amazed at his fondness for women, parties, and the belief that he can get away with anything.

The relationship between John F. Kennedy and Judith Campbell will last for two years. Their dalliance will be kept secret—or so JFK thinks. It all begins with their flirtation in the Copa Room tonight. Frank Sinatra's guess has proven correct: despite the "bimbos and showgirls" flocking around the table, in the words of newsman Blair Clark, the candidate only has eyes for Campbell. Coincidentally, she bears an amazing resemblance to Kennedy's wife, Jackie.

The whole thing is a setup. The Mafia knows JFK's weakness for women and means to use Judy Campbell as a source of blackmail, if necessary. There is speculation that Sam Giancana himself ordered Campbell to Las Vegas, using Frank Sinatra as the go-between.

"They deliberately fed her to Jack," actor Brad Dexter, a good friend of Sinatra's, will recall. "And Frank was part of it. Very serious."

After the show, JFK and Campbell join the raging party in Sinatra's suite, with free-flowing alcohol, cocaine, and a bevy of beautiful showgirls. Campbell is popular with most men because she still projects the healthy image of a young, wholesome girl. But, at the Sands, she is "notorious in the sense that we knew who she was and that we considered her a high-class call girl who could be bought," in the words of one gaming dealer.

Kennedy does not know this, nor is he aware that Campbell was procured specifically for him.*

Campbell will later claim Kennedy does not force himself on her this first night—nor does she offer herself. In her version of events, they just make conversation.

"When you talked to Jack," Campbell will later recall, "he talked just to you. He was endlessly curious about everything and everybody. He loved gossip. That night he did not want me to leave his side."

FBI director J. Edgar Hoover will eventually get a detailed memo on Kennedy's "sex activities" from this Vegas weekend, but Campbell

---

* This is not the first time Campbell and Kennedy met, so it was known at the time that JFK had an eye for her. Their first encounter came months earlier at Puccini Restaurant in Beverly Hills. Senator Kennedy was dining with Sinatra when the two spied Campbell sitting with actress Angie Dickinson.

will long state that the candidate does not sleep with her on this occasion. She claims she returned to her own room in the early morning hours and he went alone to his suite at the El Rancho hotel farther down the Strip.

According to Campbell, the first voice she hears the following morning is that of JFK, calling to invite her to lunch in Sinatra's suite. This is the first of many phone calls between the two as Kennedy campaigns around the country. "He called almost every day," she will later write. "No matter where he was, or how tired."

One month later, as the race takes Kennedy through New York City, he and Campbell rendezvous once again, this time at the Plaza Hotel. It is March 7, the eve of the New Hampshire primary and the first crucial step on John Kennedy's road to the White House, when Campbell claims the couple first consummates their relationship.*

✦

Just two weeks after Campbell and Kennedy meet in New York, Frank Sinatra once again invites the young beauty to take a trip with him. And once again, despite the callous manner in which she has been treated, Judy says yes.

This time, the destination is the Fontainebleau in Miami. The singer has been a regular headliner in the luxury hotel's La Ronde nightclub since 1954, but on this occasion he is taping a television special welcoming Elvis Presley back from his two years in the army. The performance takes place on March 26, 1960, and is bathed in irony. Once upon a time, Frank Sinatra was the skinny young teenage idol for whom all the girls screamed. Now his hair is thinning and his voice husky from constant smoking and drinking Jack Daniels. Elvis Presley is the new icon. His rock 'n' roll sound has revolutionized modern music, replacing the standards for which Sinatra is known best. In effect,

---

* Judith Campbell Exner wrote a memoir in 1977 entitled *My Story*, about her affair with JFK. At first, it was disputed by the Kennedy family, and Campbell weakened the veracity of her claims by changing details of her story several times. But as more details about Kennedy's womanizing came to light, Campbell's story turned out to be mostly true—at least according to FBI wiretaps. However, to this day, some historians believe Campbell exaggerated to make money.

Frank Sinatra is welcoming home his replacement. Within a few short years, Las Vegas will be one of the only venues where Sinatra's sound will reign—and Presley is soon to make his mark there, too. Thus, the television broadcast six weeks from now will become a seminal moment in entertainment television history.

But even more interesting than the show are the actions taking place behind the scenes in Miami. Frank Sinatra has brought Judy Campbell here to be his plaything, considering her a "hooker." In the beautiful and willing young woman, Sinatra also sees a means of expanding his personal empire by keeping his powerful friends happy.

"I don't think it takes a great deal of imagination," Campbell will write years later, "to think there is a possibility I was used."

So, during a private party, Sinatra "introduces" Campbell to a gentleman. "Come here, Judy," she will write in her memoir. "I want you to meet a good friend of mine, Sam Flood."

Campbell will long claim that this is her first meeting with Sam Giancana, as he is actually named. The fifty-two-year-old widower is twice Campbell's age, a dour and physically unattractive man, but his tailored sharkskin suit, expensive alligator shoes, silk shirt, and powerful bearing signal a man of means.

In truth, there is a good chance Judy Campbell already knows the gangster, even if they have not been properly introduced. For Giancana is the best friend of her former lover, Johnny Roselli. And it is already a well-known fact that she has had several relationships with Mafia figures. Rat Pack member Peter Lawford specifically refers to Campbell as a "Mob moll."

What Judy Campbell does not know is that, on this night in March, she is about to become the center of a complex maelstrom of sex, politics, and crime.

Sex: Judith Campbell is having an affair with John Kennedy and is about to begin another with Sam Giancana.

Politics: Joseph Kennedy recently had lunch with Johnny Roselli and Sam Giancana at Felix Young's restaurant in New York City to discuss ways in which the Mafia could assist JFK's campaign. This comes less than eight months after Bobby Kennedy famously grilled Giancana before the McClellan hearings. The Mob boss tells a nervous

Joe Kennedy that he does not have a problem with JFK, but he is still angry about Bobby's public attacks on him. Joe Kennedy argues that his son's disrespect is in the past and reminds Giancana that "it's Jack who's running for president, not Bobby." Kennedy also tells the mobster that if he helps get JFK elected, the president will owe him a favor. "This is business, not politics," Kennedy concludes before leaving the dinner early so that Roselli and Giancana might discuss the matter alone.

Crime: Sam Giancana has bribed and blackmailed politicians and law enforcement officials throughout Illinois, a state vital to winning the presidency. He has the power to rig an election—but he's still not sure JFK should be supported.*

So it is that Judith Campbell sleeps with Sam Giancana, even as she continues to speak with JFK on the phone every day and bed the candidate whenever his schedule allows. All of these private actions take place in the midst of the very public spectacle of the 1960 presidential campaign. At first, JFK does not know about Giancana. But the Mob boss surely knows all about Campbell and the senator—and is thrilled that JFK has "a regular" who might prove a source of blackmail and insider knowledge.

Judy Campbell is now a conduit, providing a direct connection between a man seeking the most powerful office in the world and a man that commands the *under*world.

And, all the while, J. Edgar Hoover is listening in.

---

* Nick Sevano, a member of Frank Sinatra's inner circle, will go on record as stating that JFK also dined with Giancana while still a member of the Senate. "Jack was very respectful to Giancana," Sevano will recall.

PART III

THE SUBVERSIVES

CHAPTER FOURTEEN

JULY 11, 1960
LOS ANGELES, CALIFORNIA
5:00 P.M.

The most powerful man in Hollywood is on the phone.

Fifteen miles away, in the heart of downtown Los Angeles, the entertainment capital of the world is on display for all to see.

The day has been hot, and the City of Angels is wreathed in smog. Now, as evening falls, more than seven thousand Democrats from all across America crowd into the Sports Arena, soon to be the home of the Los Angeles Lakers basketball team. They are here to select a presidential nominee. Sixteen primary elections have been held in the past four months, with John F. Kennedy winning ten of them. The Massachusetts senator appears to be the front-runner among those vying to gain the nomination.* Joseph Kennedy, leaving nothing to chance, has stopped in Las Vegas en route to the convention and placed a massive $1 million bet on his son to win the presidency, thus ensuring that the oddsmakers will tout JFK as the favorite.

Ironically, the Kennedy patriarch will not be making an appearance at the convention. His strong anti-Semitic beliefs have made him a

---

* They are Senators Stuart Symington of Missouri, Hubert Humphrey of Minnesota, Wayne Morse of Oregon, and George Smathers of Florida. Lyndon Johnson, Adlai Stevenson, and Governor Robert Meyner of New Jersey will join them.

political pariah. At such a pivotal moment in the campaign, his son cannot risk the controversy Joe Kennedy's presence will elicit.

For while John Kennedy may appear to be the front-runner, recent developments are endangering his candidacy. The popular Texas senator Lyndon B. Johnson announced his own run two days ago, as did Democratic candidate Adlai Stevenson from Illinois. The winner will be decided over the next two days of argument, debate, and roll calls in Los Angeles.

But before the politicking begins, it is time to entertain the delegates, Hollywood-style.

At 5:00 p.m. the crowd grows quiet as a military color guard brings forth the American flag. Alaska and Hawaii were admitted to the union just one year ago, so the standard has a unique new look, with fifty stars instead of forty-eight.

In addition to delegates, the crowd is packed with movie stars—among them three members of the Rat Pack. Last night, at a one-hundred-dollar-per-plate gala at the Beverly Hilton Hotel, Frank Sinatra, Sammy Davis Jr., and Dean Martin entertained a crowd of twenty-eight hundred enthusiastic Kennedy backers. For the closing night of the convention, the three singers have arranged for an all-star chorus consisting of thirty major Hollywood stars to serenade the delegates.*

For the city of Los Angeles, hosting the convention is a bid at seeking world-class legitimacy. L.A. is mostly known for making movies and for whimsical attractions like nearby Disneyland. Indeed, the delegates are treated to backstage tours at the Hollywood studios and have flocked to the Magic Kingdom during their brief stay. Late night parties at watering holes like Chasen's and Romanoff's will include icons like Henry Fonda, Jack Lemmon, Gary Cooper, and Lauren Bacall. The connection between Hollywood and Washington that will soon become pivotal to national politics can be said to have begun with the glamour and glitz of the 1960 Democratic National Convention.

✦

---

* Among those appearing were Shirley MacLaine, Myrna Loy, Vincent Price, Nat King Cole, Shelley Winters, Janet Leigh, Charlton Heston, and Edward G. Robinson.

To mark the beginning of the proceedings, Frank Sinatra, Sammy Davis Jr., and Dean Martin are introduced, along with a dozen other celebrities. Democratic Party leaders hope to dazzle the audience watching on national television with this display of Hollywood wattage. The spectacle backfires temporarily when Davis is booed by pro-segregation southern delegates—because he is openly dating the white actress May Britt.

But Frank Sinatra ends the rancor. He is given a prolonged round of applause as he steps onstage. The house lights are brought all the way down. Then, under a lone spotlight, Sinatra performs "The Star-Spangled Banner."*

Thus begins three nights of democracy in action as the deeply divided delegates argue and feud before eventually choosing their candidate. With so few states holding primaries, the majority of voters are free to select whomever they want. And as the delegates battle, John Kennedy stays above the fray, cavorting with Marilyn Monroe and Judith Campbell in an apartment on Rossmore Avenue borrowed from actor Jack Haley. But by July 13, it is done. John Fitzgerald Kennedy wins a majority on the first ballot. In the Hollywood mansion of Marion Davies, where Joseph Kennedy and Frank Sinatra get the news together, the singer jumps up and down, shouting, "We're going to the White House!"

Thus, the man whose father assured Sam Giancana that the president of the United States would owe him a favor is now just one general vote away from taking up residence in the White House.

Yet, on this historic night, Kennedy is *not* the most powerful man in Hollywood.

That distinction belongs to a shadowy figure known as the Fixer.

✦

Very few people know the name Sidney Korshak, a.k.a. the Fixer, which is exactly how he wants it.

The tall, immaculately dressed Mafia attorney lives in the wealthy Los Angeles enclave of Bel Air. Korshak is fifty-three years old, a

---

* It is worth noting that Sinatra also sang the national anthem at the Democratic National Convention in 1956. He later became a Republican.

Chicago-born Jew of Lithuanian descent. His FBI case file number is 92-789. He and his wife, Bernice—Bee, to friends—live lavishly. The walls of their newly purchased home on Chalon Road are decorated in original works by Renoir and Chagall. Their wine cellar is stocked with the most expensive vintages. Their exclusive annual Christmas party is attended by the likes of Peter and Patricia Kennedy Lawford, Dinah Shore, Robert Evans, Tony Curtis, and Cubby Broccoli—the producer currently working on his first movie about a British secret agent named James Bond.

Like most homes in Bel Air, the Korshak property is ringed by an impenetrable wall of shrubs and towering trees, offering complete privacy. Unlike other homes in the neighborhood, however, the front door is answered by a security guard armed with a loaded pistol.

Korshak's garage is filled with a Rolls-Royce, Jaguar, Mercedes, and a Cadillac, but he prefers to hire a car and driver when traveling to meetings with top mobsters like Sam Giancana. The actions of Sidney Korshak are veiled in secrecy and are difficult to document, but his success hinges on his uncanny ability of convincing people to do what they don't want to do.

An example of his influence is the time comedian Alan King attempted to check in to a plush Paris hotel but is turned away by the front desk citing lack of availability. A frustrated King calls Korshak from a lobby pay phone. Before the comedian can even hang up, a clerk is standing outside the phone booth, ready to guide King to a suite.

But more frequent are calls no one knows about, thus Korshak's reputation as the Fixer. "A nod from Korshak," Hollywood producer and Korshak protégé Robert Evans will later write, "and the Teamsters change management. A nod from Korshak and Vegas shuts down. A nod from Korshak, and the Dodgers can suddenly play night baseball."

Six years from now, in 1966, it will be a call from Korshak that will elevate Robert Evans to the position as the chief executive at Paramount Pictures.*

---

* The signature film during Evans's time at Paramount was *The Godfather*. Director Francis Ford Coppola was determined that Al Pacino play the role of Michael Corleone. But Pacino was contractually obligated to another film, whose producer would not release him from the contract. Korshak made a phone call on Evans's behalf, and within twenty minutes Pacino was free to play Michael Corleone.

In a city like Hollywood, where fame is the calling card most residents crave, Sidney Korshak shuns the spotlight. He never allows his picture to be taken. As the Outfit's legal counsel, Korshak not only consorts with mobsters like Sam Giancana and Johnny Roselli, but also with labor leaders like Ronald Reagan, currently president of the Screen Actors Guild. By controlling unions such as SAG, the Mafia runs Hollywood. It is Korshak, in a conversation with Lew Wasserman, Reagan's agent, who insists that Reagan seek a second term as SAG president—which he does.

And it is not just the Hollywood labor unions. Korshak has deep ties to Jimmy Hoffa and the Teamsters. In show business there are many who believe that the dapper lawyer is more powerful than the union president. This will be clearly evidenced in October 1961, when Korshak travels to Las Vegas and checks in to the Riviera Hotel during a national conference for the International Brotherhood of Teamsters. Korshak requests the presidential suite, even though it is currently occupied by Jimmy Hoffa. Within moments, the labor leader's belongings are moved to smaller accommodations.

The truth is, Korshak's influence is everywhere. A decade ago, it was the lawyer who presented Senator Estes Kefauver with photographic blackmail—pictures of him with a mistress—thus bringing about an abrupt end to the Kefauver hearings against organized crime. And it is Korshak who knows the names and motivations of Bugsy Siegel's killers, even as the Los Angeles police struggle to find a single clue.

✦

Organized crime has been a fixture on the Hollywood scene since the early days of cinema. Cedric Belfrage, a British writer who arrived in the 1920s, described the pervasive "gangster element" in the movie world. The Jewish movie moguls of Eastern European birth are like the Sicilian mobsters in many ways, in particular their tight ethnic culture, immigrant origins, and outsider status in America. Traditional banks do not lend money to people like that.

Thus, the studio heads turn to the Mafia. As Sidney Korshak well knows, the film industry needs the Mob for financing. Traditional banks are loathe to make loans to movie studios because the success or failure of a film is never certain and, as stated, they don't like "the element" in charge.

However, organized crime could not care less about that. It is looking for ways to launder cash accrued illegally, so investing in a motion picture offers an ideal opportunity. In addition, just like in their Las Vegas casinos, the Mob adds to its bottom line by skimming money off a film's profits. In some instances, actors are not paid their full salary, a brutal yet effective way for the Mob to make even more money. Few actors complain because those who do soon find themselves unable to work.

"Nobody can skim as well as Las Vegas, because they invented it," director Richard Brooks will comment, "but Hollywood is second."

New York mobster Henry Hill will one day write of Hollywood: "On the surface, this world seems as far away from the gangster life as you can imagine. But the slime below the surface is sickening. It recently occurred to me that my adventures [in the Mob] prepared me nicely for swimming with the sharks on Wilshire Boulevard."

Organized crime in Los Angeles began just after the turn of the twentieth century, with an Italian American gang making big money bootlegging alcohol. In time, the gang grew in power, enabling its boss, Tom Dragna, born in Sicily, to secure a spot on the Commission—the national crime syndicate founded by Lucky Luciano in 1931. No other individual west of Chicago was so honored.

But the arrival of Bugsy Siegel in 1937 spawned a rivalry. The Los Angeles crime family was slowly replaced by Siegel and his New York connections. The first Hollywood labor unions were just beginning to organize and Dragna was slow to insert himself. But Siegel managed to do so almost immediately. A Hollywood film is a cooperative effort requiring writers, carpenters, painters, electricians, teamsters, and many more skills specific to motion pictures. Movies do not get made without these artisans. By controlling the unions as well as providing movie funding, the Mafia effectively runs Hollywood.

In fact, big stars like Debbie Reynolds, Dinah Shore, and Jill St. John are just a few of the many celebrities benefiting—at least indirectly—from the power of organized crime. Kirk Douglas is among Sidney Korshak's closest celebrity friends, a list that also includes Warren Beatty, Jack Benny, Cyd Charisse, David Janssen, and Vincente Minnelli. It pays to be a friend of the Fixer: when Frank Sinatra's acting career appeared to be over in the early 1950s, it was a phone call to Columbia Pictures president Harry Cohn that secured him the supporting role in *From Here to Eternity* that won Sinatra an Oscar. Likewise, when Korshak entered into a sexual affair with Ms. St. John, he convinced the actress to buy shares in a Las Vegas casino operation. This meant that when making the film *Diamonds Are Forever*, she will actually be part owner of the casino where the movie is being filmed. Korshak's insider information eventually makes the actress very wealthy when the Parvin-Dohrmann casino group is purchased by the Stardust Hotel.

No group benefits more than the Mafia when union membership in Los Angeles leaps from 20,000 in 1936 to 125,000 in 1938. Actor George Raft, who is very often cast as a mobster, is one of Bugsy Siegel's best friends and helps the newcomer navigate the world of Hollywood politics.* Though the territory still technically belongs to Tom Dragna and his L.A. crime family, Siegel slowly assumes control.

After Siegel is murdered in Beverly Hills, a man named Mickey Cohen seizes power, but he is sent to prison in 1951 for tax evasion. Dragna, in turn, dies of a heart attack in 1956.

The demise of Tom Dragna and Mickey Cohen presents an opening for the Chicago Mob. The Outfit is represented by Johnny Roselli, taking orders from Sam Giancana. And while Giancana has been head of the Chicago Mob since 1957, he prefers the sizzle of Hollywood to life in the Windy City and spends a great deal of his time consorting with movie stars and his singer girlfriend, Phyllis McGuire of the famous McGuire Sisters. Roselli and Giancana are both enamored with celebrity nightlife, preferring to let someone else manage day-to-day business arrangements.

That someone is Sidney Korshak.

There is nothing the Mob boss does not control in Hollywood—craft unions, casting, talent agencies, and even studio heads. Columbia Pictures president Harry Cohn, a longtime associate of Roselli,

---

* George Raft modeled his on-screen gangster persona on the voice and style of dress of New York City mobster Joey Adonis.

borrowed half a million dollars from the Mob to obtain control of the studio. The deal was structured in a way that the Mob secretly retained one-third ownership. Roselli and Cohn were such good friends that they wore the similar pinky rings as a sign of brotherhood. Upon Cohn's death in 1958, Sidney Korshak was appointed legal adviser to the mogul's estate.*

"It was well known in the industry," FBI agent Mike Wacks will later recall to journalists, "that if you were going to make a movie, the talk around the town was that you'd have to use the Teamsters. Of course, you better get it straightened out with Sidney before you get those Teamsters over there, or you could have problems. He'd get a consulting fee from both ends—the producers as well as the Teamsters. I wish we could have proven that."

In fact, Korshak's name has come up in more than twenty investigations of organized crime, yet he has never been indicted. This is a credit to his discretion. When other Mafiosi gathered in New York for the Apalachin Summit, Korshak thought it too public a gathering and stayed away. When the FBI succeeded in bugging the Outfit's Chicago headquarters, Korshak's voice is never heard on tape because he refuses to go there. In fact, Korshak is so cautious about security that he will never use a telephone he believes might be tapped. On one occasion, federal agents watch in amazement as he enters a phone booth carrying a large bag filled with loose change to make a number of calls. To frustrate law enforcement officials even further, Korshak does not use credit cards, often carrying as much as $50,000 on his person in large bills.

On occasion, however, investigators are successful in peeling back the layers behind Korshak's activities. During a federal extortion trial

---

* Harry Cohn was one of the most volatile individuals in the history of Hollywood, with a manic and profanity-laced style that would become the caricature for movie mogul behavior. He also made liberal use of his Mafia ties. When African American singer Sammy Davis Jr., who lost his left eye in an automobile accident, began dating the white actress Kim Novak, Cohn threatened to have Davis's other eye put out unless the affair ended. The biracial relationship eventually halted, but only when Sidney Korshak intervened and reminded Davis that his career would effectively be over if he did not comply.

concerning Mafia involvement in the motion picture industry and organized labor, union official Willie Bioff testifies that he was told by the Chicago Mob that "Sidney is our man, and [we] want you to do what he tells you. He is not just another lawyer, but knows our gang and figures our best interest. Pay attention to him, and remember, any message he may deliver to you is a message from us."

In the recording of one FBI wiretap, federal agents overhear members of the Chicago Mob giving directions to mobster Leslie "Killer Kane" Kruse: "never personally contact Sidney Korshak, hoodlum attorney."

Which points to the very reason Sidney Korshak remains a free man, even as other Mafiosi are being sent to the penitentiary: he protects himself. The Justice Department will refer to the attorney as "the most significant link in the relationship between the crime syndicate, politics, labor, and management."

In time, Korshak's client list will expand to include Hilton and Hyatt Hotels, the Los Angeles Dodgers, and the Madison Square Garden Corporation in New York, owner of the New York Knicks and New York Rangers hockey team.

Yet lower-level mobsters are forbidden from even speaking to him. "Sidney was up on a plateau we never really got to," one law enforcement officer will later remember. "It never came down to our level; we never ran across him. We never saw Sidney meeting with the guys . . . Sidney was always meeting with lawyers, with legitimate people."

This is how the secretive Sidney Korshak runs Hollywood.

✦

Desi Arnaz does not take Korshak's call, much to his peril.

The Cuban-born star of the sitcom *I Love Lucy* is one of the biggest names in television—so famous and powerful that he fears no one in Hollywood. In addition to taping his own show with his wife, the comedienne Lucille Ball, he now produces several other television programs. Among them is a crime drama called *The Untouchables*. Based on a true figure—Treasury agent Eliot Ness, played by Robert Stack—the production follows fictitious Prohibition battles in Chicago. The law enforcement group headed by Ness is made up almost entirely of white males, with the agent known as Rico the only individual with obvious ethnic Italian heritage. Ironically, this agent is played by an actor of Greek ancestry.

The bad guys in the show are almost all Italian American. In addition, the actor portraying Al Capone, Neville Brand, acts like a vicious psychopath. This not only enrages Capone's widow, Mae, but also makes Sam Giancana very angry. Coincidentally, Desi Arnaz was once a good friend of Sonny Capone, the gangster's only son. The Capone family believes they were instrumental in helping the Arnaz family flee Cuba in 1933 and are wounded by the depiction of their late father.

The pressure begins. In New York, union leader Tony Anastasia, brother of the assassinated Albert, orders longshoremen not to unload crates of cigarettes manufactured by Liggett & Myers, a sponsor of the program.

In Hollywood, Frank Sinatra moves his production company off the lot at Desilu-Gower Studios, owned by Arnaz. "What do you want me to do?" Arnaz screams at a furious Sinatra, "make them all Jews?" The two men nearly come to blows when Arnaz calls Sinatra "a television failure." But the singer knows better than to punch him. Through the many highs and lows in his career, Sinatra has learned that challenging power is not a recipe for success.

In Chicago, the pressure also builds. Sam Giancana actually orders Desi Arnaz killed! Jimmy "the Weasel" Fratianno, just released after six years in San Quentin, is assigned the job.

"Have you seen that TV show, *The Untouchables*?" asks Johnny Roselli when he sits down with Fratianno to discuss the situation.

"I don't have time to watch that shit," replies the Weasel.

"Let me tell you something, Jimmy. Millions of people all over the world see this show every fucking week. It's even popular in Italy. And what they see is a bunch of Italian lunatics running around with machine guns, slopping up spaghetti like a bunch of fucking pigs."

"Nobody pays attention to that shit," Fratianno says. "It's like a comic book. A joke. Who cares?"

Roselli responds immediately: "I'll tell you, Jimmy: Sam cares . . . what

I'm about to tell you has been decided by our family. The top guys have voted a hit ... we're going to clip Desi Arnaz, the producer of this show."*

A stunned Fratianno knows he must follow orders. But he is wary of the publicity surrounding the murder of a celebrity. The police investigation is sure to be intense. A return to the penitentiary is the last thing he wants right now.

So Fratianno stalls, hoping that Sam Giancana might somehow have a change of heart and call off the hit.

Meanwhile, unaware that his life is in danger, Desi Arnaz begins to realize that *The Untouchables* is losing money. Sponsors are backing out, refusing to purchase commercial time. Hollywood unions are also threatening to not allow their members to work on *The Untouchables*, which would shut down production entirely. These setbacks are carefully orchestrated by Sidney Korshak.

So in an act that will save his life, a desperate Arnaz schedules a meeting with Johnny Roselli and Frank Sinatra. The three gather in the Polo Lounge at the Beverly Hills Hotel.

"This is getting crazy," Arnaz begins. "What do you want me to do? How can I make this work for you?"

"Stop every week with these terrible Italian mobsters," says Roselli. "It's an insult to the good Italian people."

"Okay, we'll change all the names," Arnaz replies. "We'll call them Smith and Jones from now on."

"And while you're at it, make one of the good guys an Italian," Roselli responds.

"I already got an Italian Untouchable. His name's Rico," Arnaz tells the mobster.

But Roselli is ahead of him. "Not so fast. That actor's Greek. You got to get an Italian actor."

---

* The source of this conversation is Fratianno's biography, *The Last Mafioso*, and is repeated in Gus Russo's *The Outfit*. It does not appear that Lucille Ball, wife of Desi Arnaz and the most famous individual in television at the time, had any knowledge of the pending Mafia hit. Fratianno would later go on to become acting boss of the L.A. crime family, then enter the Federal Witness Protection Program in 1980 after agreeing to testify against the Mafia because he was facing murder charges. The Weasel would be dropped from the program after publication of his autobiography. He died of Alzheimer's disease in 1993.

"Who do you want me to put in?"

"Well, let me think a minute," Roselli responds. "There's a pal of mine . . . he'd be great in there."*

Arnaz complies. Roselli's friend is cast. The hit is called off. And while members of the Mafia will recount the details of the ordered murder for years to come, Desi Arnaz will never know how close he came to death.

✦

The Democratic National Convention ends with John F. Kennedy in triumph. Hollywood and Sidney Korshak return to business as usual. But, in Illinois, Sam Giancana gets set to enter a different business— politics. The mobster throws his support—and power—behind the Kennedy campaign.

That will alter history.

---

* The actor's name was Paul Percini.

CHAPTER FIFTEEN

R ichard Nixon is beginning to sweat.
Sitting under the hot lights of a television studio, the vice president of the United States wears a thin coat of cheap pancake makeup known as Lazy Shave, designed to hide Nixon's five-o'clock shadow. "I can shave within thirty seconds before I go on television and still have a beard," he lamented to television journalist Walter Cronkite two weeks ago.

The forty-seven-year-old presidential candidate wears a light gray suit for this televised presidential debate. It has been yet another long day on the campaign trail and Nixon is exhausted. He has just lost twenty pounds after suffering a staphylococcus infection in his left knee that required a hospital stay. Between August 29 and September 3 he was laid up in Walter Reed Army Medical Center, the injured leg immobilized by traction weights as antibiotics were administered to battle the infection. Then, shortly after his release, Nixon endured a crippling bout of flu from which he has not completely recovered. This combination of light suit, pale face, and wan complexion gives Nixon a sallow and unhealthy appearance. "My God," Chicago mayor Richard J. Daley exclaims at the televised sight of Nixon, "they've embalmed him even before he died."

The next morning, Nixon's mother will call to inquire about her son's health.

Now, Richard Nixon perches on the edge of his chair, legs splayed, left hand betraying his anxiety by flitting nervously from an armrest to his lap and back again. His eyes also shift, as Nixon is unsure whether to stare into the camera lens or at his opponent. Making matters even worse, he bumped his bad knee hard against a car door as he arrived at the CBS broadcast center in Chicago for tonight's debate. The pain radiates up and down his leg, even as Nixon unsuccessfully tries to appear at ease.

Opposite the vice president, looking the very picture of health, is John F. Kennedy. The Democratic candidate for president sits calmly, legs crossed, hands folded in his lap. Journalist Howard K. Smith moderates the debate from a desk placed between the two candidates.

The endocrine disorder known as Addison's disease, which causes Kennedy so much pain, also has the positive side effect of making his skin glow with a healthy tan. Kennedy takes steroids to combat this degenerative condition, which have added a few pounds to his 175-pound frame, imbuing JFK with a strong and rugged look. The boyishly handsome Kennedy's blue suit and greenish-gray eyes make him appear a decade younger than his opponent, though their actual age difference is just four years. And unlike Nixon's long day of donor speeches and campaign appearances, JFK has spent the entire weekend holed up in a hotel suite with his staff, resting and preparing answers to potential questions.

"This is a great country, but I think it could be an even greater country," Kennedy says in his opening remarks. He stares directly into the camera lens with an unwavering gaze. JFK's hair is parted perfectly, and his patrician Boston accent makes him sound confident instead of just rich. "This is a powerful country, but I believe it could be even more powerful."

Richard Nixon quickly echoes those opening lines, stating, "I subscribe completely to the spirit that Senator Kennedy has expressed tonight."

There are one hundred million Americans following the debate, some listening on the radio while others watch on television. Those who could not see the candidates will later agree that the final result is a toss-up between Nixon and Kennedy. But the seventy million TV viewers will overwhelmingly choose Kennedy as the winner.

Nineteen sixty is a time when a frivolous-minded America is enthralled with the hula hoop and singers like teen sensation Fabian. But beneath that escapist exterior, the nation is frightened. The United States is in the midst of a cold war for world domination with the Soviet Union. Communist Cuba's Fidel Castro is said to be aligning with the Soviets just ninety miles south of the American mainland. And the civil rights movement is sparking radical division between blacks and whites in America. It is a turbulent year and some see Senator Kennedy as the answer—a politician capable of standing up to USSR leader Nikita Khrushchev.

In Vice President Nixon, many viewers see a nervous man with a gray pallor and perspiration leaving trails through his makeup as the sweat rolls down his face.

As the debate continues for the next hour, both candidates articulate their policies with intelligence and clear knowledge of the subjects. Each is well aware that Election Day is just six weeks away. Pollsters are currently calling the race a draw. Tonight is very much about appearances, but the truth is that most viewers will vote along party lines, no matter how ill at ease Richard Nixon may appear.

So each candidate seeks the slight advantage that will lead to victory.

Which is why, after apparent setbacks with Senate hearings, the Apalachin Summit, and the FBI's forced acknowledgment of organized crime, the Mafia now rises stronger than ever. Hoodlums like Chicago's Sam Giancana, Tampa's Santo Trafficante, Teamster boss Jimmy Hoffa, and even the incarcerated Vito Genovese secretly possess the power to influence who will be the next occupant of the White House.

✦

In fact, the Mafia in America now has few adversaries on the federal level. So its power is almost unchecked. And, as always, the Mob is looking for new ways to make money, as well as influence not only the political landscape but also the social tempo of America.

At the dawn of the 1960s, that means rock 'n' roll.

Disc jockey Alan Freed coined that term after bringing his radio program to New York City's WINS radio. Previously based in Cleveland, the thirty-eight-year-old Freed rose to fame playing rhythm and blues records, formerly popular only with black audiences. Freed used the alter ego Moondog as he opened the mic to howl along with the music, speaking to his audience in hipster patois. But as Alan Freed transfers his act to New York, he is sued by another artist who goes by the name Moondog. After losing the case and being forced to pay $6,000, as well as being banned from using the name ever again, Freed is forced to rename his show.

He settles on "Alan Freed's Rock 'n' Roll Dance Party," well aware that most white Americans will not understand the reference. Since black singer Trixie Smith released the song "My Man Rocks Me with a Steady Roll" in 1914, the term *rock and roll* has become a frequently used euphemism for sex in black neighborhoods.

Though Bill Haley and His Comets' hit single "Rock Around the Clock" should have clued in many listeners to the illicit nature of rock 'n' roll music, this mixture of rhythm and blues, gospel, and country music is seen as a threat to the American way of life for other reasons. Unlike crooners such as Andy Williams and Perry Como, whose soothing tones are a holdover from Frank Sinatra's 1940s heyday, the edgy nature of rock performers encourages a sense of teen rebellion. And unlike the large orchestras featuring musicians in suits and ties, a typical rock 'n' roll band is a singer backed by guitars, drums, and sometimes piano or a saxophone—each displaying their own frenetic energy. In this way, the entire band generates a following, not just the lead singer.

But most controversial is the fact that rock 'n' roll music appeals to both white and black audiences. That leads bigots to brand it seditious—and a threat to racial segregation.

The rebellious nature of rock only makes America's young people listen all the more. By the time of the 1960 presidential election, rock 'n' roll is a $100 million industry, and a huge cultural force.

Alan Freed may have been at the forefront of this phenomenon, but none of it happens without the transistor radio and the television set. Rather than the cabinet-sized radio found in most homes of the 1940s and '50s, the advent of the portable handheld transistor in 1954 allows listeners to hear music on AM radio almost anywhere.

The invention of the transistor coincides precisely with the birth of rock'n'roll, as does the growing number of American households owning a TV. In 1954, that number was 65 percent of U.S. homes. By 1960, that figure has leapt to almost 90 percent, with many now watching in color instead of black and white.

It is typical of television programming at the time to include musical shows once popular on the radio, such as country sensation *Grand Ole Opry*. In keeping with this theme, Philadelphia TV station WFIL creates *American Bandstand*. The host is Bob Horn, a radio announcer making his TV debut. But when Horn is removed from the show after being arrested for drunk driving, as well as cavorting with a prostitute, a new host is introduced. That man is Dick Clark, a boyishly handsome radio and television personality who is not yet thirty years old.

Clark quickly takes the show national on the ABC network, featuring a stable of regular dancers as well as games like "Rate-the-Record," in which audience members choose the best songs of the day. Featured artists often appear on *Bandstand* lip-synching their hits. As the show explodes in popularity, a single appearance on *American Bandstand* is enough to make any young entertainer into a star. When black singer Chubby Checker debuts "The Twist" on August 6, 1960, the dance craze becomes a phenomenon. And the record knocks Elvis Presley's "It's Now or Never" off the top of the charts.

Quickly, rock'n'roll becomes the leading source of revenue in the music industry, challenging motion pictures for the American dollar. As a result, many top musical performers such as Elvis Presley migrate to Hollywood to make films alongside veteran stars like John Wayne and Bing Crosby, seamlessly blending the two forms of entertainment.

Yet it is not disc jockeys, musicians, or television hosts who benefit most from these transactions—it is organized crime.

The Mob quietly bankrolls and manages the careers of many singers and songwriters. The more often a record is played on the radio, the more likely it is to become a hit. Thus, "payola"—bribing a disc jockey to play a record—is an investment that pays dividends in higher royalties, as well as guaranteeing a packed house when an artist performs in a Mob-run venue.

"That's the atmosphere I grew up in when I was a kid," New Jersey native Frankie Valli of the Four Seasons will recall many years later. "If you were in the music business, in most cases, all the places you worked for were owned by those guys. Organized crime are the guys who owned the bars and nightclubs. I came from a very Italian neighborhood and there was a lot of organized crime presence. I knew guys who dressed in suits every day and drove Cadillacs and didn't go to work. I didn't know what they did."

In Detroit, a thirty-year-old songwriter and record producer named Berry Gordy allegedly funds the start of his new Motown record label by borrowing a few thousand dollars from the Detroit Mafia. Angelo "the Chairman" Meli is the syndicate's underboss, working as part of the nationwide Commission alongside New York's five families. Meli's top lieutenants are his brother Frank and nephew, Vince. In addition to labor racketeering, the Meli family owns record labels Meltone Music, White Music Company, and Jay & Cee Music—as well as overseeing the local jukebox market and controlling the booking of musicians in local clubs.*

In Philadelphia, Bob Marcucci, the son of a labor organizer, looks for local singers to churn out hits. His efforts initially fail. When gangsters claim all the royalties for Marcucci's 1953 song, "You Are Mine," the young man leans upon his father for assistance negotiating the world of music and organized crime.

Bob Marcucci soon discovers the singers Fabiano "Fabian" Forte, as well as a trumpet player named Francis Thomas Avallone, who becomes famous as Frankie Avalon.

Robert Louis Ridarelli, a Philadelphia singer who performs under the name of Bobby Rydell, is not among Marcucci's clients. He prefers to let his father manage him. But Rydell's connection to organized crime goes right to the top.

---

* The rumors about Berry Gordy's Mafia connections were strong enough that the FBI's Detroit bureau brought him in for questioning. Now ninety years old at the time of this writing, Gordy continues to deny rumors that the Mafia was involved in the founding of Motown Records. He claims the rumors began because he hired an Italian American to head his sales department.

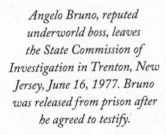

Angelo Bruno, reputed underworld boss, leaves the State Commission of Investigation in Trenton, New Jersey, June 16, 1977. Bruno was released from prison after he agreed to testify.

"He was a wonderful man," Rydell will remember of Angelo Bruno, the powerful boss of the Philadelphia crime family. Bruno took over the Philadelphia crime family in 1959 and will rule for two decades in a style so opposed to violence that he will become known as the Docile Don. "He was a Mob figure but . . . a wonderful man."

At one point, Bobby Rydell's father, Adrio, inadvertently double-books his son. One engagement is singing at the Americana Hotel in Miami. The other is making a movie in Australia. When the Americana refuses to postpone Bobby Rydell's performance—placing the film in jeopardy—Adrio Rydell places a call to Mob boss Bruno.

The results are immediate.

"There was a phone call made to a particular gentleman in Miami," Rydell will recall. "And I went and made the motion picture. I never played the Americana."*

---

* The movie Rydell made in Australia was *That Lady from Peking*.

✦

But not every machination within the music world can be solved with a simple phone call. Sometimes the dealings are so complex and duplicitous that they take years to resolve.

And it seems the Mafia always comes out on the winning end.

Morris Levy, who has deep ties with Vito Genovese, owns the famous Birdland nightclub in Manhattan, as well as the Roulette record label. Both businesses are a front for the Genovese family.

Levy makes it a practice to secure copyright control of all songs performed in his club. Artists working for Roulette are also expected to grant Levy a songwriting credit, allowing him to receive royalties as both the writer and publisher of a record. For example, the famous hit "Why Do Fools Fall in Love" was written by a fourteen-year-old named Frankie Lymon from Harlem. Again, Morris Levy receives a writing credit. Upon Lymon's death at age twenty-five from a heroin overdose in 1968, Levy has all mention of the singer's name removed from legal documents.

Later, when sued by Lymon's widow for back royalties, Levy testifies under oath that he cowrote the song. Upon being asked how a businessman with no ability to play or read music manages to write a top forty pop hit, Levy shrugs: "You get together, you get the beat together, and you put the music and words together. I think I would be misleading you if I said I wrote songs, per se, like Chopin."

After three decades of legal wrangling, Morris Levy—and the Genovese family—wins the case. The widow of Frankie Lymon walks away with nothing but legal bills.

In another instance, when Ritchie Cordell writes "It's Only Love" for Tommy James and the Shondells, Levy flexes his power by insisting that unless his name is listed as the co-songwriter, the record will never be released. For the sake of his career, James goes along.

"We ended up selling 110 million records at Roulette," Tommy James will later admit. "Of course, getting paid was impossible."

✦

Finally, public outrage about abuses in the music business surfaces in 1960. But it is not the Mob that suffers public scandal. Instead, it is disc jockey Alan Freed and *American Bandstand*'s Dick Clark who are asked to speak before a congressional subcommittee investigating payola—a combination of the words *payment* and *Victrola*, a once-fashionable record player.

The act of paying to have an artist's music played on radio and television is not technically illegal. But the notion of success being bought by promoters is disturbing to many, thus the hearings. President Dwight Eisenhower is so offended by one disc jockey's claim that payola is "the American way of life," that he feels compelled to attack the practice as "an issue of public morality."

At the time of the House hearings, Alan Freed had already been fired from WINS in 1958 and moved on to WABC in New York, where he was fired in 1959. It was well known he accepted bribes to play songs on his show. Payola had been around since the big band era of the 1930s, but Freed's high profile in the rock 'n' roll world, as well as resistance to the new music by an older generation, made him a target. It did not help Freed's case that he cowrote "Maybelline" with Chuck Berry, and played the record on his show frequently to ensure it became a hit. In 1962, Freed will plead guilty to a charge of commercial bribery and will receive a suspended sentence. Unable to find work, Freed moves to California, where he drinks himself to death at the age of forty-three.

✦

Dick Clark will be far more fortunate. Despite the heavy Mafia influence in the record business, he has come to own thirty-three different distributors, record labels, and manufacturers. "I think the crime I may have committed, if any, is that I made a great deal of money in a short time on a little investment. But that is the record business," Clark tells Congress.

Wisely, Dick Clark divests himself from each of these enterprises before testifying in the payola scandal. He will go on to a long and prosperous life, hosting *American Bandstand* well into the twenty-first century. Clark never acknowledges any connections to the Mob, any instance in which the Mafia might have helped him or altered his business practices, or any awareness that his holdings might have fallen into crime family hands.

"Obviously," Representative Oren Harris of Arkansas tells Clark at the close of his testimony, "you're a fine young man."

✦

Entertainment is one thing, but power politics is something far more serious. And while the public would be shocked to know that the clean-cut John F. Kennedy and his father, Joseph, have Mob associations that could influence the 1960 presidential election, Americans would be just as incredulous to learn that Richard Nixon has a very good friend in Jimmy Hoffa, the corrupt head of the Teamsters union.

Almost nine months ago, Hoffa arranged to meet with Oakley Hunter at the Americana Hotel in Miami Beach. Hunter is a Nixon ally, a veteran of the U.S. House of Representatives from California. As Hoffa enters the congressman's suite, he takes off his suit coat to show that he is not wearing a recording wire. Hunter does the same.

The two men sit down, and it is soon clear to Oakley Hunter that Jimmy Hoffa's hatred for the Kennedy brothers has not abated. "He feels he is being made a scapegoat and a whipping boy," Hunter will write to Richard Nixon in a memo. The Kennedy brothers, Hoffa believes, are "young millionaires who had never done a day's work in their lives."

Above all, Jimmy Hoffa wants a more conciliatory relationship between the teamsters and the federal government. Should Nixon be elected president, Hoffa is confident that will happen. But, knowing that his personal reputation could harm Richard Nixon, Hoffa delegates teamster support to local leaders across the country. Along the way, he promises the Nixon confidants that he will deliver the vote of his 1.6 million union members. In addition, Jimmy Hoffa promises that a significant amount of campaign money will flow to Richard Nixon.

On September 7, 1960, two months before Election Day, Hoffa publicly announces that JFK "presents a very real danger to our nation if he is successful in buying our country's highest office."

On September 26, an anonymous donor gives the Nixon for President campaign a suitcase full of $500,000 in unmarked bills—and a promise of another half million to come.*

In the meantime, in an act of political quid pro quo, Hoffa receives the *coincidental* news that the Justice Department, led by Republican attorney general William Rogers, has canceled a pending indictment of Jimmy Hoffa in a Florida case involving fraud with teamster pensions.

✦

"We stand today on the edge of a new frontier," John Kennedy states as he accepts his party's nomination, "the frontier of the 1960s, a frontier of unknown opportunities and perils, a frontier of unfulfilled hopes and threats."

The Democratic candidate is speaking about the United States of America.

But if the speaker was, instead, Sam Giancana or Jimmy Hoffa, they could just as easily be talking about organized crime.

As the new decade begins to unfold, organized crime seems to be an unstoppable force. The Mob has vast influence in movies, gambling, commerce, music, vice—almost every form of transaction and gratification. Criminals control the food delivered to American tables, the restaurants in which the people dine, the hotels where they sleep, and the entertainment they enjoy.

As Election Day 1960 draws near, it is a fact that organized crime will attempt to use its vast power to influence who will become the next president of the United States.

And few Americans have any idea what is happening.

---

* Hoffa aide Ed Partin, who later became a government informant, was present when New Orleans mobster Carlos Marcello presented Jimmy Hoffa with the suitcase. "I was right there, listening to the conversation," Partin will later recount. "Marcello had a suitcase filled with $500,000 cash which was going to Nixon. It was a half-million-dollar contribution. The other half was coming from the Mob boys in New Jersey and Florida."

CHAPTER SIXTEEN

January 20, 1961
Washington, D.C.
12:51 p.m.

"I, John Fitzgerald Kennedy, do solemnly swear . . ." intones Supreme Court chief justice Earl Warren.

The president-elect repeats those words back to the jurist. The two men stand on the east portico of the Capitol Building, watched by a crowd of nearly one million spectators. A severe overnight snowstorm forced the use of flamethrowers to clear the streets, and fourteen hundred cars stranded by the blizzard had to be towed from Pennsylvania Avenue this morning. Now, even at midday, the temperature, adjusted for windchill, is just seven degrees. Yet JFK does not wear an overcoat or hat for his swearing-in, preferring to depict an image of rugged youthfulness. After eight years under America's eldest president, the seventy-year-old Dwight Eisenhower, the nation has now elected one of its youngest.* As befitting that youth, both of the forty-three-year-old Kennedy's parents are in attendance, a first in presidential history.

✦

---

* Teddy Roosevelt was America's youngest president, but JFK was the nation's youngest elected president.

J. Edgar Hoover, director of the Federal Bureau of Investigation, with President John Kennedy as Kennedy arrives to address graduates of the seventh session of the FBI National Academy. Washington, D.C., October 31, 1962.

One mile away, in his office at the Justice Department on Constitution Avenue, FBI director J. Edgar Hoover watches the proceedings on television.

Hoover is surrounded by several agents and their families. The mood is festive, despite the fact that Hoover's personal choice in the recent election, Richard Nixon, was not triumphant. J. Edgar Hoover has now been in charge of the bureau in its many guises since 1925, and despite rumors that he may retire because of JFK's election, Hoover has no plans to step down.

And John F. Kennedy will not remove him. "You don't fire God," Kennedy explained to his friends.

On this afternoon, Director Hoover is keeping a secret. He is well aware that vote tampering played a key role in JFK's election. FBI wiretaps have provided Hoover with that information and a number of other things that will increase his power. For example, Hoover now has a thick file on Kennedy's extramarital affairs, including detailed accounts of his philandering with Frank Sinatra as well as the new president's ongoing relationship with Judith Campbell. After analyzing the voluminous material gathered by the FBI during the campaign, Hoover believes Sam Giancana and the Outfit in Chicago were able to falsify some votes in JFK's favor. But rather than make these explosive allegations public, the director holds them in reserve to be used when it can benefit him most.

The truth is, J. Edgar Hoover does not trust the Kennedy brothers. He is angry with JFK's decision to anoint his thirty-five-year-old brother attorney general. There is no way J. Edgar Hoover is going to answer to Bobby Kennedy.

The job of attorney general is usually given to someone with vast legal experience. But Robert Kennedy has never tried a case in court or even practiced law. In fact, RFK's primary credentials are a sibling relationship with America's new leader and the fact that Bobby successfully helmed JFK's victorious presidential campaign.

So it is that Robert Francis Kennedy is now J. Edgar Hoover's boss. Hoover has worked under five presidents and has been granted unrestricted access to the Oval Office. This has allowed him to undercut attorneys general, when necessary, in order to advance his personal agenda. But this will be impossible in the new administration. The two brothers will effectively run the nation as a team, with Hoover "outside the tent, pissing in," to use an expression used by Vice-President Lyndon Johnson.

Even so, the director is trying to be optimistic about the situation. He recently delivered a five-page letter to the new attorney general, detailing the FBI's investigations into Communism in America. Hoover believes this to be the greatest threat to the nation and hopes RFK will allow him to widen the scope of these "red" inquiries.

It is apparent that J. Edgar Hoover does not intend to be subservient. Tour guides at the Justice Department have been instructed to advise visitors that Hoover became head of the Bureau of Investigation the same year Bobby Kennedy was *born*. In addition, an agent is being posted at the door of the Justice Department gymnasium, ready to prevent access to anyone without official FBI identification—including the fitness-obsessed new attorney general.

But, for now, surrounded by friends and cronies as he watches John Kennedy complete his oath of office, J. Edgar Hoover is content. The Kennedy brothers may hold electoral power, but the thick dossier he possesses on JFK's sex life is power of a far different nature. The documents are insurance that Hoover will remain director of the FBI for as long as he likes.

However, the files are not enough, as Hoover leaves nothing to chance. Anticipating Robert Kennedy's arrival, the director has placed listening devices throughout the Justice Department. Hoover is so determined to undermine the new attorney general's authority that he not only bugs RFK's private elevator but also arranges for the speed of ascent and descent to be slowed so that the secret discussions can be recorded for longer periods of time.

Traps are being set.

✦

Bobby Kennedy does not fear J. Edgar Hoover—nor is Communism his primary interest.

America's new attorney general is eager to "hit the ground running," and to RFK that means greater focus on destroying organized crime. His work during the McClellan hearings has exposed the many tendrils of the Mob that permeate American society. In his bestselling 1960 book *The Enemy Within*, Kennedy writes: "If we do not on a national scale attack organized criminals with weapons and techniques as effective as their own, they will destroy us."

In fact, the *Wall Street Journal* anticipates "the most sweeping campaign against gangsters, labor racketeers, and vice overlords that the

New Orleans underworld boss Carlos Marcello, scheduled to appear in Federal court after allegedly assaulting Federal Bureau of Investigation agent J. Collins at the New Orleans airport on Friday, October 7, 1966.

country has ever seen." In other words, the paper believes Bobby Kennedy will go to war with the Mob.

And he does. In April 1961, after just three months in office, he authorizes the Internal Revenue Service to hire a team of new agents to investigate the tax returns of known underworld figures.

And that's just the beginning. In a display of ruthless aggression that demonstrates the extent of Kennedy's zeal, he authorizes the deportation of Carlos Marcello, the feared head of the New Orleans crime family. Born in Tunisia, the silk suit–wearing Marcello came to America as an infant but, in adulthood, never applied for citizenship.

Using this illegal alien status against him, the U.S. Immigration Service handcuffs a surprised fifty-one-year-old Marcello as he tries to renew his resident's card. The feds then place him on a "black" flight to Guatemala, on which he is the only passenger. For reasons that remain unclear, Marcello had previously obtained a fraudulent Guatemalan birth certificate. This provides American officials legal authority to deport the mobster to that nation.

The United States has been trying for a decade to deport Marcello, but until now no country would take this legendary criminal. But this time is different. The process begins when the Justice Department learns through an informant that Marcello has arranged for a forger to doctor Guatemalan birth records. The Central Intelligence Agency, which has been active in propping up the Guatemalan military regime, receives orders to search for irregularities in the official recording of births in the San José Pinula region. There they find the phony register. The U.S. Immigration and Naturalization Agency then uses this "evidence" to obtain an official entry permit from the Guatemalan government.

Marcello's woes do not end with his arrival in Central America. Not wanting him in their country, Guatemalan authorities apprehend the gangster for holding false citizenship papers. He is then driven into neighboring El Salvador under the cover of darkness, where he is released at a military camp. The soldiers quickly place Marcello on a bus to neighboring Honduras. After a lengthy journey through the jungle, chased by local men seeking to rob and perhaps murder him, Marcello finally reaches an airport, where he arranges a military flight to Miami through his good friend Rafael Trujillo, dictator of the Dominican Republic. From Miami, the gangster takes a commercial flight to New Orleans, where he is promptly rearrested for illegally entering the United States and also served with an $835,000 tax lien. But Carlos Marcello is allowed to remain in the United States as his lawyers fight the charges. All the while, Marcello seethes and plots against the Kennedy brothers, swearing he will get his revenge.

✦

Bobby Kennedy is livid that Marcello is back in America, but as the New Orleans courts debate the mobster's future, the attorney general has other things to do. Kennedy sends a team of fifty lawyers to Chicago as a special prosecution unit against the Outfit. In June, the Justice Department hands down thirteen gambling indictments. In July, RFK is successful in getting four anti-crime bills passed, which stiffen penalties against racketeering and illicit wagering. The attorney general is present in the Oval Office when his older brother signs the Interstate Wire Act of 1961 (also called the Federal Wire Act), allowing the feds to secretly monitor gambling activity. All of this, of course, is cutting into the Mob's profits.

Behind the scenes, Bobby Kennedy's hopes of establishing a national crime commission are opposed by J. Edgar Hoover. So Kennedy authorizes the Justice Department's Organized Crime and Racketeering Section to gather information on known Mob activities, bypassing the FBI. Data collected by twenty-seven government agencies is now controlled by Kennedy.

The results are almost immediate: in 1961 alone, prosecution of underworld figures nets eleven major convictions, including that of longtime Los Angeles boss Mickey Cohen. In addition, the Justice Department breaks up an international heroin smuggling ring known as the French Connection, winning eleven convictions in the process.* Impressed by this success, Congress doubles the Justice Department's budget for fighting organized crime.

J. Edgar Hoover does not like any of this and is especially offended when RFK visits the FBI field office in Chicago. The visit takes place in October 1961. Agents ask if the attorney general is interested in hearing wiretaps of local Mafiosi discussing a recent crime. Kennedy eagerly agrees.

On the tapes, the murder of a 350-pound Mob "Juice Man"—slang

---

* The French Connection was the conduit for smuggling heroin into the United States and Canada from Turkey through France. First begun in 1937, the Corsican-led operation was protected by the American Office of Strategic Services (or OSS, precursor to the CIA) during World War II, in exchange for helping defeat French Communism. Many members of the drug ring also served in the French Resistance during the war, leading to later rumors that French police were unwilling to prosecute them as thanks for their service. Despite the convictions obtained by Bobby Kennedy's Justice Department, the French Connection continued to operate into the 1970s. In 1971, a movie by the same name starring Gene Hackman became a major hit.

for debt collector—is discussed in detail by the men who did the killing. William "Action" Jackson is no saint. In the course of his work, he is fond of breaking into the homes of men who fall behind on their debts, then raping their wives as a reminder to pay up. He is arrested in the summer of 1961 while attempting to unload stolen electrical appliances in a warehouse. His five accomplices all manage to flee, but Jackson is too heavy to run. While in custody, the debt collector is asked to become a federal informant. As a lifelong member of the Outfit, Jackson refuses.

But the Juice Man's story is not believed by his fellow mobsters, who in their paranoia think he's an informer. Two months later, Bobby Kennedy listens to the killers brutally describe how Jackson is kidnapped and taken to a Chicago meat plant. The giant man is stripped. His hands and feet are bound with rope. A meat hook is inserted into his rectum. His kneecaps are broken with a baseball bat. Then his ribs. A sharp object is shoved into one ear, poking a hole in the drum. An electrical cattle prod is then shoved into his genitals.

Jackson still refuses to confess to being an informer. So his brutalizers use a blowtorch to incinerate his penis. Only then is he taken off the meat hook. The murderers leave the big man bound to bleed to death—a passing that does not take place for three long days.

In all his years of congressional hearings, Bobby Kennedy has never heard such depravity. He knows of murders and corruption, but this barbarity is too difficult for him to immediately process. The FBI agents will report to J. Edgar Hoover that a shocked Kennedy flushes with rage before he abruptly leaves their office.

As RFK flies back to Washington to continue his crusade against organized crime, he is well aware that the Outfit can murder almost anyone—at any time they choose.

Even Robert Francis Kennedy.

✦

If 1961 is triumphant for Bobby Kennedy, the same cannot be said of 1962.

It is on December 11, 1961, that the success of the attorney general's first year begins crashing down. J. Edgar Hoover writes a succinct memo to his boss, revealing the contents of a Sam Giancana wiretap. The mobster is overheard lamenting that his efforts to get John Kennedy elected have not resulted in less pressure on the Outfit. Nor has there been any significant attempt to get rid of Fidel Castro and return the Mafia to control of the Havana casinos.

In fact, because of Bobby Kennedy, the scrutiny of Mob crimes has intensified. Giancana then boasts that he will find a way to use his relationship with patriarch Joseph Kennedy to keep the Justice Department at bay, admitting on tape that he secretly—and illegally—funneled a large donation to the Kennedy campaign through the father to help JFK win the West Virginia primary. Frank Sinatra is one of the go-betweens delivering the cash.*

For the first time, the director of the FBI now has evidence that there is a connection between the Kennedy family and organized crime—at least in allegation form.

This is big. Sam Giancana's criminal empire now dwarfs that of all New York's five families combined. His enduring relationship with Johnny Roselli continues Giancana's control of Las Vegas and Hollywood. Both Kennedy brothers would be disgraced and forced out of office if the American public knew that the most powerful crime boss in the country had influence over them.

Thus, J. Edgar Hoover's memo to Bobby Kennedy is a cryptic threat that he could use the Giancana tap to bring down the Kennedys, should that become necessary. Hoover writes in the memo: "[Giancana] made a donation to the campaign of President Kennedy but was not getting his money's worth."†

This is the first time that Bobby Kennedy learns about any association between his father and Sam Giancana. Prior to this, the attorney general believed that Joseph Kennedy wanted him to avoid organized

---

* The FBI had listening devices planted in the Chicago First Ward Democratic organization (code-named Shade), in the Outfit's Michigan Avenue hangout (Little Al), and in Sam Giancana's Armory Lounge (Mo). Though providing valuable intelligence, the surveillance was in violation of the Fourth Amendment prohibiting unreasonable search and seizure, and thus kept highly classified.

† John F. Kennedy never acknowledged any Mob interference in the presidential election of 1960. And to this day, allegations remain just that—allegations.

crime controversies in order to court the labor vote. Knowing that his father may be more involved with organized crime is deeply disturbing to RFK.

What happens next is unclear. Bobby and his father often have heated discussions about sensitive matters, such as their blowout over the McClellan hearings three years ago. So it is more than likely that after being briefed by Hoover, the new attorney general brings the Giancana issue to his father.

Joseph Kennedy is vacationing at the family compound in Palm Beach and Bobby is in Washington, so the discussion, *if* it happened, is by telephone.

On December 18, just one week after Hoover's memo is sent to Bobby Kennedy, a severe stroke immobilizes the seventy-three year-old patriarch. Paralyzed on the right side of his body and afflicted with aphasia, the elder Kennedy will never speak again. A stroke is brought on by soaring blood pressure and ensuing blood vessel ruptures that cause a stoppage of blood flow to the brain. Whatever brought all that on, in Joseph Kennedy's case, will never be known.

What is known is that the patriarch no longer possesses the ability to dictate family strategy, leaving John and Robert Kennedy to chart their own paths for the first time in their lives.

Yet Joseph Kennedy is not dead—nor is the connection with organized crime that J. Edgar Hoover has in his possession.

✦

On February 27, 1962, the director sends another memo to Bobby Kennedy, this time referencing the seventy calls made to the White House by one Judith Campbell. Gleefully, Hoover tells the attorney general that this twenty-seven-year-old beauty is a known companion of Sam Giancana and Johnny Roselli. The FBI has long tapped the phone lines in Roselli's Los Angeles apartment, where Campbell often stays when the gangster is out of town. The tap provides Hoover with transcripts of all conversations made from that apartment to the White House.

Bobby Kennedy knows he and his brother are in dangerous territory. Not only does the director of the FBI know that JFK is cheating on his wife, but he also knows that Sam Giancana says he helped get the president elected. Emboldened, Hoover places a call to an associate of Walter Winchell, the legendary gossip columnist. He feeds an anonymous item about Judith Campbell as "topic number one in romantic political circles."

The Kennedy brothers get the message.

Under normal circumstances, a connection between a high-ranking individual and organized crime would warrant a criminal investigation. Instead, J. Edgar Hoover practices a form of blackmail. He places these nuggets of information in the personal file of John F. Kennedy. The director is sixty-six now, a year past suggested retirement age for civil servants. But the bureau is his life's work and he has no intention of retiring. With these explosive files, Hoover believes he doesn't have anything to worry about.

And while John Kennedy can be flippant about his private indiscretions, often acting as if they have no bearing on his presidency, he now takes immediate action to address Hoover's memos. Two years after his first association with Judith Campbell, the president instructs his secretary, Evelyn Lincoln, that he will no longer take Campbell's phone calls.

Judith Campbell is out.*

✦

So is Frank Sinatra.

The entertainer who arranged for both John Kennedy and Sam Giancana to share Judith Campbell claims to be one of the president's best friends. Yet his allegiance to the Mob runs far deeper. In an attempt to gain even more influence with the Kennedys, the singer is now having an affair with Patricia Lawford—JFK's sister and wife of fellow Rat Pack member Peter Lawford.

Sinatra still reveres Kennedy but is now in dangerous waters. The singer is insisting that JFK stay at his palatial Palm Springs home in

---

* The racist J. Edgar Hoover made wide use of the FBI's phone surveillance, both legal and illegal. In addition to gathering information about Sam Giancana and Judith Campbell, he also tapped Martin Luther King's telephone. Because Hoover had damaging information on the Kennedy family, Bobby reluctantly allowed the wiretapping that led to damaging personal information about Dr. King.

the Tamarisk Country Club, with its orange furnishings, movie theater, and enormous swimming pool. In anticipation of the president's arrival, Sinatra has even installed a new helipad, cottages for the Secret Service, and a telephone switchboard featuring twenty-five lines—fit for the most powerful man on earth.

But J. Edgar Hoover once again inserts himself into the situation, this time by playing Bobby Kennedy wiretaps of a conversation between Sam Giancana and Frank Sinatra. The mobster is clearly disappointed with the singer, who promised to influence the Kennedy family to obtain more lenient treatment of organized crime. Giancana believes Sinatra has lied to him about his discussions with Bobby Kennedy and is actually considering a Mob-style murder as revenge.

"Don't worry about it. If I can't talk to the old man, I'm going to talk to *the* man," Sinatra tells Giancana about Bobby Kennedy's relentless attacks on the Mafia, making reference to Joseph Kennedy and then JFK. In fact, before the patriarch's stroke, Frank Sinatra had met with him on three separate occasions to suggest that the president and attorney general back off from the Mob.*

But Sinatra's efforts really didn't matter. Only results would do. FBI wiretaps reveal that Giancana is deeply conflicted about having Sinatra murdered. If it was any other individual, the hit would be made immediately. But the Mafioso is so enchanted by Sinatra's singing voice that he cannot imagine a world without it. "I'm fucking Phyllis [McGuire], playing Sinatra songs in the background, and the whole time I'm thinking to myself, 'Christ, how can I silence that voice?'" Giancana admits to a fellow mobster.

So Frank Sinatra continues doing everything he can to please Sam Giancana. One FBI wiretap overhears the singer speaking in vulgar language as he displays his fealty toward the mobster, making it clear that Giancana is the friend he wishes to please most—even more than the president. Sinatra insists that he is taking extreme measures to obtain greater influence with the Kennedy brothers and their war on organized crime.

---

* The meetings were chronicled in a December 1961 FBI wiretap on the Giancana operation.

In addition, Sinatra tells Giancana about his affair with Patricia Kennedy Lawford and vows to "sleep with this goddam bitch until I get something going."

The FBI tape is shocking. When informed of it by his brother, President Kennedy immediately cuts off Sinatra. He asks Peter Lawford to phone the singer and inform him that he will not be staying at his house in Palm Springs. Instead, he will spend the night at Bing Crosby's Silver Spur Ranch, where actress Marilyn Monroe will be present.*

Upon hearing the bad news, a furious Sinatra steps outside his home, sledgehammer in hand. He then personally begins reducing the helipad to rubble, blow by blow.

✦

John and Robert Kennedy know that J. Edgar Hoover can destroy them. But there is little they can do other than avoid Campbell, Giancana, and Sinatra.

Try as they might, the Kennedy brothers cannot definitively break the link to organized crime. And in the summer of 1962, the Mob connection becomes ever more outrageous. Attorney General Bobby Kennedy is quietly informed by officials of the Central Intelligence Agency that the government has enlisted the aid of Sam Giancana and Johnny Roselli to assassinate Cuban dictator Fidel Castro.

The plan was not originally hatched during the Kennedy administration. President Dwight Eisenhower had advocated a Mafia hit on Castro years before. President Kennedy was told of the mission and gave his approval upon taking office. Bobby Kennedy is also aware of the plot and backs it enthusiastically. The Mob is the perfect group to manage such a killing, which would allow the Kennedy administration to disavow any participation.

Sam Giancana's Outfit is so eager to see Fidel Castro dead that

---

* The official version of events is that the Secret Service preferred Crosby's home because there were only four homes on the sixteen-acre Silver Spur parcel, with just one gate leading in and out, allowing greater security. As he would in Dallas just a little over a year later, the president traveled around town during his weekend stay in the back seat of an open-air Lincoln Convertible, giving little thought to security.

Johnny Roselli and Giancana initially turn down the CIA's offer of $150,000 to perform the hit. The gangsters want to do it for free. They despise Castro that much.*

Initially, the CIA preferred a gangland murder utilizing gunfire, but no mobster would take the job on because the chances of escape are nonexistent. Instead, the Mob decides to use poison, based on the knowledge that Fidel Castro frequently drinks tea, coffee, and bullion.

"The operation had two phases," the official CIA report will document, "the first ran from August 1960 until late April or early May 1961, when it was called off following the Bay of Pigs."†

But that bungled CIA operation did not stop the plot against Castro.

Instead, it was a monumental blunder taking place in a Las Vegas hotel room.

It all begins when Sam Giancana suspects that his girlfriend, singer Phyllis McGuire, is having an affair with comedian Dan Rowan. Giancana asks former FBI agent Robert Maheu, who now works as the Mob's liaison with the CIA, to place a wiretap in Rowan's Las Vegas hotel room to confirm whether or not the affair is taking place.

Hoping to keep the mobster happy, the forty-four-year-old Maheu agrees. In the name of discretion, he does not do the job himself but arranges for a private investigator named Arthur Balletti to plant the bug.

Dan Rowan is staying at the Riviera Hotel on the Las Vegas Strip. Balletti successfully places the device and then spends the next week eavesdropping. But as he takes a lunch break one afternoon, Balletti forgets to hang the Do Not Disturb sign. A hotel maid, entering to clean Balletti's room, grows suspicious when she sees a suitcase full of transmitters, wiring, receivers, and other listening devices. Notes detailing Rowan's conversations are also left in the

---

* Giancana foresees a return of Mob dominance in Cuba once Castro is killed.

† The Bay of Pigs was an attempt by the United States government to overthrow the Castro regime by landing an army of Cuban freedom fighters on the beaches of the same name. The mission was a catastrophe. Almost all the guerrillas were captured or killed, and the Kennedy administration was forced to admit culpability in this attempted invasion of a sovereign nation.

open. The Las Vegas Sheriff's Department is notified, and Balletti is arrested. The next morning, Rowan requests that all charges be dropped. It is assumed he was coerced.*

But J. Edgar Hoover is now on the case. Seeking advantage, he asks to have Balletti prosecuted in open court for the federal offense of wiretapping. He believes there is evidence to implicate Sam Giancana and Johnny Roselli—perhaps tying them to the Kennedy brothers.

The CIA steps in, protesting that Balletti's behavior is a matter of national security. Simultaneously, the murder plan against Castro is quietly shut down.

But the CIA will not stop. In May 1962, the agency revives the assassination scheme. Director Hoover is still trying to prosecute Balletti, leading to tense negotiations among the CIA, FBI, and the Justice Department. On May 7, Bobby Kennedy is briefed about the situation.

"If you could have seen Mr. Kennedy's eyes get steely and his jaw set and his voice get low and precise, you get a definite feeling of unhappiness," CIA general counsel Lawrence Houston will remember.

The attorney general's dismay has little to do with the wiretap. He does not want Sam Giancana exposed in the Castro situation because he knows the mobster could implicate the Kennedys in all kinds of things.

"I trust that if you will ever try to do business with organized crime, with gangsters, you will tell the attorney general," Bobby Kennedy orders the federal agents who have come to brief him on the Las Vegas matter.

RFK quickly covers his tracks by drafting a memo stating that the Justice Department must no longer participate in *any* CIA activities.

Two days later, Kennedy meets with Director Hoover to express his "astonishment" about the CIA aligning with the Mob.

But the damage is done.

And there is more to come.

✦

---

* **Dan Rowan will later go on to fame with his partner Dick Martin in the hit show** *Laugh-In.*

Sam Giancana has another plan.

The Mob boss remains angry that his secret payoff to get JFK elected has done nothing to ease pressure on the Mob. Giancana is also still of the belief that sleeping with a man's lover gives him personal power over that individual. Giancana now sets his sights on bedding another Kennedy consort—thirty-five-year-old actress Marilyn Monroe. Frank Sinatra has assured Giancana that the president is sleeping with the troubled Hollywood star.

On May 19, 1962, at a gala Madison Square Garden celebration, Marilyn Monroe publicly—and somewhat scandalously—serenades John Kennedy with a breathy version of "Happy Birthday." The actress is just months removed from divorcing playwright Arthur Miller, her third husband. Dressed in a backless sequined dress so skintight that she had to be hoisted into it, and wearing absolutely nothing beneath the gown, Monroe's slinky performance is a very public signal of her desire for the president.

The display reaffirms Monroe's sex symbol status at a time when age and her personal addictions are slowing a once-promising career. She has, in fact, risked her livelihood to be in New York City. Monroe abruptly took time away from filming the movie *Something's Got to Give!* to fly from Hollywood, much to the consternation of its producers.

Famously self-destructive, fond of mixing alcohol with pills, Marilyn Monroe returns home to Hollywood and begins a steady downward spiral that lasts well into July. She will be fired from the motion picture upon her return and sued for damages. Marilyn will never again make another film.

To some, this sad decline engenders sympathy. But to Sam Giancana, it presents opportunity. Making the actress even more desirable to the mobster is innuendo that Bobby Kennedy has become an ardent admirer.*

---

* Rumors about an affair between Bobby Kennedy and Marilyn Monroe have persisted for a half century. In the 1970s, the FBI declared the rumors "utterly false." The authors of this book have not been able to confirm any liaisons between Bobby Kennedy and Marilyn Monroe, despite writing *Killing Kennedy* and *Killing the Mob*.

So four months after the Palm Springs falling-out between JFK and Sinatra, Sam Giancana sets a trap.

Among the mobster's personal land holdings is a resort on the state line dividing California and Nevada. Appropriately, the casino is named Cal-Neva. But Giancana's name is not listed on the deed. Instead, it is Frank Sinatra who publicly owns this gambling den on the shore of Lake Tahoe. In addition to having an affair with Patricia Kennedy Lawford, the singer has ended his relationship with her Rat Pack husband, Peter, over the Palm Springs–JFK fiasco. And yet, for reasons unexplained, Sinatra now thaws that relationship and invites the Lawford couple to spend a few summer days at Cal-Neva.

Patricia Lawford knows that Marilyn Monroe has been quietly informed to stay away from the Kennedys by Bobby and other top insiders. She refuses. The president no longer takes her phone calls, but the actress still has limited access to RFK. Monroe is upset about JFK ending the affair and there are fears she will damage the 1964 reelection campaign by speaking to the press. Patricia Lawford hopes to calm Marilyn down. So now, at the behest of Frank Sinatra, she invites the actress to join her at Cal-Neva.

Marilyn Monroe had stayed there a year ago, while filming *The Misfits* with Montgomery Clift and Clark Gable in the nearby Nevada desert. The film would be the last for the legendary Gable, who died soon afterward. Monroe herself flirted with death during the production—her dependence upon barbiturates so strong that filming was stopped for a week so she might detox.

The actress's return to Cal-Neva is anything but restful. "I was there in '62," Las Vegas boss and partner of Meyer Lansky, Vincent "Jimmy Blue Eyes" Alo, will recall. "Peter and Frank were there with Monroe. They kept her drugged every night. It was disgusting."

Eyewitnesses will state that a photographer recorded much of the activity, with Monroe so completely under the influence of narcotics that she appears to be passed out. They will also describe the actress leaning over a toilet, covered with vomit, as Sam Giancana kneels behind her, grinning for the camera.

FBI agent William Roemer of the Chicago office will later listen to wiretap recordings of Giancana and Roselli discussing the goings-on in

Bungalow 52. "There, I had put together, she engaged in an orgy. From the conversation I overheard, it appeared she may have had sex with both Sinatra and Giancana on the same trip," Roemer will conclude.

Confirming that Sam Giancana had his way with Monroe, then bragged about it, FBI wiretaps will record Johnny Roselli's incredulous response to Giancana's relentless boasting "You sure get your rocks off fucking the same broads as the brothers, don't you?"

One week later, Marilyn Monroe ingests a lethal overdose of chloral hydrate and pentobarbital in the bedroom of her Los Angeles home. The barbiturates slow her heart and lungs until they stop altogether. By 10:30 p.m. on August 4, 1962, Marilyn Monroe is dead.

Sam Giancana seems to have gotten away with yet another atrocity. But his luck is all about to change.

CHAPTER SEVENTEEN

Joseph Michael Valachi fears for his life.

The fifty-eight-year-old member of the Genovese crime family, currently serving a sentence of fifteen years for heroin trafficking, walks quickly across the prison yard. Valachi is the cellmate of Vito Genovese, to whom he has sworn a lifetime oath of allegiance. Valachi's official Mob title is that of a low-level *soldato*—soldier—and as a "made man," he has also taken a vow of omertà—silence under questioning.

At five foot six and a heavyset 184 pounds, with a raspy voice and graying hair of an older man, Valachi does not appear to be a physical menace. But he has been a member of La Cosa Nostra for more than thirty years and knows how to deal with a threat. He does not attract attention as he wanders close to an area undergoing construction and quietly picks up a two-foot section of iron pipe.

Weapon in hand, Valachi knows he must act quickly.

This is not the first time the diminutive mobster has plotted murder. He has been a criminal since the age of nine while growing up in East Harlem, New York. At first, his specialty was driving getaway cars during robberies. But at the age of twenty-seven he became a "made man"—a full-fledged member of the Mafia—and was almost immedi-

Joseph Valachi, convicted murderer and former Cosa Nostra mobster, testifies before the
Senate Permanent Investigation Committee in Washington, D.C., October 1, 1963.
Valachi tells how he was initiated into the national crime society, La Cosa Nostra,
by having to burn a crumpled ball of paper in his hands while taking the oath to
"live by the gun and the knife and to die by the gun and the knife" and be burned
to ashes if he ever informed against his associates.

ately involved as a *soldato* in the bloody 1931 Castellammarese War for control of organized crime in New York. It was Lucky Luciano who emerged victorious, and Valachi threw his allegiance behind the young Sicilian.

When Vito Genovese took over the New York family following the 1957 murder of Albert Anastasia, Valachi had no issue switching loyalties. The actual number of deaths in which he is complicit is unknown, but the mobster is most prominently suspected of arranging the murder of fellow Mafioso Steven Franse at the behest of Genovese—luring Franse into a trap where he was strangled to death.

Joseph Valachi has prospered in organized crime, owning three restaurants, a jukebox company, and a dress factory. His ex-wife,

Millie—whom he left for another woman after twenty-five years of marriage—knows all about his illicit lifestyle. Her father was Gaetano Reina, the founder of the Lucchese crime family who was murdered by a shotgun blast to the head at age forty. Millie's brother Giacomo is Valachi's coconspirator in the drug-trafficking operation that landed the mobster in this federal penitentiary.

Joseph Valachi has one son, Donald, a twenty-six-year-old construction worker in New York who may not know what his father really does for a living.

Valachi understands completely that if he uses this iron pipe in the manner he is now contemplating on this humid summer morning, the murder charge will most likely result in the death penalty. But the specter of the electric chair is preferable to a Mob hit that would happen without warning. So Joe Valachi will take his chances.

In the past, Valachi has offered minor bits of information to federal narcotics agents, hoping it might lead to preferential treatment or even a reduced sentence. He does not believe this qualifies him as an informant—a "rat" in Mob parlance—and yet, he is under suspicion. One recent night in their cell, Vito Genovese made a rather unusual comment: "You know, we take a barrel of apples, and in this barrel of apples there might be a bad apple. Well, this apple had to be removed, and if it ain't removed, it would hurt the rest of the apples."

Sensing danger, Valachi protests immediately. "If I done anything wrong, show it to me and bring the pills," he replies to Genovese, referring to poison. "And I will take them in front of you."

"Who said you done anything wrong?" Genovese replies. Then the crime boss makes a most unusual statement. "We've known each other for a long time. Let me give you a kiss for old time's sake."

The two men kiss on the cheek. At first Valachi tries to rationalize the gesture's meaning, but eventually he realizes it is the "kiss of death" customarily offered to men about to get murdered.*

Valachi will later recall that after this gesture of false affection he "just laid on my bed. But who could sleep?"

---

* The kiss of death was meant to show friendliness toward an individual about to be murdered as a means of making him think he was not in danger.

Whatever Genovese's motives for wanting him dead, Joseph Valachi knows who will do the killing. He believes that task will go to yet another inmate connected with the Genovese family, Joseph DiPalermo—a known "enforcer" for the crime boss.

So Joseph Valachi decides to strike first. Pipe in his fist, he walks across the yard to where DiPalermo now stands.

Before his imprisonment, Joe Beck, as DiPalermo is nicknamed, had a reputation as a drug-trafficking mastermind. DiPalermo is fifty-five, and despite his reputation as an enforcer, he has long survived by his intellect rather than by pure strength.

It was Vito Genovese, at the Havana Conference sixteen years ago, who first advocated that the Mob begin selling drugs. But it is DiPalermo who has made it the Mafia's most lucrative source of income. He procures heroin, marijuana, barbiturates, cocaine, and any other pharmaceutical substance his clients request. Though he now wears prison gray, DiPalermo was well-known for his flashy behavior on the streets of New York, dressing in vivid blue suits, fedoras, and snakeskin shoes and driving a matching blue Cadillac.

As Joseph Valachi hefts the pipe in his right hand, the short, narrow frame of Joe Beck stands just a few feet away, back turned. So as Valachi steps forward to attack, his victim does not see the first time the iron pipe crashes down on the back of his skull. Or the second. Or the third.

Knowing guards will soon intervene, Valachi flails at DiPalermo's lifeless corpse until he is sure the capo is dead.

But Valachi has made a mistake. The man bleeding in front of him is not Joseph DiPalermo.

Instead, Valachi has ended the life of Joseph Saupp, a convicted forger with no criminal ties to Vito Genovese whatsoever, but whose height and build tragically match that of DiPalermo.*

In an instant, Joseph Valachi realizes he will soon be joining the unfortunate Saupp.

---

* Joseph DiPalermo—Joe Beck—was one of the most notorious drug dealers in history. Despite several stints in prison, he operated globally for more than six decades and was reputed to still be actively engaged in selling heroin when he died in 1992 at age eighty-five.

After forty years as a criminal, Joseph Valachi knows there is only one way to avoid the inevitable Mob hit—he must become a full-fledged rat.

✦

The murder of fifty-two-year-old Joseph Saupp is of little consequence, or so it seems. His remains are returned to Crawford County, Ohio, where he is buried in Mount Calvary Catholic Cemetery. The life of this small, thin felon was unremarkable, but the aftermath of his brutal death will change America forever.

Once he makes known his willingness to speak on the record about the Mafia, Joseph Valachi quickly disappears into federal protective custody. His whereabouts are unknown even to his ex-wife and son. In fact, he has been removed from the Atlanta penitentiary and relocated to the Westchester County Jail, north of New York City.

In exchange for a life sentence for murder rather than the death penalty, Valachi agrees to testify against the Mob. Meanwhile, hit men from several crime families scour the country in search of the informant, desperate to kill him before he can reveal their secrets.

Agents of the Federal Bureau of Narcotics interrogate Valachi. Among the first questions directed at the mobster is when he joined the Mafia.

"Right after the war," Valachi responds.

"World War One or World War Two?" the agents want to know.

"You don't understand," Valachi states, before clarifying. "Right after the war with Chicago."*

This glimmer of unique intelligence begins a steady stream of information about life in the underworld. When the narcotics agents have extracted as much information as they can, the FBI takes over the interrogation. In particular, Special Agent James P. Flynn makes it

---

* Valachi is referring to the Castellammarese War. From February 1930 to April 15, 1931, this clash between the Sicilian old guard and a new wave of gangsters ended with a complete restructuring of power in organized crime. The victors included many of the men who would rule the underworld for decades to come, including Lucky Luciano, Vito Genovese, Frank Costello, Bugsy Siegel, Albert Anastasia, Joe Bonanno, and Joe Profaci.

a priority to befriend the mobster and gain his trust. In January 1963, Valachi is moved from Westchester to the stockade at Fort Monmouth, New Jersey, to be closer to Flynn's office.

Agent Flynn begins his work with simple discussions about helping Valachi lose forty pounds in order to enjoy better health. Knowing that the mobster has a fondness for horse racing and has owned four Thoroughbreds of his own, Flynn arranges for Valachi to receive the *New York Daily News* every morning. Before scanning the obituary page for the names of fellow mobsters, Valachi pores over the horse racing results and then sits down with Flynn to handicap the day's races at Belmont and Saratoga. Once their friendship is established, Flynn guides their talks into crime. Over the course of eight months, the mobster submits to hundreds of hours of interviews, working three hours a day, four days per week. As information comes forth, it is shared with several governmental law enforcement agencies for fact checking. Among them are the Treasury Department, Secret Service, IRS, and Postal Service. Amazingly, all of Valachi's information checks out. He never contradicts himself or is caught in a lie.

In time, Valachi not only reveals specific details of unsolved crimes now connected to the Mob—some performed decades ago—but also reveals the specific inner structure of La Cosa Nostra and its manner of committing specific crimes. According to Valachi, the lowest level of Mafioso is the simple "associate." Above them are the soldiers, then caporegime, then underboss, then at the top, the boss. Parallel with the boss at this upper level is an adviser known as the consigliere.

As a lifelong Mafioso, Valachi has seen the rise of New York's five families and establishment of the national crime syndicate. He states for the record the names of individuals who first ran the families: Lucky Luciano, Tommaso Gagliano, Joseph Profaci, and Salvatore Maranzano.

Then Valachi gives up the names of the men *currently* running the five families: Tommy Lucchese, Vito Genovese, Joseph Colombo, Carlo Gambino, and Joe Bonanno.

Publicly admitting even one of those names ensures Joe Valachi now has a price on his head. Confessing all five is to ask for the most brutal torture conceivable before the murder takes place. Even behind prison bars, Joseph Valachi will live the rest of his life in fear.

The damage is done. The mobster's willingness to speak in detail about organized crime—heretofore basically a mystery—will forever change law enforcement's strategies for dealing with the Mafia.

✦

With more and more disclosures forthcoming, Attorney General Bobby Kennedy grows excited about sharing this information with the general public. It is arranged that Joseph Valachi will appear before a Senate subcommittee looking into organized crime. And unlike the last group of Mafiosi testifying before Bobby Kennedy's McClellan hearings four years ago, all of whom maintained their code of omertà by pleading the Fifth Amendment, Joseph Valachi is expected to reveal all.

As the date for Valachi's appearance before the Senate committee draws near, the time comes for Special Agent James Flynn to say goodbye to the mobster. The two men have become such good friends that Flynn would often bring Italian delicacies to Valachi's cell and then share a meal with the informer.

Despite this close relationship, Flynn is sanguine about the mobster and his motives. "Revenge was a large part of it, but it was also a cold, calculated move for survival. Don't think for a moment that this was a repentant sinner. He was a killer capable of extreme violence. He was devious, rebelling against all constituted authority, and he lived in a world of fear and suspicion. Fear especially marked him—fear of what he was doing and at the same time fear that nobody would believe him."

✦

The result of Agent Flynn's patient interrogation has the unlikely effect of spurring a publicity war between J. Edgar Hoover's FBI and Bobby Kennedy's Justice Department. On September 25, 1963, two weeks before Valachi is to testify before the Senate committee, a story titled "The Inside Story of Organized Crime and How You Can Help Smash It" appears in the national weekly magazine *Parade*. The byline is that of J. Edgar Hoover.

Not to be outdone, Robert Kennedy authorizes family friend Peter Maas to write a book based on Valachi's testimony. In addition, Maas authors a story for the *Saturday Evening Post* about organized crime using details given to him by Bobby Kennedy.

Director Hoover is furious when informed of Kennedy's tactics. "I never saw so much skullduggery," he writes. Then, ignoring the fact that he also personally published an article containing secret information, the director adds: "The sanctity of Department files, including Bureau reports, is a thing of the past. H."

But Hoover is not finished. Continuing the war to take credit for the Valachi disclosures, he attempts to prevent the release of Peter Maas's book *The Valachi Papers*. The matter will go to court.

J. Edgar Hoover will lose.

✦

Bobby Kennedy is finally winning the war on organized crime. His most recent triumph came this past May, when Jimmy Hoffa was indicted for charges of jury tampering. The case has not yet gone to trial, but that day will soon come. Kennedy's "Get Hoffa" squad is at last seeing results for its vendetta against the union boss.

In addition, the sheer volume of information obtained from Joseph Valachi is making a big difference for the Justice Department.

"A principal lesson provided by the disclosures of Joseph Valachi and informants is that the job ahead is very large and very difficult," writes Bobby Kennedy in a special twenty-four-page announcement on the eve of Valachi's appearance before the U.S. Senate Permanent Subcommittee on Investigations. The date is September 27, 1963.

"Evidence concerning their clandestine operation is particularly hard to uncover," Kennedy writes. "A witness who will testify in the face of threats to himself and his family is rare. This is one reason the disclosures made by Joseph Valachi are of such significance: For the first time an insider—a knowledgeable member of the racketeering hierarchy—has broken the underworld's code of silence."

As the attorney general well knows, the last decade has seen the Kefauver hearings, McClellan hearings, and Apalachin Summit investigation—all futile attempts to penetrate the inner workings of organized crime. Valachi has changed all that. The government has gone from knowing nothing about the Mafia to knowing almost *everything*.

"The picture is an ugly one," Kennedy notes. "It shows what has been aptly described as a private government of organized crime, a government with an annual income of billions, resting on a base of human suffering and moral corrosion."

Finally, the attorney general summarizes: "We have been able to make inroads into the hierarchy, personnel, and operations of organized crime. It would be a serious mistake, however, to overestimate the progress federal and local law enforcement has made. A principal lesson provided by the disclosures of Joseph Valachi . . . is that the job ahead is very large and difficult."

✦

It is October 1963 as Joseph Valachi appears before the second McClellan Committee on organized crime. His testimony goes on for six days in public and one more session in private. He rambles as he answers the questions directed at him, often taking a break to suck on a lemon when his mouth gets dry. The Valachi hearings, as they will become known, are broadcast on national television. The American public soon learns of the ritual initiation ceremonies to become a "made man," as well as the history of the Mafia going back to the early 1930s. Valachi names names, telling which individuals run which crime families. He describes wars between rival families that resulted in the murders of dozens. And to the chagrin of Vito Genovese, who has placed a bounty of $100,000 for Valachi's murder, the informant testifies that Genovese is the Boss of All Bosses and runs gambling operations in Nevada from inside his Atlanta prison cell.

Joseph Valachi's appearance makes history. Upon completion of his testimony, he is returned to federal custody to spend the rest of his life in the penitentiary.

It has taken Attorney General Robert Francis Kennedy six years of obsessive struggle to crack the secret code of organized crime. It seems nothing now stands in the way of RFK crippling the Mafia.

But something does.

The assassination of President John F. Kennedy.

✦

The president of the United States is murdered on the streets of Dallas, Texas, shortly after noon on November 22, 1963. A lone gunman named Lee Harvey Oswald is arrested and charged with the crime.

Jimmy Hoffa, awaiting trial, is eating lunch in Miami when he gets the news. As waitresses and busboys break down and cry, Hoffa stands on his chair and cheers: "I hope the worms eat his eyes."

Finding a pay phone, Hoffa places a call to his lawyer. Frank Ragano also counts Tampa crime bosses Santo Trafficante and Carlos Marcello as clients—both of whom have sworn revenge on the Kennedy brothers. Ragano and Trafficante have just raised a glass in celebration of JFK's murder when the union boss calls. "They killed the son of a bitch," chortles Hoffa.*

Given the Kennedy brothers' pursuit of organized crime and the number of high-powered Mafioso who have promised vengeance on the president and attorney general, there is every reason to believe that the Mob might have ordered the hit. The assassination has the appearances of organized crime involvement: lone gunman, high-powered rifle, shots aimed at the head.†

✦

It is a warm Virginia afternoon and Bobby Kennedy is at home, sitting by his pool. The phone rings. J. Edgar Hoover is on the other end of the line. The director tells the attorney general that his brother, the president, has been assassinated. There is no emotion in Hoover's voice when he shares the brutal news.

A shocked Bobby Kennedy places a hand over his eyes, then shares the news with the small crowd of friends on hand. His wife, Ethel, puts her arms around him.

Within minutes, RFK is convinced that Jimmy Hoffa and the

---

* In his 1994 book, *Mob Lawyer*, Ragano will claim publicly that Jimmy Hoffa requested that Ragano contact the Mafia about murdering the Kennedy brothers.

† The authors of this work investigated a possible Mob connection to JFK's assassination for the *Killing Kennedy* book. No hard evidence was found.

226 ✦ BILL O'REILLY and MARTIN DUGARD

Mafia might be involved—perhaps working together with Carlos Marcello or Sam Giancana.

But no matter who carried out the hit, the attorney general believes it is *his* fault. He has long believed that the Mob would try to kill him, but RFK never anticipated they might go after his brother. "I thought they'd get me," he confides to his press secretary, Ed Guthman.

The attorney general immediately asks Walter Sheridan of his "Get Hoffa" squad if he knows of any connection among Hoffa, the Mafia, and the assassination.

The chain-smoking Sheridan and RFK have worked together since the first investigations of Teamster activities began several years ago. His official role is that of special assistant to investigate federal crimes, but his real talent is infiltrating the Teamsters union by cultivating informants.

Coincidentally, Sheridan recently learned from insiders the alarming news that Jimmy Hoffa has openly discussed the possibility of shooting Robert Kennedy. The job would be conducted with a high-powered rifle as he, the attorney general, drives his convertible—the very same scenario that just transpired in Dallas. Walter Sheridan tells the attorney general there is a very good possibility that Hoffa might have played a role in JFK's assassination.

Bobby Kennedy immediately orders Sheridan to Dallas to oversee the investigation. J. Edgar Hoover is already there and sees to it that the FBI controls the crime scene. Just two days later, there's another shocking occurrence: a sleazy Dallas nightclub owner named Jack Ruby somehow manages to infiltrate the security detail protecting the accused assassin Oswald and shoots him dead. Immediately, rumors fly that Ruby—birth name: Jacob Leon Rubenstein—has ties with organized crime. A subsequent congressional inquiry into the Oswald murder will later confirm this, revealing that Ruby, originally from Chicago, "had a significant number of associations and direct and indirect contacts with underworld figures."

In the end, Walter Sheridan will return to Washington to inform Bobby Kennedy that he was not successful in finding a connection among Jimmy Hoffa, the Mafia, and the president's murder.

And so, suspicion lingers—who really killed John F. Kennedy?

The nation wants to know.

✦

Among Jimmy Hoffa's first comments to his attorney after the Kennedy assassination is an expression of relief: "Bobby Kennedy is out as attorney general."

But Hoffa is wrong. New president Lyndon Johnson requests that RFK stay on at the Justice Department. A grieving Bobby Kennedy agrees. His work is not done, and he has a very old score to settle.

Hoffa.

On March 4, 1964, Jimmy Hoffa is convicted of attempting to bribe a grand juror and sentenced to eight years in prison. A separate conviction for fraud boosts that total to thirteen years. His appeals process will continue for three years, but on March 7, 1967, Jimmy Hoffa begins serving his sentence at the Lewisburg federal penitentiary in Pennsylvania.

Robert Francis Kennedy has finally gotten his man.

Kennedy has not finished the job of eradicating the Mafia, but his efforts and investigations have severely damaged America's "alternate government," as he once referred to the Mob.

✦

Bobby Kennedy's relationship with J. Edgar Hoover has always been tense, but having the president as a brother gave RFK the upper hand. That changes immediately after the assassination. "[Hoover] no longer had to hide his feelings," Kennedy will acknowledge to friends. "And he no longer had to pay any attention to me."

One of the first RFK orders when he took over the Justice Department was that a special phone be installed in J. Edgar Hoover's office. This direct line to Kennedy's own desk was to only be answered by the director. Hoover long chafed at the appearance of being the attorney general's subordinate and loathed the intrusion of that special phone.

That direct line now goes unanswered.

So while RFK was still Hoover's boss, Hoover "would never deal directly or through me" any longer, according to RFK. Both men are aware that John Kennedy had plans to replace Hoover during his second term in office when reelection would no longer be a factor.

Now, J. Edgar Hoover makes sure that the new president, Lyndon Johnson, has no such plan. Hoover has a special relationship with Lyndon Johnson, to whom he has been funneling information about the sexual peccadilloes of congressmen and senators for many years. Before Johnson became vice president and was serving as Senate majority leader, the Texan was fond of using this political dirt to influence votes. John Kennedy's personal secretary, Evelyn Lincoln, will even claim that Johnson used Hoover's secret files to obtain the nomination for vice president. "LBJ had been using all the information Hoover could find on Kennedy—during the campaign, even before the convention," Mrs. Lincoln told an interviewer.

In May 1964, President Johnson returns Hoover's favors, perhaps knowing that the director most likely possesses a file of Johnson's own numerous indiscretions. Standing in the White House Rose Garden, before a podium bearing the presidential seal, Johnson directly addresses Hoover. "Edgar, the law says you must retire next January when you reach your seventieth birthday. And knowing you as I do, Edgar, I know you won't break the law."

Hoover stands just behind the president, hands clasped before him.

"But the nation cannot afford to lose you," LBJ continues in the twang of his native Texas, "and by virtue of, and pursuant to the authority vested in the President of the United States, I have just now signed an executive order exempting you from compulsory retirement for an indefinite period of time."

J. Edgar Hoover is now director for life.*

✦

On September 3, 1964, Robert Kennedy resigns as attorney general of the United States. During his time in office, the Justice Department

---

* The cozy relationship between President Johnson and Director Hoover will reach its zenith just a few months later during the 1964 presidential campaign. At Johnson's orders, FBI agents will spy on Republican candidate Barry Goldwater's campaign by illegally wiretapping his plane and headquarters. That was not known until Hoover revealed it to Assistant Attorney General Robert Mardian in 1971.

has indicted 687 organized crime figures, with a conviction rate of 90 percent.*

But those triumphs are soon to be a thing of the past. Since JFK's assassination, J. Edgar Hoover has ordered the FBI to stop focusing manpower on investigating organized crime. With the conflict in Vietnam escalating into actual war, he now prefers to focus on political violence, the civil rights movement, and foreign espionage.

Thus, the war on organized crime is over—for now.

Meanwhile, the Mafia quickly moves to monetize their sudden advantage.

A primary target: the heavyweight championship of the world.

---

* RFK had his eye on politics. There was considerable pressure on Lyndon Johnson to name Kennedy as his running mate in 1964, despite the fact that both men distrusted each other. Instead, on August 24, Kennedy leased a house in New York. The following day he declared his candidacy for the U.S. Senate. On November 3, 1964, Kennedy defeated incumbent Republican Kenneth Keating in a landslide.

CHAPTER EIGHTEEN

M uhammad Ali is under armed guard.
       The twenty-three-year-old heavyweight champion of the world is about to defend his title in this small ice hockey arena. His opponent is former champ Sonny Liston, whom Ali beat by technical knockout one year ago. At the time, Ali went by his given name of Cassius Clay. But he has since converted to Islam and become a follower of Elijah Muhammad, leader of the militant Nation of Islam group. Just three months ago, three NOI members assassinated a rival cleric named Malcolm X, shooting him twenty-one times. There are now fears that Ali will be the target of a revenge killing, thus the unlikely cordon of FBI agents and bow tie–wearing Nation of Islam bodyguards protecting the fighter as he prepares to enter the ring.

       Though it is ludicrous for a boxing match of this magnitude to be held in such a small, out-of-the-way location, fears of organized crime influence over the event forced it to be relocated from Boston. Boxing fans and gamblers can watch via closed-circuit television, which will be flashed around the world. Now, as thick clouds of tobacco smoke waft through the arena, the paid crowd of 2,434 takes their seats alongside a rowdy band of students from nearby Bates

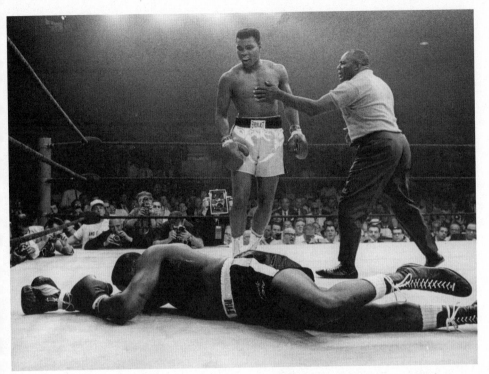

Triumphant boxer Muhammad Ali (Cassius Clay) being stopped by referee Walcott as he looks at his opponent, Charles "Sonny" Liston, who is lying on the ground during their bout in Lewiston, Maine, on May 25, 1965.

College—all of whom received free tickets as part of a giveaway to fill the house. Two hundred police officers are also in the arena to ensure maximum security.*

Photographers press against the ring, taking photos of the muscled, athletic Ali as he steps through the ropes wearing white shorts and calf-high boxing shoes. Liston is the exact opposite, wearing black shorts and shoes. Prior to their first match, held in Miami Beach, Liston entered the ring as not just the undisputed champion of the world but also a fighting force that redefined heavyweight boxing.

---

* The fight was originally scheduled for the Boston Garden but was moved because of Liston's arrest record and the lack of a Massachusetts promoting license by Inter-Continental, the company organizing the bout. Inter-Continental was in the business of promoting fights and was suspect in the eyes of state authorities.

Known as the Big Bear, the six-foot-one and 213-pound Liston was lightning fast, his fists measuring fifteen inches around, so large that he needs custom fighting gloves. One former manager, the Mafia-connected Frank Mitchell, describes him as having "the mind of a 12-year-old child. He has no finesse, tact, whatsoever."

But for all his fame, Sonny Liston lives a life shrouded in trouble. His actual date and place of birth are unknown, shifting from 1929 to 1932 over the course of his career. He is fond of drink, and there are even reports that he had alcohol on his breath during his first fight with Ali. His Arkansas childhood was brutal—he was born the twenty-fourth child of a twice-married sharecropper of whom Liston went on record as stating "the only thing my old man ever gave me was a beating." The boxer is illiterate and took up fighting while serving time for burglary in the Missouri State Penitentiary. Released in 1952, he was sent back to prison for six months in 1956 after breaking a police officer's leg and stealing his gun.

That incident has not been forgotten by the general public. In fact, Liston is such a polarizing figure that Congress openly debated whether he should be allowed to fight Floyd Patterson, then the heavyweight champion of the world. There were fears that a Liston victory would undermine the gentleman's sport of boxing. Liston was even called to appear before the Senate to explain himself on December 13, 1960. Baseball great Jackie Robinson spoke out publicly in favor of Liston, while President John Kennedy urged Patterson to find an opponent "with better character."

Little did JFK know about Liston's connections with the Mob.

The former champ has such a high-profile history of associating with mobsters that *Sports Illustrated* magazine exposed him in a 1961 profile. The story proved to be so accurate that it was admitted as evidence in a case before the New York State Athletic Commission, which denied Liston a license to fight.

"It would be unrealistic to deny that [John] Vitale and [Blinky] Palermo, a Carbo lieutenant, control Liston," the *Sports Illustrated* story states.* "There was ample testimony at the Kefauver hearings to indicate

---

* Frankie Carbo was a member of the Lucchese family who went on to become a leading boxing promoter—even while serving a twenty-five-year prison sentence. Attorney General Robert Kennedy was chief prosecutor in the case against him.

that Vitale and Palermo shared in Liston's purses. In 1958 the Mob moved Liston out of St. Louis to Philadelphia and got him a new manager, Joseph (Pep) Barone (two arrests), who had never managed a fighter until he was given Liston to handle. Barone is a longtime associate of Palermo's."*

The magazine went on to document Sonny Liston's sordid life.

Phone company records indicate that several of Liston's previous opponents were in touch with John Vitale, the Sicilian-born underboss of a St. Louis crime family who has served time in prison for narcotics trafficking. Because of that, and other circumstantial evidence, some in the boxing world believe that Liston was involved in a number of fixed fights.

On September 25, 1962, Sonny Liston and Floyd Patterson finally squared off in Chicago. Liston took the title from Patterson in stunning fashion, hammering him to the canvas just two minutes into the first round. Patterson was so embarrassed that he donned a fake beard to disguise himself from reporters on his way out of town.

A subsequent rematch in Las Vegas one year later went the same way, with Liston knocking Patterson down three times before he was counted out with a minute left in the first round.

In between the first and second Patterson fights, Sonny Liston made the acquaintance of a bookie named Ash Resnick. The forty-eight-year-old, six-foot-one former college basketball star from New York is a professional gambler and Las Vegas fixture. Resnick made it a point to become Liston's personal assistant, "offering Sonny everything from fine clothes to escorts," in the words of one friend. Resnick is also close friends with legendary boxer Joe Louis, who has fallen on such hard times that he serves as an enforcer when Resnick calls upon clients whose wagers are past due.

On February 25, 1964, Sonny Liston defends his title against twenty-two-year-old Cassius Clay in Miami Beach. The Louisville

---

* John Vitale became head of the St. Louis crime family and died of natural causes. Blinky Palermo, who had previously testified before the Kefauver Committee on organized crime, was sentenced to twenty-five years in prison for Mob activities related to boxing. Pep Barone died of a heart attack at the age of sixty-six, also having testified before Congress about racketeering in boxing.

Lip is an Olympic gold medalist with a penchant for showboating and a reputation as a light puncher. Liston, now in his mid-thirties, despises Clay. The root of the angst is that Clay, who was fond of showing up in Las Vegas while Liston was training for the second Patterson fight, then publicly taunted the champ, saying he would destroy him once they got in the ring. In one altercation, Clay confronted Liston at the Thunderbird Casino. Liston was playing craps and the two began jawing. Pulling himself up to his full height, Liston pressed his face close to Clay's. He is surprised that the younger man is two inches taller but insults him anyway, in a voice heard by the crowd: "Listen, you nigger faggot, if you don't get out of here in ten seconds I'm gonna pull that big tongue out of your mouth and stick it up your ass." Liston allegedly then drew a handgun and aimed it at Clay to make his point.*

So in the lead-up to the first Clay-Liston fight, the confident heavyweight champ had no fear of the Louisville Lip. Having won most of his recent fights in the first or second round, Liston sees little need to train. Rather than run five miles a day, he does just one mile. Prostitutes visit his training camp. He seldom enters the gym, preferring to drink beer and eat hot dogs.

Nevertheless, bookie Ash Resnick advises his gambler friends to put big money on Liston, a 7-1 favorite.

But by fight time, serious money is being directed toward Clay. The odds plummet to 2-1. Resnick, very quietly, puts his own wager on the Lip.

There are two ways to fix a fight: the most common—and legal—is mismatching opponents, pitting a top boxer against another with much less ability. The other is to pay one of the fighters to "take a dive"—fall down and accept the loss by pretending to be knocked out. The Mafia prefers the second method because it controls the outcome, allowing wagers to be placed with the certainty of winning.

This appears to be what occurs during the first Liston-Clay fight. After six rounds of fighting, Sonny Liston spits out his mouthpiece. He is exhausted and looks old. Liston remains sitting on his corner

---

* That incident was recounted by promoter Harold Conrad to Thomas Hauser, an Ali biographer.

stool as Cassius Clay strides to the center of the ring. By choosing not to answer the bell for the seventh round, Liston hands Clay a stunning victory by technical knockout.

When Liston's mother calls him at his hotel afterward, he explains: "I did what they told me to do."*

Almost immediately, allegations surface that the fight was fixed. A U.S. Senate subcommittee opens an investigation. Acting on direct orders from J. Edgar Hoover himself, the FBI also looks into the matter, specifically rumors that a well-known Las Vegas gambler and friend of Sonny Liston, Ash Resnick, is involved in rigging the contest.

All findings are to be sent to Hoover's desk.

But the FBI comes to no conclusions before a lucrative rematch is booked.

✦

In Maine, the audience cheers as Sonny Liston enters the ring followed by four police officers. Ali is next, booed as his protection force flanks him. The audience settles in as Robert Goulet sings "The Star-Spangled Banner," forgetting many of the words. Lines at the concession stand are long and slow, leaving many seats unoccupied as the fight begins.

Almost all those waiting to buy their food will miss the most controversial punch in boxing history.

Just a few weeks before the fight, a Las Vegas boxing gym owner named Johnny Tocco runs into John Vitale, the St. Louis crime boss who is among the Mafia figures controlling Sonny Liston. Vitale jokes that Tocco should be happy that he's watching the fight on television rather than traveling all the way to Lewiston, Maine. When Tocco asks why, Vitale responds that the fight will end in the first round.

Which is exactly what happens.

The odds are 8-5 in favor of Liston as the bell rings to start round one, but the "smart" money is betting against him.

FBI special agent William Roemer, who specializes in organized crime and was the man responsible for planting listening devices in the

---

* The quote comes from E. B. Ward, Sonny Liston's oldest brother, who was also on the call.

headquarters of the Chicago Mob, will state that the bureau "learned that there very definitely had been a fix in the fight."

✦

Muhammad Ali is an intelligent man, but never did he envision what is about to happen in this small Maine building.

One minute and forty-four seconds into the first round, Muhammad Ali snaps a right hand toward Sonny Liston's chin. It does not appear to connect, but Liston immediately slumps to the canvas.

Ali stands over his fallen opponent, bicep curled as he screams at Liston: "Get up and fight, sucker!"

Looking over at his corner, a confused Ali asks: "Did I hit him?"

Referee Jersey Joe Walcott, himself a former heavyweight champion, stops the fight at 2:12 into the first round.

"Fake, fake, fake," chants the audience. Boos and cries of "fix" then rain down from the crowd as Muhammad Ali raises his hands in triumph.

The fallout is immediate. Some call for the abolition of professional boxing in America. The FBI is now under extreme pressure, and its investigation intensifies.

It will lead nowhere.*

✦

As Muhammad Ali leaves Maine with the heavyweight crown, millions of wagers have been lost. But the Mob knows that the outcry over the second Ali-Liston fight will soon die down. Bobby Kennedy no longer leads the Department of Justice, and no one else there will aggressively look into organized crime.

That estimation will be proved correct. The FBI focuses its entire investigation on gambler Ash Resnick, who allegedly made $1 million

---

* An FBI memo concluded of Ash Resnick: "[He] is the fix point of two heavyweight title fights—both Liston. He has been and always will continue to be a corruption source for professional sports." However, the federal investigation went no further, although the FBI continued looking into Resnick for another decade. It is important to note that Muhammad Ali knew nothing about any efforts to fix the fights with Sonny Liston, according to the FBI.

from the first Liston-Clay fight. But the inquiry goes no further. In June 1965, the FBI is told by United States attorney Alton Lessard that no criminal charges will be filed. The bureau is "advised" that further investigation will be fruitless.

So it is that the Liston-Ali scandal simply disappears.

But the murder of Bobby Kennedy is not so easily forgotten.

CHAPTER NINETEEN

JUNE 5, 1968
LOS ANGELES, CALIFORNIA
12:15 A.M.

Juan Romero hears the deafening celebration.

The seventeen-year-old busboy works in the kitchen at the Ambassador Hotel, a legendary local landmark long frequented by Hollywood celebrities. But on this night, it is not a movie star holding center stage. An entirely different sort of famous individual is galvanizing the hotel's Embassy Ballroom with his words of hope and reconciliation.

His name is Robert Kennedy and he is running for president of the United States.

It is election night for the California presidential primary. The polls closed four hours ago. All evening long, Romero has borne witness to the Kennedy faithful in their white "Kennedy for President" Panama hats nervously awaiting results, then finally cheering with elation as RFK is crowned the winner just before midnight. The room is in a frenzy as Bobby Kennedy addresses the audience in a lengthy and personal victory speech, his supporters on their feet and reporters standing in a large crush on the stage surrounding the candidate.

Kennedy speaks about all that is now dividing America—the new-found realization that the Vietnam War is unwinnable after the disastrous Tet Offensive, the race riots in major cities in the wake of the murder of Dr. Martin Luther King, the division between poor and affluent. "We can start to work together. We are a great country," Kennedy tells the crowd. "A compassionate country. And I intend to make that my basis for running."

As the crowd cheers Kennedy off the stage, Juan Romero is startled to see the candidate enter the kitchen. The awestruck busboy stretches his arm out as far as he can to get a handshake from this famous man. To Juan's delight, he feels Bobby Kennedy's palm and fingers wrap around his own. The handshake is brief but one that Juan Romero will never forget.

Then, in an instant, the deafening sound of gunfire echoes off the kitchen walls. Bobby Kennedy falls backward and sprawls onto the floor, his eyes closed and arms outspread.

Romero, wearing black pants and a white collarless busboy shirt, immediately kneels. He puts his hand under Kennedy's head to keep it from the cold concrete floor. The senator's lips are moving, so the busboy places his ear to Kennedy's mouth to hear what he's saying. "Is everybody okay?" RFK asks.

"Yes, everybody's okay," Romero answers.

The busboy feels a warm stream of Kennedy's blood flowing through his fingers. From the Embassy Room comes a cry over the same microphone the candidate used just moments ago, asking if there is a doctor in the room.

Juan Romero has a string of rosary beads in his shirt pocket. He wraps them around Kennedy's right hand. "He would need it more than me," the busboy later remembers thinking.

"Then they wheeled him away."*

✦

---

* Juan Romero died of a heart attack in 2018 at the age of sixty-eight. A twenty-four-year-old Palestinian immigrant named Sirhan Sirhan was convicted of murdering Robert Kennedy and is serving a life sentence at the Richard Donovan Correctional Facility in California. Robert F. Kennedy Jr. told Bill O'Reilly in an interview that the Kennedy family believes that Sirhan did shoot his father but likely had help. RFK Jr. stated: "Because an eight-chamber revolver cannot fire nine shots, much less thirteen, we know that a second gunman must have been firing in the Ambassador Hotel party on the night my father died." However, an FBI investigation into the assassination could produce no compelling evidence that another person was involved. It is worth noting that J. Edgar Hoover oversaw the investigation.

One year after the murder of Bobby Kennedy, on the other side of America, a member of the Genovese crime family named "Fat Tony" Lauria wonders if his secret gay lifestyle will get *him* assassinated. Lauria and other members of the Mob have no connection to the changing social morays of America in 1969. Organized crime remains what is has always been: a moneymaking machine, not interested in ideological politics.

Lauria owns a bar catering to homosexuals on Christopher Street in Manhattan's Greenwich Village. This is not unusual in the Mafia, for almost all gay establishments in New York are controlled by the Mob. Fat Tony bought the Stonewall Inn, as it is known, in 1966 for $2,000. His partner is Matty "The Horse" Ianniello, who also owns the Hay Market in Times Square, the Gilded Grape favored by cross-dressers, and the Peppermint Lounge—all gay bars in Manhattan.

The Stonewall Inn was a low-earning straight establishment at the time of Fat Tony's purchase, but Lauria reopened it as a gay bar. The establishment's name likely came from a memoir, *The Stone Wall*, which featured graphic depictions of lesbian love and was published in 1930, the same year the original Stonewall Inn opened as a speakeasy masquerading as a tearoom. "Stonewall" was a code the gay crowd knew well.

Now, on the night of June 27, the Stonewall is packed with its usual mix of drag queens, openly gay men, and homosexuals still "in the closet." Thick cigarette smoke hangs over the narrow room and a jukebox plays dance music. There are two bars and the walls are painted black. Plywood covers the windows to prevent the prying eyes of the police from seeing inside. The Stonewall is known as a great place to socialize, although some consider it too uptight.

Most important, a bouncer stands at the double doors of the main entrance, not letting anyone inside until they have been scrutinized through a peephole to ensure that they are regular customers or at least have the appearance of being gay. Raids by Lily Law—the New York City Police Department—occur at least once a month and Fat Tony is extremely cautious about letting undercover officers inside his club.

Tony more than lives up to his nickname, once weighing in at 420 pounds. He was married and divorced but now lives with a gay Italian man, though the two have never revealed the true nature of their relationship.

Sex with another man is forbidden in the Mafia world, and Fat Tony could take a bullet to the head if his true sexual inclinations are ever discovered.

Yet while the Mob forbids homosexual relations among their own, they are more than happy to profit from the gay lifestyle. The Mafia's involvement in prostitution is not limited to women. "Keep your zipper open and your mouth shut" is a saying often used among male prostitutes controlled by organized crime.

It is establishments like the Stonewall Inn that provide the Mob a lucrative source of income. However, it is a tricky business. Homosexuality is not against the law, but serving alcohol to openly gay customers is said to be a violation of the State Liquor Authority's ban on "disorderly houses," and the SLA refuses to license such establishments.

To the Mafia, this presents a unique business opportunity. Instead of seeking a legal permit to sell alcohol, a "private bottle club" is formed. All patrons are "members" and must sign in—most often using an alias. Fat Tony takes full advantage of his clientele. Because there is no running water behind the bar, glasses are dumped into a sink after each use and simply wiped clean before reuse, sometimes leading to hepatitis. Everything in the house, from the cigarette machine to jukebox, goes to the Mob. And the bottled liquor is watered down, then resold at exorbitant prices.

✦

Like the rest of the Mafia, Tony Lauria never had any use for Bobby Kennedy or Martin Luther King, the civil rights advocates slain within two months of each other in 1968. Kennedy was an avowed opponent bent on bringing down the Mob, and the racial equality preached by MLK is totally rejected by La Cosa Nostra. In fact, the Mob is so racist that many of its social clubs have a strict "no blacks" policy.* And while

---

* In an extraordinary departure from this policy, hit man Gregory "the Grim Reaper" Scarpa of the Colombo crime family was approached by the FBI in 1964 about helping find missing civil rights workers James Chaney, Andrew Goodman, and Michael Schwermer in Mississippi. J. Edgar Hoover was under media pressure to locate the graves of the three individuals, who were thought to have been murdered. After the FBI's legal methods failed, Scarpa was secretly paid $5,000 to do the job. He was already connected to the FBI as a sometime informant. After flying to Mississippi, Scarpa located a known member of the Ku Klux Klan, forced a gun barrel down his throat, and demanded to know the location of the bodies. The terrified Klansman immediately told Scarpa the precise burial spot.

the Vietnam War may impassion others—for and against—the conflict represents just another way of making money for organized crime. An estimated 15 to 30 percent of American soldiers fighting in the war actively use illegal narcotics. The Mafia is only too happy to continue providing them drugs upon their return home.

✦

Things do not end well for Fat Tony Lauria. His lifestyle eventually leaks out. Lauria's father, also a Mob boss, disowns him. Eventually, Tony simply disappears.

A message has been sent.

✦

The assassination of Robert Kennedy in Los Angeles once again opens the door to a growing number of conspiracy theories, much like what happened after the murder of JFK in 1963. Some of these involve organized crime. Mob leaders like Santo Trafficante and Carlos Marcello become the subject of scrutiny. But it is in New York that Mob turbulence reaches an all-time high.

Shortly after the assassination of President Kennedy, Joseph Bonanno, leader of the crime family bearing his name, attempts a total takeover of the five families. But when this ambition is discovered, the nationwide coalition of organized crime known as the Commission takes action, declaring all-out war on Bonanno. Mob underbosses Gaspar DiGregorio and Paul Sciacca are promoted to replace him.

Joe Bonanno fights back. The deaths pile up, one by one.

Carlo Simari, a Bonanno soldier, is gunned down outside his home in Brooklyn. Another soldier, Joe Badalamonte, is shot to death in Brooklyn, as well. Vince "Jimmy Lefty" Cassese and Vince "Vinnie Carroll" Garofalo are gunned down in front of a bakery. Bonanno's bodyguard, Salvatore "Big Hank" Perrone, is shot dead while purchasing cigarettes at a candy store.

But it is not just Joe Bonanno's loyalists who die. At the 1967 Cypress Gardens Massacre, three DiGregorio-Sciacca family capos are machine-gunned to death in a Queens restaurant. Other soldiers from that family are also murdered.

The bloody gang war lasts six years. It becomes so intense that Joe Bonanno flees to Arizona. But that does not stop the fighting. It is only after a series of bombings in Tucson targeting the crime boss that he officially steps aside in November 1968. He has led the family since 1931. At the time, Bonanno was the Commission's youngest-ever boss. He was in charge when J. Edgar Hoover's attention was focused on names like John Dillinger, Pretty Boy Floyd, and Bonnie and Clyde rather than the Mafia. He has been in power long enough to have played a role in every major underworld event since then: Havana, Apalachin, and Bobby Kennedy's Senate hearings. Joe Bonanno has seen it all but is now forcibly retired.

✦

The beginning of the 1970s marks a dramatic time for organized crime. The Bonanno wars have just ended. The disarray and uncertainty that marred the conflict have led to a destabilization of the Commission—a breakdown of its authority.

Soon, the code of silence, omertà, will be overlooked by some high-ranking Mafia criminals, even though the death penalty for talking is still in effect. As traditional Mob power changes, so does behavior.

However, one thing does not change. Talking about organized crime in public can get you killed.

CHAPTER TWENTY

DECEMBER 23, 1971
DETROIT, MICHIGAN
8:00 P.M.

J immy Hoffa still talks too much.

Teamster leadership is gathered with their families here at Carl's Chop House for a Christmas celebration. The dance floor is full and drinks flow freely. A polka band clad in ruffled shirts and tuxedos provides the music. A brightly decorated Christmas tree and inflatable Santa Claus centerpiece add to the holiday spirit.

It is a night for merriment, and nothing raises the crowd's spirits more than the news that James Riddle Hoffa was released from prison at 4:00 p.m. today. President Richard Nixon commuted his sentence to the five years already served. Nixon is running for reelection in the coming year and has been assured he will receive Teamster support for this act of largesse.*

Already, the revelers here at Carl's—a regular Teamster hangout—are showing their colors. "I'm very happy," one official tells the reporters who have crashed the party. "I think President Nixon has done us a great service."

Another Teamster joyfully adds: "With Jimmy out of jail it's going to be the best Christmas ever."

---

* You can view the party at Carl's Chop House on YouTube.

But not all are so happy. Current Teamster president Frank Fitz-simmons does not believe Jimmy Hoffa is capable of staying out of Teamster affairs. He has formed his own "Get Hoffa" squad, this one consisting of union members told to be on the lookout for Hoffa meddling in local affairs.

A key proviso of Hoffa's prison release is that he refrain from participating in Teamster leadership until 1980. Fitzsimmons, fearing Hoffa will once again take control of the union, insisted that Nixon include these terms. However, speaking to reporters outside the Lewisburg federal penitentiary, Hoffa makes it clear that he will not let the president of the United States or the president of the International Brotherhood of Teamsters dictate what happens next. "*I* will determine whatever I'm going to do politically after I learn what the restrictions are," Hoffa boldly states.

When pressed by reporters about "the restrictions Nixon put on you, forbidding you from running for union office," he pleads ignorance.

"I am unaware of any restrictions," Hoffa states firmly.

The union boss wears a gray suit, blue tie, and brown shoes. He is visibly thinner and suffers from a mild case of diabetes. It is known that his wife, Josephine, has developed a heart condition. But other than health issues, the future appears bright for Jimmy Hoffa.

As the interviews wind down, Hoffa turns to look at the penitentiary one more time. He thrusts a defiant fist into the air for the inmates to see.

Then he steps into a car to be driven to the airport, where a private plane awaits. As the revelers at Carl's Chop House know, Jimmy Hoffa is alive, well—and on his way.

✦

FBI director J. Edgar Hoover is late for breakfast.

It is May 2, 1972, five months after the release of Jimmy Hoffa. Annie Fields, the director's longtime live-in housekeeper, has already poached the eggs, prepared the slice of white toast, and brewed the black coffee Hoover prefers each morning. But she does not hear the sound of a running shower from upstairs or Hoover's footsteps padding around his bedroom. She last saw her boss yesterday, when he returned from dinner with FBI associate director Clyde Tolson.

James Crawford, until recently one of the bureau's few African American agents, arrives to do some gardening and oversee household remodeling. Crawford worked as Hoover's driver from 1934 until 1972, when he was forced to retire from the FBI due to ill health. Hoover immediately hired him as a helper. A concerned Annie Fields asks Crawford to tap on the bedroom door to check on the director.

✦

It has been a troubling time for the FBI and J. Edgar Hoover. Congress recently enacted a law making the FBI leadership subject to Senate approval. Despite the endorsement of current president Richard Nixon, there are cries for the seventy-seven-year-old Hoover to resign. Critics cite his abuse of wiretaps, which Hoover has blamed on the late senator Robert Kennedy, stating that RFK gave his approval for those breaches of the Fourth Amendment. Hoover is also publicly feuding with former attorney general Ramsey Clark, whom the director is quoted as calling a "jellyfish" for his flexible code of morality. Hoover's unwillingness to investigate civil rights violations and refusal to prosecute unlawful police conduct have also fanned controversy.

In addition, the director is being criticized for placing antiwar activists under criminal investigation, an action that many believe falls beyond the bureau's purview. Hoover recently made claims that radical elements were attempting to kidnap Secretary of State Henry Kissinger, whom many believe to be an architect of the Vietnam conflict. These charges were proved false, prompting a new round of demands that Hoover retire. And just yesterday, political reporter Jack Anderson published an exposé revealing that the FBI used illegal wiretaps on Dr. Martin Luther King's telephones in order to investigate his sex life.

Yet J. Edgar Hoover hangs on to his job, recently assuring a House Appropriations subcommittee that he is very much in charge and that the bureau is prospering. However, there is talk that Hoover will be asked to resign if Richard Nixon wins reelection in 1972. Hoover sees that as yet another storm to be weathered.

He is, after all, director for life.

James Crawford knocks on Hoover's bedroom door. Hearing nothing, he steps inside. A naked J. Edgar Hoover is slumped on the floor atop an oriental rug. Crawford does not touch the body, with the exception of confirming that the director's hands are ice cold. The cause of death will be listed as "hypertensive cardiovascular disease" by Washington medical examiner Dr. James Luke. No autopsy will be performed.*

The news is flashed to FBI offices around the world. Only then is the American public informed of Hoover's death by acting attorney general Richard Kleindienst. Congress immediately votes that Hoover's body be allowed to lie in state within the Capitol Rotunda. This honor has been allowed for just twenty-one persons in American history. President Nixon himself will give Hoover's eulogy at the National Presbyterian Church two days from now.

From the discovery of J. Edgar Hoover's body to the many public condolences now pouring in, just three hours elapse.

Yet the urgency of those events hardly compares with the lightning-fast dispatch of J. Edgar Hoover's secret files. Upon discovering the director's lifeless corpse, Agent Crawford instructs housekeeper Annie Fields to call Assistant Director Clyde Tolson, Hoover's confidant and second in command. Tolson then phones Helen Gandy, the director's personal secretary. The seventy-five-year-old, an avid trout fisherman and spinster who has worked fifty-five years for Hoover, immediately begins the destruction of the "Official and Confidential" files.

Among the memos that will mysteriously escape the shredding is a teletype from the Los Angeles field office, stating that Bobby Kennedy borrowed a white Lincoln Continental convertible from Special Agent William Simon in order to visit Marilyn Monroe on the night she died, potentially placing RFK at the scene of her suicide.

To Hoover, these files were not blackmail but a valuable means of keeping his power. Among the data now being destroyed is the long list of congressmen having ties to organized crime. Hoover has never

---

* The lack of an autopsy on J. Edgar Hoover, the fact that his remains were embalmed within hours of his death, and his own doctor's admission that the director's heart condition was not serious enough to cause death were extremely unusual and have never been explained by the federal government.

once leaked this information or sought prosecution of these corrupt politicians.

In 1992, twenty years after J. Edgar Hoover's death, Gambino crime family capo Carmine "the Doctor" Lombardozzi will explain why: "J. Edgar was in our pocket. He was no one we ever needed to fear."*

✦

Hoover's death brings to an end one era of law enforcement, even as the 1970s usher in a changing time for organized crime.

As it has been since the Kefauver hearings two decades ago, the secret world of the Mob is a source of endless fascination to Americans. *The Godfather*, a novel loosely based on New York's five families, sells

Organized crime boss Joseph Anthony Colombo Sr. at an unknown location in 1971.

---

* It is alleged that Mafia financier Meyer Lansky had been blackmailing Hoover since 1935 over homosexual acts. At the time, Hoover was known to frequent a Havana gay nightclub known as Cocktail while wearing a fake mustache as a disguise.

more than nine million copies and remains on the *New York Times* best-seller list for sixty-seven weeks. The subsequent film and sequel of the same name make organized crime even more accessible to the general public. Not surprisingly, the Mafia tried to shut down filming of *The Godfather* before it even began.

The Mob-connected Frank Sinatra sang at a Madison Square Garden fundraiser for the Italian-American Civil Rights League, a group of which crime boss Joe Colombo Sr. is a member. Monies were to be used to battle negative media depictions of Italian Americans, particularly *The Godfather*. But eventually, after producer Al Ruddy secretly paid Colombo for the privilege of filming in New York, production was allowed to commence.

But Colombo's very public entanglement with *The Godfather* was heavily frowned upon by other New York crime families. In a vivid instance of art imitating life, on the same day director Francis Ford Coppola films a scene depicting the murder of a Mafia boss in New York, actual crime boss Joe Colombo Sr. is shot in the head just four blocks away. The hit occurs during the Italian-American League's public rally in Columbus Circle.*

✦

After the film's release, the Mafia is so taken with *The Godfather* that some mobsters adopt many of the rituals seen on film. The cheek-to-cheek kisses of made men, the act of kissing the Godfather's ring, and even use of the term *Godfather*—all long ago abandoned by crime families—once again become part of the Mafia ritual.

The movie wins three Academy Awards, including Best Picture. Dangerous and violent men revel in its success. But reality will soon intrude.

✦

---

* It is alleged that Joseph "Crazy Joe" Gallo ordered the hit. The Mob used an outside individual to do the shooting, an African American named Jerome A. Johnson, who was immediately killed by Colombo's bodyguards, even though he was already in police custody and surrounded by policemen. Johnson got close to the mobster by posing as a credentialed reporter. Amazingly, Joe Colombo survived the bullet to the head but was paralyzed for life and had little ability to communicate.

In January 1975, the Senate Select Committee to Study Governmental Operations with Respect to Intelligence Activities begins investigating the inner workings of the FBI and CIA. Led by Senator Frank Church of Idaho, this Church Committee is soon stunned to discover that they are uncovering some of the most tightly held secrets in America.

In addition to learning that the FBI and CIA are opening the mail of average citizens, eavesdropping on their telephone conversations, and even breaking into their homes to gather evidence, the Church Committee confirms that the CIA actually hired Mafia killers to assassinate Fidel Castro.

The committee hastily works to put a real-life Mafioso on the stand. That man is Sam Giancana. The American public's fascination with the Mob leads Senate majority leader Mike Mansfield to warn against turning the hearings into a "television extravaganza" rather than a serious investigation. But it's too late. Giancana's pending appearance ensures enormous publicity for the proceedings.

At Giancana's last appearance before a Senate committee, he famously sparred with Bobby Kennedy but chose to take the Fifth to maintain his code of omertà. But that was long ago. This time, the mobster promises to speak on the record.

It has been a decade since Giancana was a force in organized crime. His flashy lifestyle and unwillingness to share the profits of his worldwide casino operations caused a rift between himself and other top crime bosses. In 1966, he endured a short prison sentence for refusing to testify before a grand jury. Immediately upon his release, knowing that another jury subpoena—and prison sentence—would be forthcoming, he fled to Cuernavaca, Mexico. This would be his home for the next eight years, a time when he traveled to Asia, Europe, and the Mideast for business and pleasure.

But on July 19, 1974, Mexican officials forcibly enter Giancana's home as he sleeps, dragging him from his bed and sending the mobster back to the United States. He soon returns to his home in Oak Park, Illinois, and attempts to ingratiate himself with the Outfit.

"Sam thought nothing had changed, but everything had changed," a Mob informant will tell the *New York Times*.

Sam Giancana is expelled from the Mob for good because he still refuses to share casino profits. And so he agrees to testify before the Church Committee. That seals his fate.

On the night of June 19, 1975, two police bodyguards mysteriously abandon their post outside Giancana's house. The mobster is not informed. He is entertaining his youngest daughter, Francine, and her husband, Jerome DePalma. There are others in the house as well, but soon they depart.

As the evening grows late, Sam Giancana goes up to his bedroom but finds that he cannot sleep. He then walks down the steps to his basement kitchen and prepares a dinner of sausage, peppers, escarole, and chickpeas.

It is a meal Sam Giancana never gets the chance to eat.

The gunshot to the back of his head comes without warning, killing the mobster instantly.

But the murderer is not finished.

Sometimes, in the world of the Mafia, it is not enough to shoot a man dead; a message must be sent.

So the killer rolls Giancana onto his back. The .22-caliber pistol equipped with a silencer is placed between his lips and shoved deep into his throat. A bullet into the mouth is the Mafia manner of death for those choosing to testify against them.

The gunman fires six times.

Robert Maheu, the CIA operative who once colluded with Giancana over the Castro assassination, gets the message. "The Mob knew Sam wouldn't keep his mouth shut," Maheu will comment, "so it silenced him for good."

✦

Johnny Roselli also talks too much.

On June 24, 1975—just five days after the shocking murder of Sam Giancana—the sixty-nine-year-old mobster testifies before the Church Committee. Roselli is rattled by the murder of Giancana and is plotting revenge against a member of the Chicago Outfit, Butch Blasi, whom Roselli suspects of assassinating his old friend. "I'd like to cut his fucking balls off and shove them up his ass," Roselli fumes to Jimmy Fratianno, a longtime Mob acquaintance.

Nevertheless, Johnny Roselli is talking. He has spent time in a federal penitentiary and finding himself completely unsuited for a life behind bars, Roselli will do whatever it takes to make sure he never returns. "If they're going to kill me, they're going to kill me," the mobster says with a fatalistic smirk, referring to the Mob.

The testimony in Washington will be the first of three appearances before the Church Committee, covering topics ranging from the Fidel Castro assassination attempt to whether or not the Mob played a role in the murder of John F. Kennedy. Roselli will reveal the shocking love triangle among Sam Giancana, JFK, and Judith Campbell. The Mafia is not happy about that. "When you're called before a committee like that you have to go to your people and ask them what to do," a confidential Mob source will tell the *New York Times*. "Roselli not only did not come to us, he went to the committee and shot his mouth off all over the place."*

So, even before he gives testimony, Roselli's murder is approved by the twenty-six top crime families in America.

In truth, Johnny Roselli has fallen on hard times. He was sentenced to prison for a card-cheating operation.† Since his release he has been reduced to owning a gift shop at the Frontier Hotel in Las Vegas. But it is too dangerous for Roselli to live in that town, so he resides with his sister and brother-in-law, Edith and Joseph Daigle, in Plantation, Florida. Roselli spends most days reading by the pool, walking his poodle, and then watching television in the evenings. He never plays the same golf course twice, for fear of getting murdered. On those occasions that he does make dinner reservations, Roselli always books under his sister's name.

---

* Judith Campbell's testimony was meant to be secret but was leaked to the media in December 1975. This marked the first time John F. Kennedy was publicly accused of marital infidelity, and Campbell was pilloried as a liar. It was only months and years later, as more stories of the president's philandering became news, that Campbell was believed.

† Peepholes were drilled into the ceiling above the high-stakes poker tables in Beverly Hills, allowing conspirators to see the cards being played. Signals were then sent to those in on the cheating, telling them whether to hold or fold. The FBI eventually was alerted and served search warrants, leading to a six-month trial and the conviction of Roselli and four other cheaters.

The mobster believes this caution protects him from being killed. But he is wrong. The hit team from Chicago is patient and methodical, carefully monitoring Roselli's scant activities.

Upon completion of his testimony, Roselli tries to make amends with the underworld. He meets with Santo Trafficante of the Tampa crime family, whom Roselli testified was heavily involved in the plot to murder Fidel Castro. As a result of that testimony, Trafficante himself is subpoenaed to appear before the Church Committee. Trafficante is among the most private crime bosses, and Roselli's actions have placed him in jeopardy.

But all appears forgiven. Roselli and Trafficante have dinner at the Landing's Restaurant in Fort Lauderdale in mid-June. Despite the obvious fact that dining with a crime family boss that he has betrayed could be dangerous, Roselli does not feel uncomfortable. Josie, Trafficante's wife, and Roselli's sister, Edith, are also present. Edith will later report that it was a polite evening and "no business was discussed."

But on July 28, 1976, Johnny Roselli finds out what happens to those who defy the Mob. After a late breakfast with his sister, Roselli borrows her year-old silver Impala. The mobster tells Edith he is going to play golf and puts his clubs in the trunk. But instead, Roselli drives to a North Miami marina. He parks the Impala and walks to the dock, where he greets an old friend. He is also introduced to a visitor from Chicago, whereupon the three men board a waiting boat for a quiet afternoon at sea.

For the debt-ridden Roselli, who longs for a return to the action, this is perhaps a chance to reinsert himself into the upper levels of organized crime. If he suspects anything is amiss, he does not show it. The dinner with Santo Trafficante has assured Roselli that he has made amends and his Senate testimony is forgiven. After months of caution and looking over his shoulder, Roselli steps aboard the boat and accepts the offer of a cocktail. He asks for vodka, then settles into a deck chair to enjoy the cruise.*

---

* The description of Roselli's murder on the boat was provided by an anonymous source to the *New York Times*.

As soon as the boat pushes off and motors toward the Intracoastal Waterway, a man hiding onshore steals the silver Impala and drives it to the Miami airport, where it is parked in a busy garage and abandoned.

Meanwhile, Johnny Roselli is enjoying his drink and the warm sea breeze. He does not pay attention as the visitor from Chicago maneuvers around behind him. Without warning, a powerful hand is clamped over Roselli's mouth and nose. He drops the vodka and struggles to free himself, but his emphysema does not allow effective resistance. He also has arthritis of the spine, making it difficult to fight back. Johnny Roselli is dead in less than a minute.

It is not enough to dump his body overboard. The mobster might bob back to the surface before the sharks can eat him. Instead, the killers tape a wash cloth over Roselli's mouth to ensure he cannot breathe if he somehow comes back to life. Then his legs are sawed off. A rope is tied around Roselli's neck and large tow hooks are inserted into his abdomen just below the ribs. The two murderers then lift the body with the rope and hooks, placing it inside a metal oil drum measuring three feet high and twenty-two inches across. Holes have been drilled into the metal so it will sink. After the torso is inside, both severed legs are shoved on top. Heavy iron chains are wrapped around the mangled corpse. Only then is the body thrown overboard.

Johnny Roselli had a running joke with his brother-in-law, Joe Daigle, that if he ever goes missing, the best place to look for his body would be an airport parking lot. So it is that when Roselli is not home by dark, Daigle drives to the Fort Lauderdale airport in search of the silver Impala. Not finding it, he then searches the Miami airport. On the third floor of a parking garage Daigle locates his wife's Chevy, with the golf clubs inside.

But no sign of Roselli.

However, the world has not seen the last of him.

Ten days after the mobster's murder, three fishermen spot the oil drum washed up on a sandbar in Dumfoundling Bay near North Miami Beach.

Roselli's brutalized and waterlogged remains are found inside. The mobster will be cremated. And while there will be no grave site for family to visit, the mystery of her brother's disappearance is solved for his sister, Edith.

But the family of another high-profile man will not be so fortunate.

✦

Jimmy Hoffa is nervous and angry.

"I'm being stood up," he shouts into a pay phone.

It is July 30, 1975, just a month after the murder of Sam Giancana, and Johnny Roselli's first appearance before the Church Committee. Hoffa has been out of jail for three and a half years now. Per the terms of his release, he is not allowed to hold union office until 1980, but his lawyers are working hard to get that time reduced. To keep himself busy, Hoffa has been touring the country, visiting local unions and gathering support for what he hopes to be a successful 1976 run for the Teamster presidency.

But Jimmy Hoffa is well aware that the Mafia has gained greater authority over the union since he was forced to step down. They control his handpicked successor, Frank Fitzsimmons, who was never meant to be more than a caretaker until Hoffa's release. However, Fitzsimmons has proven pliant in his relations with the Mob, more than willing to make Teamster pension funds available for loans and other deals to enrich the Mafia. As a result, he is a most formidable opponent.

Tony Provenzano is the leader of the powerful New Jersey Local 560. But Tony Pro, as he is known, also holds the rank of capo in the Genovese crime family. His enemies have a way of disappearing, among them Armand "Cookie" Faugno and Anthony Castellitto, whose bodies are thought to be entombed in a sixty-acre New Jersey landfill known as Brother Moscato's Dump.*

Making the situation even more unpredictable, Hoffa and Provenzano knew each other while serving time in Lewisburg penitentiary, where they were not on friendly terms. "It's because of people like you that I got into trouble in the first place," Hoffa said to Tony Pro, alluding to Bobby Kennedy's successful public unveiling of the relationship between the Teamsters and the Mafia.

---

* It is believed by some that the dump may contain the body of Jimmy Hoffa.

But today is a chance for a new beginning, though it is off to a bad start. Hoffa was due to have lunch with Provenzano and Detroit Mafioso Anthony Giacalone at 2:00 p.m. this afternoon. Both men are late.

The meal is supposed to take place at the Machus Red Fox restaurant in Bloomfield Hills, seven miles northwest of Detroit. Hoffa knows it well. Like Carl's Chop House, the Red Fox is a frequent Teamster hangout. Hoffa's son, James, held his wedding reception here. Normally, Hoffa would never bring Mafia members to this highbrow establishment, but due to the sensitive nature of today's meeting, the union leader makes an exception. This is to be a "peace meeting" between Hoffa and Tony Pro, an attempt to achieve reconciliation between the two men and discuss the future relationship between the Mob and Teamsters if, and when, Jimmy Hoffa takes back his old job.

Nevertheless, Jimmy Hoffa is uncomfortable. He suspects something isn't quite right. So Hoffa is not himself today. His wife, Josephine, will later recall how tense Hoffa looked as he left the house, as if he had a premonition of bad things happening.

In fact, Hoffa is so ill at ease that en route to the lunch he makes an impulsive visit to the limousine company owned by good friend Louie Linteau hoping he might come along as an ally. But Linteau is out and Hoffa must proceed alone. Dressed in blue pants, blue shirt, white socks, black Gucci loafers, and sunglasses, Hoffa arrives and then waits in the parking lot across from the restaurant.

It is 2:15 when Hoffa phones Josephine, who tells him no one has called to explain the delay. He tells her he will be home by 4:00 p.m. to barbecue steaks. Hoffa hangs up, then resumes pacing. Despite the fact that he has not yet been restored to Teamster leadership, Jimmy Hoffa is popular and famous among Detroit union members. So even as he frets in the parking lot, Hoffa is approached by two local men eager to say hello and shake his hand.

They leave. By 2:30, Jimmy Hoffa is still waiting for Tony Pro and Anthony Giacalone.

Sometime between 2:45 and 3:00 p.m., Hoffa's wait comes to an end.

A maroon sedan pulls up. Three men sit inside. Jimmy Hoffa steps into the vehicle, taking a seat up front on the passenger side. At the age of sixty-two, with a lifetime on the fringe of the murky world of organized crime, Hoffa is well aware that he has chosen a perilous place to sit. It was Al Capone rival Hymie Weiss, during the days of Prohibition, who invented the manner of execution known as "taking a ride." The victim sits in the front seat, unable to see the actions of the man sitting directly behind him, who then shoots him in the head. Another version is for the individual in the back to loop a rope or piano wire around the neck of the person sitting in front, then strangle the victim.

That scenario was used in the movie *The Godfather*.

Jimmy Hoffa must have completely trusted the driver of the sedan, thought to be either a Lincoln or Mercury as described by an eyewitnesses who saw Hoffa get in. And he must have felt at ease with the men in the back seat. Nervous, alone, and battle-hardened, Hoffa would never put himself in the hands of adversaries.

As Jimmy Hoffa settles into the front seat, events unfold that still remain a mystery. Only one thing is certain: Hoffa vanishes.*

✦

And so it is that in 1975 and 1976, major crime figures Giancana, Roselli, and Hoffa are off the board. They will be replaced by young blood, organized crime members who are even more ruthless than their predecessors. But one of these men is not who he appears to be.

His name is Donnie Brasco.

---

* The authors of this book investigated thoroughly but could find no authoritative account to explain what happened to Jimmy Hoffa. Various scenarios have been portrayed in books and movies, but to this day the FBI has never solved the case. On December 9, 1982, a Michigan judge declared Hoffa legally dead, despite the absence of a corpse. Charles "Chuckie" O'Brien, a longtime friend of Hoffa, believed the union boss was killed over fears he might give testimony to the Church Committee. There is an allegation that O'Brien, trusted by Hoffa, actually drove the car that picked him up. Before he died on February 14, 2020, O'Brien denied any knowledge of Hoffa's disappearance.

CHAPTER TWENTY-ONE

August 3, 1982
Federal District Court
Manhattan, New York
10:00 A.M.

The Mob's worst nightmare takes the witness stand.

It has been six years since FBI special agent Joseph D. Pistone, a.k.a. Donnie Brasco, went under deep cover to infiltrate the Bonanno crime family. Now, he prepares to testify about his life inside the Mob. Agent Pistone is forty-three, with a confident demeanor. He wears a dark blue sports coat, light blue slacks, and a striped red tie as he takes the oath. The jury is composed of four men and eight women. Across the courtroom, which is filled with 150 spectators, are men "Brasco" once considered brothers during his life as a Mafioso: Benjamin "Lefty Guns" Ruggiero, John Cerasini, Nicholas Santora, and Antonio Tomasulo. All are on trial for racketeering conspiracy.

Special Agent Pistone is the key witness in this trial. That is evident by the fact that the Mob has placed a $500,000 bounty on his head.

✦

It is the spring of 1976 when Joseph Pistone volunteers to expose the Mob. He has been an FBI agent for almost seven years, with a wife and three daughters, living in New York City. Never before has the bureau successfully placed an agent inside the Mafia, and Pistone's chances of

Joseph D. Pistone, a.k.a. Donnie Brasco, an FBI agent who worked undercover to infiltrate organized crime families from 1976–81.

success in this clandestine world are slim. And yet, if ever there is an ideal candidate to pull this off, it is Joseph Pistone.

The special agent grew up in Paterson, New Jersey—a "street guy," in his own words—where he hung out in Mob-run social halls and witnessed Mafia life firsthand. "I knew how wiseguys acted," he will write in his autobiography. "I knew the mentality. I knew the things to do and not to do. Keep your mouth shut at certain times. Don't get involved in things that don't concern you."

Pistone brings special skills to his job. He speaks fluent Italian, born into a family of Sicilian heritage. He looks the part, powerfully built at six feet tall, 180 pounds, with broad shoulders, high forehead, and the tough, streetwise confidence of a man who can handle himself under pressure. On the surface, Joe Pistone easily passes as a Mob foot soldier.

The FBI under J. Edgar Hoover rarely used undercover agents. The director believed they might be compromised in the criminal world full of vice and money. However, Joe Pistone has already proved himself a capable operator, having just spent two years inside a vehicle theft ring. It is his ability to drive an eighteen-wheel truck that landed Pistone that assignment. But now the stakes are far higher—the special agent must convince the ferocious Bonanno crime family to trust him with secrets, a daunting task to say the least.

Before going undercover, Pistone spends months immersing himself into his persona as a small-time jewel thief named Donnie Brasco. He attends FBI gemology classes, learning about precious stones and how they are illegally bought and sold.

Pistone's name and employment record are erased from all FBI files. Coworkers and even good friends are not told of his assignment. His wife and daughters are relocated to a home in a different state, with a new last name and the realization that they will not see Joe for months at a time—and, even then, he will only be home for a day or so.

At first, the family is fine. Maggie Pistone and the girls all welcome their new circumstance. But in time the strain of Pistone's job and the long periods of separation will lead Maggie to deeply resent her husband's job. To escape questions, his teenaged daughters tell friends their parents are divorced. He will miss all the family birthdays and graduations. Making matters even worse, Pistone is not allowed to tell his family about his assignment, leaving them completely in the dark as to why he is abandoning them for such long periods of time.

The FBI gives Pistone two apartments, one in Miami and one on the Upper East Side of Manhattan. He also possesses, under his new name, credit cards, social security identification, a driver's license, and a monthly stipend of spending money so he can look and act like a gangster.

Joe Pistone is a driven man but feels enormous guilt over leaving his family.

✦

In September 1976, "Donnie Brasco" goes into action. He is on his own, unable to make immediate contact with the bureau if things go wrong. The agent meets once a month with an FBI official who replenishes his cash. But as far as protection is concerned, Brasco has none. The chances of taking a bullet behind the ear are very high.

The undercover operation is supposed to last six months. Instead, it continues for five perilous years.

✦

"You got a beef?" Donnie Brasco asks the mobster known as Patsy.

Brasco's immersion into the underworld begins by frequenting bars and restaurants known to be Mob hangouts and befriending small-time gangsters. For the most part, Brasco finds it tedious. "I'd play cards, drink a little, hang around," he will remember. The agent refrains from asking too many questions to avoid suspicion. He soon becomes part of a crew of hijackers in Brooklyn, knowing that his first order of business each day is to check in with the crew boss, sometime between 10:00 and 11:00 a.m.

On this particular morning, Brasco's outspoken behavior and brash reputation become sources of irritation to crew boss Jilly Greca, who asks his second in command, a Mafioso nicknamed Patsy, to see if Brasco is legitimate.

"You say you pulled off all those scores down in Miami before you came here," Patsy says to Brasco. "But we don't know nothing about that . . . So Frankie and me wanna know somebody you did those jobs with, so we can check you out."

"You don't need to check me out," Brasco responds. "I don't have to satisfy you just because you were in the can."

"Yeah, you do," Patsy replies. "Let's go back inside and sit down."

The two men walk into a clothing store on Fifteenth Avenue where Jilly maintains an office. Its name is ACERG—Jilly's last name spelled backward. The front section features racks of low-priced clothing procured by hijacking garment trucks and burglarizing other establishments.

The back room features a desk and card tables where Jilly's crew hangs out. "When they got up in the morning they didn't think about going to work and punching a time clock," Pistone will write. "The mob was their job. You got up, went to the club or wherever you hung out, and spent your day with those guys."

Patsy pulls a loaded pistol from a drawer and places it on the desk. "You don't leave here until you give me a name."

Brasco knows he cannot give in—at least for a while. His under-cover status means that he actually *does* possess the name of a low-level informant in Miami who will vouch for the agent's "criminal" reputation, but passing along a name too quickly will mark Brasco as a potential snitch.

So, in this first dangerous confrontation, Brasco blusters. "I'm not giving up the name just to satisfy your curiosity," he tells Patsy.

"You got a fucking smart mouth. You don't give me a name, the only way you leave here is in a rolled-up rug."

"You gotta do what you gotta do, but I ain't giving you a name."

A short time later, after calculating the odds, Brasco takes a chance and gives up a name. He is then locked in a room with several other mobsters, where they play cards and smoke while Patsy checks out Brasco's story.

"We sat there for hours. Everybody but me was smoking. We all sat and breathed that crap, played cards, and bullshitted," Joseph Pistone will later write. He is nervous, knowing there is no way out of the room. The gun is still on the table but the roomful of Mafiosi all have their own guns anyway.

Finally, Patsy returns, wearing a relieved look. "We got an answer. And your guy okayed you."

✦

After a year of surreptitiously recording conversations and memorizing the names and license plates of New York Mafiosi, Donnie Brasco is finally introduced to the higher-ups in the Bonanno family. He quickly befriends mobsters Anthony Mirra and Dominick Napolitano, who eventually trust him so thoroughly that his Mob membership is a fait accompli. Brasco not only gets on the inside but, incredibly, becomes a trusted companion of Benjamin "Lefty Guns" Ruggiero, a rising member of the Bonanno outfit.

"I'm telling you now, pal, you belong to me alone," Ruggiero tells Brasco as he brings him into the family. "I'll die with you."

"I know that," Brasco replies.

"Now you are affiliated officially," Ruggiero tells him, cementing Joseph Pistone as the greatest undercover agent in FBI history.

But one that may perish at any time.

Lefty Ruggiero is a vicious killer, known to have at least twenty-six confirmed murders. Brasco's initial role is to assist Ruggiero's book-making operation, but in time their friendship grows so strong that Brasco dines often at the Ruggiero home in Manhattan. He counsels Lefty in dealing with the mobster's stepson—who is addicted to heroin.* Ruggiero, himself, is a gambling addict and Brasco covers some of his debts. On a daily basis, Donnie Brasco's life becomes a long sequence of Mafia social clubs, bars, parties, and card games.

"As a wiseguy you can lie, you can cheat, you can steal, you can kill people—legitimately," Ruggiero tells Brasco. "You can do any goddamn thing you want and nobody can say anything about it. Who wouldn't want to be a wiseguy?"

Through it all, Donnie Brasco's friendship with Lefty Ruggiero grows deeper. The two men become so close that the mobster even asks the special agent to serve as best man for his 1977 wedding to his second wife, Louise.

✦

By February 1980, the connection between Brasco and Ruggiero escalates into a dangerous situation. Lefty is pushing for Brasco to become a "made man" inside the Mob. That means Donnie Brasco would have to execute someone in service to the Bonanno family.

The FBI, of course, could never sanction that. Agents are prohibited from committing acts of violence other than self-defense.

The undercover operation is now in its fifth year. But problems are starting to accumulate. One March afternoon, Brasco and Ruggiero are sitting in a Miami restaurant, with Lefty flipping through a copy of *Time* magazine. The mobster notices an unusual photograph of a yacht

---

* Thomas Sbano, Benjamin Ruggiero's stepson, was found shot to death in the front seat of a Lincoln Continental convertible parked in a garage on the Lower East Side of Manhattan on January 15, 1984. Also dead in the car was Joseph Chilli, son of a top Bonanno family capo, leading police to believe the killing was a Mob hit.

named *Left Hand*. The vessel is part of a story about the FBI and its undercover assets.

Several months prior, Donnie Brasco had used that yacht to entertain a group of Mafiosi and their wives in Biscayne Bay. Ruggiero was part of the outing.

The killer looks up from the magazine and immediately demands an explanation. Brasco is caught by surprise but is glib enough to say he knows nothing about any FBI involvement with the yacht. Maybe, Brasco says, he was scammed.

Ruggiero is skeptical but puts the matter aside, at least for the moment.

✦

Joseph Pistone will later write that mobsters are thieves first, and "not primarily an organization of murderers." But in the midst of his new life comes a stark reminder of what happens when the Mob turns on one of its own. On March 21, 1980, just two weeks after the *Left Hand* incident in Miami shatters the agent's belief that he is invincible, a major Mafia hit becomes national news. Powerful Philadelphia crime boss Angelo Bruno—known as the Docile Don for his unwillingness to use violence—is murdered by a single shotgun blast to the head while sitting in the passenger seat of a vehicle parked in front of his home.

It quickly becomes apparent that the Docile Don's close friend and consigliere, Antonio Caponigro, also known as Tony Bananas, ordered the assassination without the Commission's approval. Within weeks, the sixty-seven-year-old Caponigro is kidnapped and murdered—his beaten corpse found nude in a car trunk in the Bronx.

Agent Pistone well knows he could be next in the trunk of a car.

✦

In May 1981, the Bonanno family begins to fracture. An intramural war breaks out after Carmine Galante, head of the family, is shot dead. During the ensuing power struggle, three top members are lured to the 20/20 nightclub in Brooklyn, under the pretense of a peace meeting. The unarmed capos are led into a storeroom, where they are machine-gunned to death. Their bodies are subsequently wrapped in drop cloths and transported to the border of Queens, to a place known as the Hole, where a number of murdered gangsters are buried.

In court, Agent Pistone will later describe the bloody scene inside the storeroom, particularly how one of the mobsters, Dominick "Big Trin" Trinchera, met his demise: "Nicky," referring to defendant Nicholas Santora, "said you should have seen when they shot him. Fifty pounds of his stomach went flying."

✦

The Bonanno gang war spelled the beginning of the end for Pistone as a Mob undercover. But before he could extricate himself, the family ordered him to kill a man named Bruno Indelicato. Once that was accomplished, Donnie Brasco would be a "made man."

In his time as a member of the Bonanno family, Donnie Brasco has committed all manner of crimes, ranging from loan sharking to racketeering. But murder is too much.

So, on July 26, 1981, Donnie Brasco disappears from the Mob and returns to the FBI. He receives a $500 bonus for all the years of risking his life.

Thirty-three days later, Lefty Ruggiero is taken into custody by federal authorities for his "own protection." The feds tell Ruggiero a contract has been taken out on his life because of his association with Donnie Brasco.

Hoping to instill paranoia, FBI agents also inform Bonanno crime family members that their longtime confidant, Brasco, will soon testify against them. On July 30, Agent Doug Fenci meets with Dominick Napolitano at a Mafia social club known as the Motion Lounge in Brooklyn. As proof, the agent holds a photograph of himself and two other agents standing in a New Jersey hotel room with none other than "Donnie Brasco."

Dominick Napolitano knows his fate is sealed. On August 17, realizing that a death sentence has been issued in his name because Brasco served on his crew, Napolitano hands a favorite bartender all his personal jewelry and the keys to an apartment, hoping that his pet pigeons will be cared for after his demise. Napolitano is not seen again for almost a year, when his decomposing body is located in a Staten Island creek by a seventeen-year-old boy. The mobster's hands have been cut off, signaling his designation as a snitch.

Anthony Mirra, the other mobster who brought Brasco into the Bonanno family, is also murdered. He is shot in the head several times by his own cousin, under orders from the Mob.

✦

After Joseph Pistone's shocking court testimony, Benjamin "Lefty Guns" Ruggiero is sentenced to twenty years in prison. Two hundred indictments and more than one hundred convictions come about as a result of the undercover operation.

"If you're a bad guy, my job is to put you in the can," Pistone will later write. "Simple as that."

But still, there is a half-million-dollar bounty on his head. A few days after the trial ends, a number of Mafia dons in New York City are surprised when they are visited by FBI agents. The conversations are very similar; the mobsters are informed that if anything should happen to Joseph Pistone and his family, they will pay dearly.

A few days later, the bounty on Pistone is lifted.

✦

By the mid-1980s, organized crime in America has been badly damaged. The code of silence is no longer sacred. One of the most powerful families, the Bonannos, has been infiltrated, and local drug gangs are challenging the Italians for control of the narcotics industry. No longer is the Mafia the dominant crime force in America. Now the Mob is diminished, although still armed and dangerous, preying on human weakness.

For decades, the Mafia ran entire cities and industries all over America. Its power rivaled that of elected officials and the police. But those days are over, largely because people like Bobby Kennedy and Joseph Pistone risked their lives in order to crush evil.

Today in America, the Mob continues to operate and corrupt. But there is little security or safety for those participating in organized crime and they all realize that change has come—they know their "brotherhood" has been rendered obsolete.

Now, it is every "made man" for himself.

POSTSCRIPT

On January 26, 1962, **Charles "Lucky" Luciano** meets with American film producer Martin Gosch to discuss a motion picture based on his life. The conference takes place at the airport in Naples, Italy. Italian police, suspecting that Luciano is actually there to smuggle narcotics, are on hand to monitor his activities. So they are stunned when the mobster suddenly collapses from a heart attack and dies. A funeral attended by three hundred mourners is held in Naples three days later, but after U.S. authorities allow the return of Luciano's remains to American soil, the actual burial takes place at St. John's Cemetery in Queens, New York, two weeks later.

✦

Ironically, given their profound hatred for each other, Luciano's grave site is very close to the tomb of **Vito Genovese**. The mobster continued to run his crime family from inside the Atlanta federal penitentiary for ten years. After suffering bouts of ill health, Genovese was transferred to the United States Medical Center for Federal Prisoners in Springfield, Missouri, where he died of a heart attack on Valentine's Day 1969, at age seventy-one. Despite his passing, the Genovese crime family lives on to this day, controlling Manhattan and the Bronx, with extended ties to organized crime in Connecticut, Massachusetts, and Florida.

✦

Meyer Lansky is acquitted on charges of federal tax evasion in 1974. Lansky died in Miami of lung cancer at the age of eighty and is buried at Mount Nebo Miami Memorial Gardens. Lansky left behind an estate of just $57,000, but the FBI believes the Mob's most accomplished accountant stashed an estimated $300 million in secret bank accounts around the world. That money has still not been found

✦

Joseph Valachi, the former Genovese family soldier and infamous cellmate of Vito, remained in prison the rest of his life. As FBI special agent Flynn once encouraged him, Joseph Valachi took up an exercise regimen and lost forty pounds. However, he did not quit his habit of smoking sixty cigarettes a day. Valachi suffered a heart attack and died on April 3, 1971, while serving his sentence at the Federal Correctional Facility in La Tuna, Texas. He was sixty-seven. Valachi is buried at the Gate of Heaven Cemetery in Lewiston, New York.

✦

Tampa crime boss **Santo Trafficante**, New Orleans don **Carlos Marcello**, New York family leader **Joe Bonanno**, and former head of the Luciano crime family **Frank Costello**—all longtime cohorts in the nationwide crime syndicate—lived long enough to die of natural causes. Trafficante passed at the age of seventy-two after undergoing unsuccessful heart surgery in Houston. He is buried at the L'Unione Italiana Cemetery in Ybor City, Florida. Though he's been dead since 1987, his crime family exists to this day.

Marcello suffered a series of strokes in 1989 and lived out his days as a retired capo at his home in Louisiana before passing away. He is buried at the Metairie Cemetery north of downtown New Orleans.

Joe Bonanno spent his retirement in Arizona, where he wrote his autobiography, *A Man of Honor*. Bonanno died in 2002, one year before its publication. He is buried at Holy Hope Cemetery in Tucson, Arizona.

Frank Costello lived to the age of eighty-two, enjoying sixteen years of senior citizen activity in Manhattan. Although officially retired, he remained in touch with New York's crime bosses and was consulted on many activities. Costello suffered a heart attack and died on February 18, 1973. He is interred in a mausoleum at St. Michael's Cemetery in Queens, New York.

✦

The death of **Sonny Liston** was just as tumultuous as his life. He passed on January 30, 1970, alone in his Las Vegas home. It is only when his wife, Geraldine, returned from a long trip that Liston's decomposing body was discovered. The former world heavyweight boxing champion, thought to be thirty-eight years old, had been dead six days. The official ruling was natural causes, specifically poor circulation. But a balloon of heroin was found in his bedroom, leading some to suspect he received a Mafia "hot shot," in which a lethal injection is given to a target. The truth will never be known.

✦

Muhammad Ali, Liston's opponent in two of boxing's most famous matches, fought professionally until 1981. By the end of his career, having absorbed an estimated tens of thousands punches, the champ began suffering from palsy and speech difficulties. This was later diagnosed as Parkinson's disease, from which Ali died on June 3, 2016, at the age of seventy-four. He is buried in his hometown of Louisville, Kentucky.

✦

The passing of **Judith Campbell Exner** went almost unnoticed. She was promised confidentiality in exchange for appearing before the Church Committee. But when her identity was leaked to the media in 1975, Campbell retreated from the public eye, wounded by the criticism over her extramarital affair with John F. Kennedy and fearful that a Mafia hit was imminent. Judy eventually married golf pro Dan Exner in 1975 but was long divorced when she died of cancer in 1999 at age sixty-five. Her ashes were scattered at sea.

✦

As for the Rat Pack, actor and former Kennedy brother-in-law **Peter Lawford** died of a heart attack in 1984. **Sammy Davis Jr.** died of lung cancer in 1990. **Dean Martin** succumbed to the same cancer in 1995. And **Joey Bishop** suffered multiple organ failure in 2007. But it was the passing of **Frank Sinatra** that received the most attention. Many, including Sinatra himself, believed that he was the inspiration for the Johnny Fontane character in *The Godfather*, written by Mario Puzo. When the two accidentally met at Chasen's restaurant in Hollywood, Sinatra berated the author as a "pimp."

The legendary crooner first retired from singing in 1971, only to resume his career almost immediately thereafter. Sinatra continued performing until 1995, when the onset of undiagnosed mental health issues and use of various narcotics caused him to forget song lyrics while onstage. Frank Sinatra died of a heart attack on May 14, 1998, at age eighty-two. He is buried with a bottle of Jack Daniels and pack of Camel cigarettes in the Desert Memorial Park in Cathedral City, California.

✦

Over the decades, a number of laws have been passed to crack down on organized crime. But it was the RICO statute in 1970 that forever altered the balance of power between law enforcement and the Mob. The Racketeer Influenced and Corrupt Organizations Act makes it illegal to run a criminal enterprise, allowing prosecution of a crime family boss for actions he authorized but did not personally commit. In essence, RICO is the first act outlawing organized crime rather than specific Mob activities. It has since been applied to a wide-ranging number of groups and individuals such as the Hells Angels, financier Michael Milken, and even the Key West, Florida, Police Department, which ran a protection racket in exchange for cocaine in the 1980s.

✦

In February 1985, United States attorney **Rudolph Giuliani** indicted nine Mafiosi, including leaders of New York's five families, for labor racketeering, extortion, and murder for hire. The Commission, the crime syndicate first formed by Lucky Luciano in 1931, was dealt a severe blow when nine bosses were convicted. Anthony "Bruno" Indelicato, capo of the Bonanno crime family and the man Donnie Brasco was asked to execute in 1981, was sentenced to forty years in prison and fined $55,000—the most lenient of the sentences. All the other mobsters were sentenced to one hundred years and fined a minimum of $240,000. With the exception of Indelicato, all have since died in prison. Bruno was released in 1998, only to be arrested again for parole violations. He was subsequently charged with murder and sentenced to twenty years in prison. Anthony Indelicato is due to be released in 2023.

✦

During the course of the Mafia Commission Trial, as the proceedings would become known, a new boss took over the Gambino family. **John Gotti**, forty-five at the time, brutally assassinated acting leader **Paul Castellano** to take control. Gotti quickly consolidated power, taking over an empire raking in an estimated $500 million each year. Rather than hide from publicity, Gotti courted it—wearing expensive suits and affecting a public persona that earned him the nickname the Dapper Don.

This was revised to the Teflon Don after three indictments against Gotti failed to result in convictions. Later, it was revealed that jury tampering played a role in his acquittals. On June 23, 1992, Gotti was finally convicted on five counts of murder, as well as loan-sharking, obstruction of justice, bribery, and tax evasion. His sentence was life imprisonment without possibility of parole. Gotti died in prison of throat cancer on June 10, 2002, at the age of sixty-one. His crypt is at St. John Cemetery in New York, near the graves of Lucky Luciano and Vito Genovese.

✦

Joseph Pistone, whose years undercover as Donnie Brasco presented a major coup for the FBI, still lives in seclusion with his wife, Maggie. Their daughters are grown. Pistone has written three books based on his experiences, one of which was made into the 1997 movie *Donnie Brasco*, starring Al Pacino and Johnny Depp. Pistone is still active in law enforcement, serving as a consultant to agencies around the world, as well as testifying before the U.S. Senate on organized crime.

Benjamin "Lefty Guns" Ruggiero, the Mafioso with whom Pistone was most closely associated during his time inside the Mob, was released from prison in April 1993 after serving a little more than ten years of his sentence. Ruggiero died of cancer on November 24, 1994, at the age of sixty-eight. He is buried in Calvary Cemetery in Queens, New York.

✦

To this day, the Mafia in New York City is still powerful. The September 11, 2001, terror attacks played a key role, shifting FBI manpower away from organized crime in order to surveil possible terrorists. The number of agents on the bureau's organized crime task force was reduced from four hundred to fewer than thirty. Since then, the American Mafia has become more international, forging links with Mexican and Colombian drug cartels, as well as organized crime elements in Italy's Calabria region. In 2008, Operation Old Bridge, a joint FBI–Italian operation, confirmed this connection, leading to dozens of arrests in both countries.

✦

Today, the FBI estimates there are currently three thousand members of the Mafia in America. But organized crime is under siege from other criminals. Russian, Chinese, and Vietnamese organizations, Mexican cartels, and homegrown African American drug gangs have encroached on the Mob's turf. However, none have succeeded on the same level as La Cosa Nostra. This is due, in part, to the tight hierarchical structure and constant recruitment of new soldiers who are threatened with death should they inform.

The Mafia has also prospered by outsourcing much of its illegal activity, a recent development that would never have occurred in the days of Lucky Luciano and Vito Genovese.

Also, the Mob has now become high-tech savvy. The Internet is a major source of revenue, using offshore shell corporations as a front for illicit gambling. The same is true of identity theft. Stealing credit card numbers and personal information from Internet porn and wagering sites is big business for organized crime.

As they have for decades, Mob-linked companies still control some of the nation's major construction projects, particularly in New York City. In Bill O'Reilly's book, *The United States of Trump*, the president openly discusses the Mafia's power. Mr. Trump needed concrete and waste management to build the Trump Tower in Manhattan. So he had to deal directly with the Mob.

✦

Gone are the days when crime families used restaurants and clubs to socialize publicly. Today, Mafia meetings are much more clandestine, and cell phones are never allowed, eliminating the risk of taping or filming the proceedings.

And so the fight against organized crime continues.

And, sadly, the war will never be won.

Very simply, there is too much money in criminal activity, especially narcotics.

And too many bad people willing to harvest it.

NOTE ON SOURCES

What follows is a primer on how to write and research a *Killing* book—or any work of popular history, for that matter.

Start with the topic and outline. The authors of this series share many tasks, but those two jobs belong to Bill O'Reilly and officially start the ball rolling. Then comes the research, which falls to Martin Dugard. The overarching subject matter is first observed at a distance, with the reading of books telling the story in broad strokes. Wikipedia is often consulted for context before beginning the deep dive into a topic. The idea is to get an initial picture of the story that is about to be told.

As the writing process begins, the research becomes line by line, with the authors poring over every word for flow and accuracy. It used to be necessary to travel the world in search of newspaper libraries and archives, but that task is now almost completely possible with a simple Google search.

Over the course of the ten *Killing* books, the research has followed a simple formula consisting of travel to places of interest, archives, books, newspapers, primary sources, and relentless Internet searches to obtain as many specific details as possible.

Killing the Mob was researched in the same manner, yet proved far more difficult. Due to the shadowy nature of organized crime, there are few records of time and place and very few accurate firsthand accounts of life in the Mob. There is also the matter of separating truth from legend, which is incumbent in any lifestyle fraught with such secretive tension. Such a unique historical record made this the most daunting book of the series, requiring endless cross-referencing of facts and dates between those sources that do exist in order to divine the truth. During the writing process, the authors made a point to present the facts, but to also note opposite theories if the details are too vague to support one viewpoint or another.

Not to say that the authors are the first to travel down this path. Of note, the Mob Museum in Las Vegas is not only a fascinating place to visit, but its comprehensive website offering details and chronology into the Mafia is extremely well researched and well written. So too the FBI website, known as the Vault, which offers thumbnail sketches into criminals and historic gangland events. The digitizing of many archives and newspaper libraries makes it possible to read federal case files and quote verbatim from congressional testimonies.

And it needs to be said that if you're ever in Gibsland, Louisiana, make the time to pay a visit to the Bonnie and Clyde Ambush Museum.

As noted in the subsequent bibliography, the authors pored through a small library of books on organized crime. All are worthy. Special thanks to Thomas Maier for an advance copy of *Mafia Spies*.

The authors would also like to thank Robert F. Kennedy Jr. for his personal insights.

BIBLIOGRAPHY

Adler, Tim. *Hollywood and the Mob: Movies, Mafia, Sex, and Death.*

Bernstein, Lee. *The Greatest Menace: Organized Crime in Cold War America.*

Bonanno, Bill. *Bound by Honor: A Mafioso's Story.*

Bonanno, Rosalie, and Beverly Donofrio. *Mafia Marriage.*

Borne, Ronald F. *Troutmouth: The Two Careers of Hugh Clegg.*

Bosworth, Richard J. B. *Mussolini.*

Cain, Michael. *The Tangled Web: The Life and Death of Richard Cain—Chicago Cop and Hitman.*

Cashill, Jack. *Sucker Punch: The Hard Left Hook That Dazed Ali and Killed King's Dream.*

Collier, James Lincoln. *Louis Armstrong: An American Genius.*

Collins, Max Allan, and A. Brad Schwartz. *Scarface and the Untouchable: Al Capone, Eliot Ness, and the Battle for Chicago.*

Dallek, Robert. *An Unfinished Life: John F. Kennedy, 1917–1963.*

Dannen, Frederic. *Hit Men: Power Brokers and Fast Money Inside the Music Business.*

DeStefano, Anthony M. *Gotti's Boys: The Mafia Crew That Killed for John Gotti.*

Dickerson, James L. *Dixie's Dirty Secret: The True Story of How the Government, the Media, and the Mob Conspired to Combat Integration and the Vietnam Antiwar Movement.*

Eghigian, Mars, Jr. *After Capone: The Life and World of Chicago Mob Boss Frank "the Enforcer" Nitti.*

Fulsom, Don. *The Mafia's President: Nixon and the Mob.*

Gambetta, Diego. *Codes of the Underworld: How Criminals Communicate.*

Gentry, Curt. *J. Edgar Hoover: The Man and the Secrets.*

Gorn, Elliott J. *Dillinger's Wild Ride: The Year That Made America's Public Enemy Number One.*

Gosch, Martin A., and Richard Hammer. *The Last Testament of Lucky Luciano.*

Guinn, Jeff. *Go Down Together: The True, Untold Story of Bonnie and Clyde.*

Hack, Richard. *Puppetmaster: The Secret Life of J. Edgar Hoover.*

Hauser, Thomas. *Muhammad Ali: His Life and Times.*

Horne, Gerald. *Class Struggle in Hollywood 1930–1950: Moguls, Mobsters, Stars, Reds, and Trade Unionists.*

Humphrey, Hubert H. *The Education of a Public Man: My Life and Politics.*

Jacobs, James B. *Mobsters, Unions, and Feds: The Mafia and the American Labor Movement.*

Kaplan, James. *Sinatra: The Chairman.*

Kessler, Ronald. *The Secrets of the FBI.*

———. *The Sins of the Father: Joseph P. Kennedy and the Dynasty He Founded.*

King, Jeffrey S. *The Life and Death of Pretty Boy Floyd.*

Lehrer, James. *Tension City: Inside the Presidential Debates.*

Levy, Shawn. *Rat Pack Confidential: Frank, Dean, Sammy, Peter, Joey, and the Last Great Showbiz Party.*

Maas, Peter. *The Valachi Papers.*

Madinger, John. *Confidential Informant: Law Enforcement's Most Valuable Tool.*

Mahoney, Richard D. *The Kennedy Brothers: The Rise and Fall of Jack and Bobby.*

———. *Sons and Brothers: The Days of Jack and Bobby Kennedy.*

Maier, Thomas. *Mafia Spies: The Inside Story of the CIA, Gangsters, JFK, and Castro.*

Mappen, Marc. *Prohibition Gangsters: The Rise and Fall of a Bad Generation.*

McNicoll, Susan. *Mafia Boss Sam Giancana: The Rise and Fall of a Chicago Mobster.*

Mee, Bob. *Ali and Liston: The Boy Who Would Be King and the Ugly Bear.*

Moldea, Dan E. *The Hoffa Wars: The Rise and Fall of Jimmy Hoffa.*

Newton, Michael. *The Mafia at Apalachin, 1957.*

Norris, John. *Mary McGrory: The Trailblazing Columnist Who Stood Washington on Its Head.*

O'Brien, Michael. *John F. Kennedy's Women: The Story of a Sexual Obsession.*

Oliphant, Thomas, and Curtis Wilkie. *The Road to Camelot: Inside JFK's Five-Year Campaign.*

Palmero, Joseph A. *In His Own Right: The Political Odyssey of Senator Robert F. Kennedy.*

Pietrusza, David. *1960: LBJ vs. JFK vs. Nixon.*

Posner, Gerald. *Motown: Music, Money, Sex, and Power.*

Purvis, Alston. *The Vendetta: Special Agent Melvin Purvis, John Dillinger, and Hoover's FBI in the Age of Gangsters.*

Raab, Selwyn. *Five Families: The Rise, Decline, and Resurgence of America's Most Powerful Mafia Empires.*

Reavill, Gil. *Mafia Summit: J. Edgar Hoover, the Kennedy Brothers, and the Meeting That Unmasked the Mob.*

Remnick, David. *King of the World: Muhammad Ali and the Rise of an American Hero.*

Reppetto, Thomas. *Bringing Down the Mob: The War Against the American Mafia.*

Roemer, William F., Jr. *Accardo: The Genuine Godfather.*

———. *The Enforcer: Spilotro: The Chicago Mob's Man Over Las Vegas.*

Rovner, Eduardo Sáenz. *The Cuban Connection: Drug Trafficking, Smuggling, and Gambling in Cuba from the 1920s to the Revolution.*

Russell, Thaddeus. *Out of the Jungle: Jimmy Hoffa and the Remaking of the American Working Class.*

Russo, Gus. *The Outfit: The Role of Chicago's Underworld in the Shaping of Modern America.*

———. *Supermob: How Sidney Korshak and His Criminal Associates Became America's Hidden Power Brokers.*

Schlesinger, Arthur M., Jr. *Robert Kennedy and His Times.*

Server, Lee. *Handsome Johnny: The Life and Death of Johnny Rosselli: Gentleman Gangster, Hollywood Producer, CIA Assassin.*

Short, Martin. *The Rise of the Mafia: The Definitive Story of Organized Crime.*

Sifakis, Carl: *The Mafia Encyclopedia.*

Skousen, W. Cleon. *True Stories from the Files of the FBI.*

Sloane, Arthur A. *Hoffa.*

Sneddon, Rob. *The Phantom Punch: The Story Behind Boxing's Most Controversial Bout.*

Stewart, Tony. *Dillinger, the Hidden Truth: A Tribute to the Gangsters and G-Men of the Great Depression Era.*

Summers, Anthony. *Official and Confidential: The Secret Life of J. Edgar Hoover.*

Summers, Anthony, and Robbyn Swan. *Sinatra: The Life.*

Theoharis, Athan. *From the Secret Files of J. Edgar Hoover.*

Theoharis, Athan, Tony G. Poveda, Susan Rosenfeld, and Richard G. Powers, eds. *The FBI: A Comprehensive Reference Guide.*

Thomas, Evan. *Robert Kennedy: His Life.*

Thompson, Douglas. *The Dark Heart of Hollywood: Glamour, Guns and Gambling—Inside the Mafia's Global Empire.*

Thompson, Julia A. *The Hunt for the Last Public Enemy in Northeastern Ohio: Alvin "Creepy" Karpis and His Road to Alcatraz.*

Tosches, Nick. *The Devil and Sonny Liston.*

Tuohy, Brian. *The Fix Is Still In: More Corruption and Conspiracies the Pro Sports Leagues Don't Want You to Know About.*

Tye, Larry. *Bobby Kennedy: The Making of a Liberal Icon.*

Vaccara, Stefano. *Carlos Marcello: The Man Behind the JFK Assassination.*

Waldron, Lamar, and Thom Hartmann. *Ultimate Sacrifice: John and Robert Kennedy, the Plan for a Coup in Cuba, and the Murder of JFK.*

Wallis, Michael. *Pretty Boy: The Life and Times of Charles Arthur Floyd.*

Wannall, Ray. *The Real J. Edgar Hoover: For the Record.*

Watts, Steven. *JFK and the Masculine Mystique: Sex and Power on the New Frontier.*

Williams, Paul L. *The Vatican Exposed: Money, Murder, and the Mafia.*

ACKNOWLEDGMENTS

Bill O'Reilly would like to thank the Macmillan/St. Martin's Press publishing team of Jon Sargent, Don Weisberg, and George Witte. In addition, thanks to Rick Pracher for the cover design.

Martin Dugard would also like to thank Eric Simonoff, Chris O'Connell, and, as always, Calene Dugard.

ILLUSTRATION CREDITS

INDEX

Page numbers in *italics* refer to illustrations.

ABOUT THE AUTHORS

Bill O'Reilly is a trailblazing TV journalist who has experienced unprecedented success on cable news and in writing sixteen national bestselling nonfiction books. There are currently more than seventeen million books in the *Killing* series in print. He lives on Long Island.

Martin Dugard is the *New York Times* bestselling author of several books of history, among them the *Killing* series, *Into Africa*, and *The Explorers*. He and his wife, Calene, live in Orange County, California. They have three sons.